(Refresher B1)

English Elements

*12 units with
back-up material
for homestudy –
including 1 CD*

*Sue Morris
Annie Roth*

Max Hueber Verlag

Das Werk und seine Teile sind urheberrechtlich geschützt.
Jede Verwertung in anderen als den gesetzlich zugelassenen
Fällen bedarf deshalb der vorherigen schriftlichen
Einwilligung des Verlages.

3.	2.	1.	Die letzten Ziffern
2008	07 06	05 04	bezeichnen Zahl und Jahr des Druckes.

Alle Drucke dieser Auflage können, da unverändert,
nebeneinander benutzt werden.
1. Auflage
© 2004 Max Hueber Verlag, 85737 Ismaning, Deutschland
Verlagsredaktion: Rebecka Howe, München
Zeichnungen: Reinhard Wendlinger, München
Satz: Petra Obermeier, München
Herstellung: Doris Hagen
Druck: aprinta Druck GmbH & Co., Wemding
Bindung: Ludwig Auer GmbH, Donauwörth
Printed in Germany
ISBN 3-19-202733-9

Introduction to the coursebook Refresher B1

More and more people are learning English nowadays:
- at school
- in company courses
- at the Volkshochschule
- at private language schools.

Most people, however, stop learning at some point in time for a variety of reasons:
- They didn't like English at school.
- They had no time.
- They changed jobs and moved away.
- They didn't have a baby-sitter for the children.
- They were more interested in Maths and Computer Studies.
- They liked English at school but forgot a lot of vocab and they are now frightened to speak.

Then some time later they become interested in English again because
- they need it for work.
- they want to be able to communicate with people they meet on holiday.
- they want to do a school-leaving certificate at night school and need to brush up their English quickly.
- they realise how important English is in our day and age.
- they like English and feel sorry they've neglected it.
- their son/daughter is getting married to an English-speaking person.
- they would like to have a recognised certificate in English.

Are you one of these people? Even if the portrait doesn't fit you completely, don't worry! The important thing is that you did have a basic knowledge of English at some time, that you're really interested in taking up English again and that you are prepared to do some work.

To be successful you need four ingredients: 1. your own motivation, 2. your textbook, 3. your teacher and 4. your fellow students.

Your own motivation

Think carefully about why you're taking this English course and what you expect of it. Be sure that you have enough time to attend the class regularly, not just for a few weeks, but for the two semesters you will need to complete the course. And if you're attending an intensive course, then it's even more important not to miss any of the sessions. Remember, too, to allow some time for homework which helps you to consolidate what you have learnt in class. Perhaps you can also find some time to watch an English film or listen to the news or do some extra reading in English.

Your textbook

We have tried to write a textbook which will help you to reactivate the English you thought you had forgotten. For this reason there is a clear grammatical progression through the 12 main units. The four revision units revise work done in the previous three units, but also give you practice in completing the type of task you will need to understand if you are going to take the European Language Certificate B1 exam. This certificate is on the equivalent level of a "Realschulabschluss" in English and is one of the language certificates recognised by the Common European Framework of the Council of Europe (http://www.sprachenzertifikate.de).

Take a little time to look through the book to see how it can help you. You can start with a look at the list of contents on pages 5–7. In each unit there is work on vocabulary (**V**), grammar (**G**), functions (**F**), one or more of the skills (**S**) of speaking, listening, reading and writing. Throughout the book there are also tips on learning vocabulary, how to improve your listening and reading comprehension and other aspects of learning English successfully (**T**). Work on pronunciation is also important because we are sure you want to sound friendly when you speak English. If you miss a lesson, don't worry. You can listen to the recording and you can check the answers to the exercises you missed in the key at the back of the book starting on page 172.

In addition we would like to prepare you for real-life English-speaking situations, and so we've tried to include the kind of English that you will hear in everyday life. Don't panic if you hear or read some words or expressions that you don't understand immediately. This is all part of the preparation. Try not to reach for the nearest dictionary or ask your teacher/a fellow student as soon as you see or hear a new word. Try to concentrate on the context first of all. We also hope that the topics we have chosen will interest you and that the literary extracts will motivate you to do some more reading of your own.

Your teacher

Your teacher will give you the opportunity to hear and speak as much English as possible not only by speaking English to you in the classroom but also by playing the recordings so that you can hear other English-speaking people with a variety of accents. Again this will prepare you for real-life situations. In addition the recordings have the advantage that you can listen to them again and again, which is a lot easier than asking people to keep repeating what they have just said!

In this course you will have a lot of speaking practice by not only talking to the teacher but also by working with a partner or in small groups. The teacher doesn't forget you when you are doing pair work or group work but listens to you and is there, of course, to help you if necessary.

Don't be surprised if your teacher sometimes changes the order of exercises in a unit or even leaves out an exercise. She/He will have a good reason for that. Your teacher will also suggest what you can do at home from one lesson to the next.

But do remember that your teacher is only one of the four main ingredients in the recipe for your learning success.

Your fellow students

Since you've all learned English at some time, you can pool your resources by working together. Just think of all the knowledge the group will have if everyone helps each other. And don't miss this wonderful opportunity to speak as much English to the others as possible. Who knows, perhaps you'll also arrange to meet outside the classroom or go over the last lesson and do the exercises the teacher suggested for the next lesson.

We also want you to have fun learning English in a relaxed classroom atmosphere. You will only feel relaxed if you are happy with the people you are working with. For this reason we have included a number of exercises in the first unit which give you the chance to get to know the other people in the course a bit better.

Now that you've got everything together, all that remains to be said is
Get started!

Table of Contents

1 Getting Started
page 8

- V   names; likes and dislikes; family relationships; daily routine
- G/F   introducing people; question patterns; simple present; have/has got; there is/there are
- S   listening for missing words; jigsaw reading; listening for details; marking word stress; spelling
- T   listening; word trees and word bank; reading; writing e-mails and letters; dictionaries; word stress

2 Sports and Hobbies
page 20

- V   sports; hobbies; telephoning; food and drink; shopping; quantities
- G   simple present and present continuous in contrast; some-any; much-many
- S   listening for key words; listening for details; telephoning
- T   listening; vocabulary; reading

3 Behaviour in Society
page 30

- V   daily routines; living together; tolerance
- G   simple present; adverbs of frequency; past tense of regular and some irregular verbs
- S   reading for gist; guessing unknown words in a reading text; identifying word stress
- T   reading; listening

Revision 1
page 38

4 Holidays
page 42

- V   holiday experiences
- G   question and negative forms in the past; past tense of irregular verbs; simple past vs. past progressive
- S   jigsaw reading; listening for details; being an interested listener; writing a postcard
- T   verb forms; intonation in question tags

5 Law and Order
page 48

- **V** crime and punishment; lost property office
- **G** present perfect for indefinite past and to show the present result of a past action; present perfect vs. simple past; possessive pronouns and adjectives
- **S** predictive reading; predictive listening; using clues in a text; using contracted forms
- **T** word stress; listening

6 Ecology Down Under
page 56

- **V** Australia and the environment
- **G/F** future forms: going to, will, present progressive; suggestions and invitations; agreeing and disagreeing; appropriate responses
- **S** listening for specific information; reading for details; telephoning
- **T** unstressed sounds

Revision 2
page 64

7 A Question of Luck
page 68

- **V** weather and forecasts; betting; lottery
- **G/F** if-sentences type 1+2; agreeing and disagreeing; expressing opinions; discussing; giving advice
- **S** working with word trees; listening for details; reading for details
- **T** inferring meaning from context

8 Childhood
page 74

- **V** changes in routine; notices for rules and regulations
- **G/F** used to; modals: must vs. have to; mustn't vs. don't have to; may, might, must, can't for deductions
- **S** listening for details; making deductions; predictive reading
- **T** practising grammar outside the classroom

9 The World of Work
page 82

- **V** jobs; careers; modern office communication
- **G/F** present perfect simple and progressive for unfinished actions; for and since; asking for clarification
- **S** listening for details; jigsaw reading; predictive reading; reading for specific information; recognising word stress
- **T** word partnerships; grammar

Revision 3
page 90

10 Transport & Technology
page 94

V   transport; likes and dislikes; technical improvements
G   comparative and superlative of adjectives; gerund and infinitives; passive verb forms
S   listening for details; reading for details
T   listening; personalisation

11 Health and Environment
page 102

V   healthy habits; safety tips; environment
G/F   if-sentences type 3; modal verbs; making polite suggestions
S   interviewing; listening for details; note-taking
T   sounding natural; diary writing

12 Entertainment
page 110

V   forms of entertainment; films
G   reported speech; past perfect
S   reading a literary extract; listening for clues; listening for details; telling a true story; writing a little scenario
T   reading for pleasure; exchanging information; writing a story

Revision 4
page 118

Appendix

File Section   page 122

Grammar Reference Section   page 129

Tapescripts   page 164

Key   page 172

Vocabulary (Unit by Unit)   page 181

Vocabulary (Alphabetical Order)   page 200

Acknowledgements   page 204

V   vocabulary
G/F   grammar & functions
S   skills
T   learning tips

(Unit 1)

Getting Started

1 Who's in my course?

a By now you'll have heard the names of all the people in your English course. Write as many of them as you can remember on a note pad.

Sylvie

b Compare your list with a partner:

- ☐ Have you got Sylvie on your list?
- ○ Sylvie? No, who's that?
- ☐ The dark-haired lady in the red jumper over there.
- ○ Oh, right. Is that Sylvie with "ie"?
- ☐ I think so.
- ○ Have you got Daniel?
- ☐ No, I haven't. Who's that?
- ○ The man to the right of Sylvie.

2 What's in a name?

a

My name's Hamish. That's scottish.

My name's John James after my two grandfathers.

MY NAME'S CAROLYN – WITH A "Y".

Hi, I'm Marcy. That's short for Mary Carlyle.

Hello, my name's Jennifer, but everyone calls me Jenny.

I've got two first names – Alexandra and Ann. At school they called me Ann, but now everyone calls me Alex.

b What's behind **your** name?

Names are very interesting things. Parents choose names for their children for different reasons, and these names sometimes take on a different form as you can see in **2a**. Some people even have a dual identity (e.g. Ann for school friends and Alex for other friends).

Why don't you ask some of the others in the course about their names? Count off groups of three or four in your circle and find out what is behind your names.

Here are some questions to help you:
- Is that Spanish?
- Are you called after someone?
- Is that short for …?
- Is that your proper name?
- Does everyone call you …?

▷ Ask other people in the group or your teacher about words you don't know in English.

When you've finished, introduce one of the people in your mini-group to the rest of the course:

> This is … She's / He's called …
> Let me introduce you to … Her / His name …

3 There's more to a name

a   This is Gisela.

This is what she likes:

G eraniums
I reland
S unny days
E nglish films
L udo
A thletics

And this is what she doesn't like:

G reen shoes
I cy pavements
S occer
E ggs
L azy people
A dditives

b   Now do the same with your partner's name. Then check to see how well you know your partner.

> Are you fond of …?   Yes, I am.
>   No, I'm not.

> Do you like …?   Yes, I do.
>   No, I don't.

c   Tell the others about one of the things your partner likes and something he/she's not fond of:

> Mark likes maccaroni, but he doesn't like red ties.
> Helga is fond of horse-riding, but she isn't fond of English beer.

Unit 1   9

(Unit 1)

4 Names aren't everything

a You now know most of the names in the class – in fact, the name list (on your note pad) should be quite full by now. You also know one or two things about some of the people in your course, but maybe there are still some other questions you would like to ask, questions that you would probably ask in your own language when you are sitting waiting for the course to begin.

Listen to this group of people on the first day of their English course and fill in the opening words of the questions you hear.
But have a look at the questions first and try to think of some of the missing words.

		done an English course before?
		was that?
		have English at school?
		your first English course?
		learn to speak English?
		ever been to England?
		need English at work?
		taking this course?
		the book?
		get it?
		was it?
		know the teacher?
		speak any other foreign languages?
		live near here?
		get here?

b What are the patterns for the two kinds of questions in this exercise?

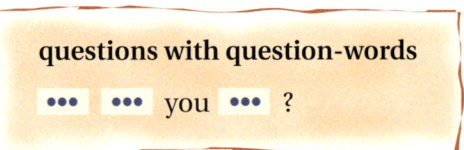

▷ Check with the grammar reference section on **pages 132–133**.

c There are perhaps some things you don't want to tell others about yourself, at least not at first. But there are probably other things you are happy to talk about.
Look at this list of three short pieces of information about Werner. There are a number of possible questions to fit each answer. Look at the boxes in **4b** to help you with the question forms if you are unsure.

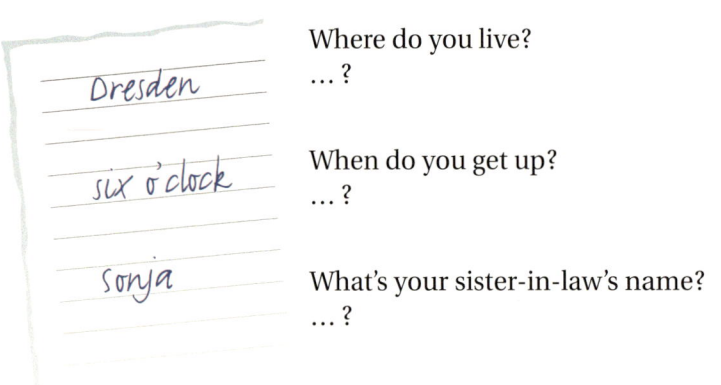

Where do you live?
… ?

When do you get up?
… ?

What's your sister-in-law's name?
… ?

d Now make a list of short answers about yourself and exchange it with a new partner. Ask each other questions like in **4c** about the things on the list.

e When you have exchanged your information, make a foursome and introduce your partner to the other pair. – Listen carefully to what your partner says about you. You may want to correct something!

> Sorry, that's wrong.
> I | don't …
> | wasn't …
> | haven't …
> | 'm not

f In **4c** we said that more than one question can fit one answer and in **4d** you asked a partner questions. How do we make questions if we want to ask about someone else, about a student who is not in class today, for example?

So what questions with "does" could we ask if the answer is "Dresden"?

○ Where does Werner live?   *Dresden*
○ Where does he work?

5 BMW world-wide

You know the people in your group a little better, but do you know anything about life in the USA or South Africa? Is life in these countries different from life in your country? You are going to read two short texts to find out. One is about a worker from Rosslyn, South Africa and one about a worker from Spartanburg, South Carolina.

Work with a partner. Partner **A** reads the information on this page and partner **B** looks at **page 122**. There is some information printed in bold in the text about Oscar Sigasa. Ask your partner questions to find out similar information about Betsy Chan. Use the prompts to help you.

○ How old / Betsy?
○ Who / work for?
○ Is / married?
○ Husband's name?
○ Children?
○ Where / live?
○ What sort of house / live in?
○ How much / pay for the house?
○ What sort of car / Betsy / drive?
○ How / get / to work?
○ How far / house / from the factory?
○ How many shifts?
○ How long / each shift last?
○ How many hours a week / Betsy work?
○ How many days' holiday / Betsy have?
○ How much / Betsy earn?

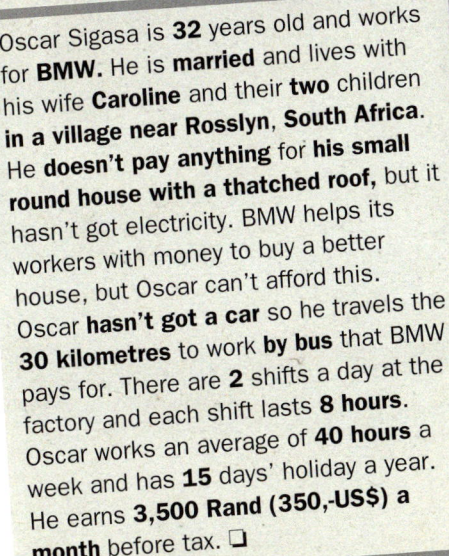

Oscar Sigasa is **32** years old and works for **BMW**. He is **married** and lives with his wife **Caroline** and their **two** children **in a village near Rosslyn, South Africa**. He **doesn't pay anything** for **his small round house with a thatched roof**, but it hasn't got electricity. BMW helps its workers with money to buy a better house, but Oscar can't afford this. Oscar **hasn't got a car** so he travels the **30 kilometres** to work **by bus** that BMW pays for. There are **2** shifts a day at the factory and each shift lasts **8 hours**. Oscar works an average of **40 hours** a week and has **15** days' holiday a year. He earns **3,500 Rand (350,-US$) a month** before tax. ❏

Now can you say something about the differences between Germany, South Africa and USA using Oscar and Betsy as examples?

> The average worker in USA **doesn't live** in a flat.
> The average worker in Germany **doesn't work** 40 hours a week.

▷ Check negative statements in the grammar reference section on **page 130**.

Unit 1   **11**

(Unit 1)

6 Commuters

a Oscar and Betsy both travel to work. They are commuters. You are now going to hear about a commuter's routine. Before you listen, look at the text and decide which verbs are missing.

David Carr _____ the sixty miles from his home Finstock in Oxfordshire to London to give his family a better life. He _____ with his wife Hilary and their three teenage children and two poodles in a four-bedroomed house worth about £300,000, and they have a large garden that he _____ in at the weekend. "It _____ me to relax", he says. He _____ up early, at 6 o'clock, and _____ the house at 6.25 and _____ into Oxford. There isn't a bus at that time in the morning. His first class train ticket _____ him £431.20 a month, just over £5,000 a year. The time he _____ on train journeys _____ up to 39 days a year!

Now listen and see if you were right.

> He **lives** in a four-bedroomed house.
> It **helps** him to relax.

▷ Remember the **s** for he/she/it. Check the forms of the present tense again in the grammar reference section on **page 130**.

b Mr Carr says he gets up early. Is 6 o'clock early for you? What time does 'Mr or Ms average' get up in your country? Does anyone in the group commute?

_____ Atmosphere
_____ Activities
_____ Facilities
_____ Schools
_____ Area
_____ Tourist attractions

c The commuter's wife

Now listen to the commuter's wife talking. Why does she like life in the village?

> **There's** a primary school in the village.
> **There are** comprehensive schools in Witney and Chipping Norton.

▷ Check "there is" or "there are" in the grammar reference section on **page 133**.

d Your home

Why do you like living in your town, city or village?

7

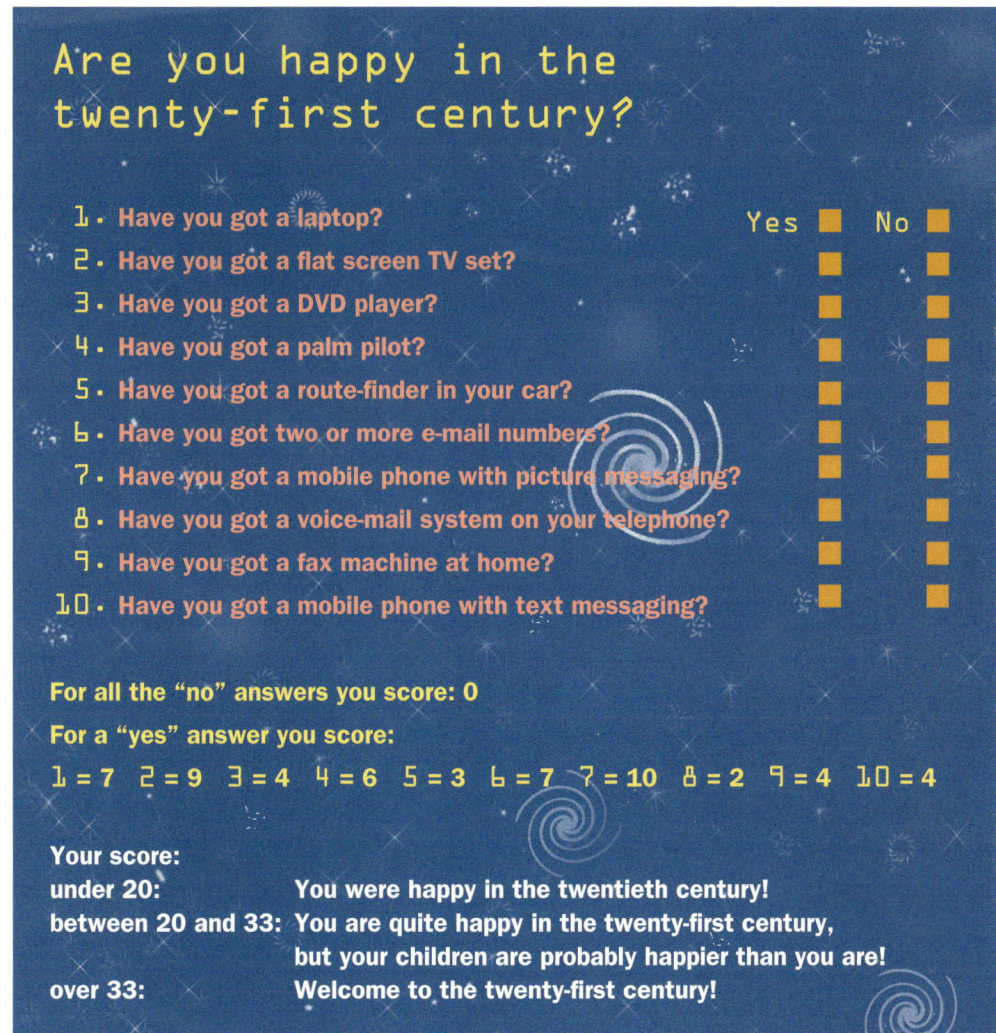

Are you happy in the twenty-first century?

1. Have you got a laptop?
2. Have you got a flat screen TV set?
3. Have you got a DVD player?
4. Have you got a palm pilot?
5. Have you got a route-finder in your car?
6. Have you got two or more e-mail numbers?
7. Have you got a mobile phone with picture messaging?
8. Have you got a voice-mail system on your telephone?
9. Have you got a fax machine at home?
10. Have you got a mobile phone with text messaging?

Yes   No

For all the "no" answers you score: 0
For a "yes" answer you score:
1 = 7 2 = 9 3 = 4 4 = 6 5 = 3 6 = 7 7 = 10 8 = 2 9 = 4 10 = 4

Your score:
under 20:   You were happy in the twentieth century!
between 20 and 33:   You are quite happy in the twenty-first century,
                       but your children are probably happier than you are!
over 33:   Welcome to the twenty-first century!

8 A phone call

Listen carefully to this phone call between Sheila and Jane and decide whether these statements are true, false or possible.

1. Sheila has got a sore leg.
2. Emily is older than Roddy.
3. Jane and Sheila are sisters.
4. Mum lives with Sheila.
5. Roddy is at least five years old.
6. Bill is Jane's husband.
7. He is on a business trip.
8. Mum is playing with Emily in the garden.
9. David is Jane's husband.
10. Mum doesn't drive.

Learning tip – Listening
Don't worry if there are some words in the dialogue that you don't understand. It's possible to do this exercise without understanding every single word. Just listen for the information you need.

Unit 1 13

(Unit 1)

9 Family relationships

a There are 12 members of the Lyle family in 3 generations. Ten are married, and two are single.
Use the following information to find out who is married to whom and to make up the Lyle family tree. Work with a partner.

- ☐ John is Richard's grandfather and Robert's father-in-law.
- ☐ Richard is Isobel's cousin and Daniel's nephew.
- ☐ Robert is William's father and Daniel's brother-in-law.
- ☐ Isobel is Helen's daughter and Agnes' niece.
- ☐ Daniel is John's son and William's uncle.
- ☐ William is Isobel's brother and Annie's grandson.
- ☐ Annie is Helen's mother and James' mother-in-law.
- ☐ Agnes is Daniel's sister and Janette's mother-in-law.
- ☐ Helen is Richard's aunt and James' sister-in-law.
- ☐ James is John's son-in-law and Isobel's uncle.

Compare your version with your partner and then answer the following question:

Who is Tom?

Here are some useful expressions when comparing answers:

> What have you got for/in ...?
> Who do you think ...?
> Shall we compare?
> Can I have a look at what you've got?

And when you can't read your partner's writing:

> Sorry, what does that say?
> Sorry, I can't read your writing.

b In the clues there are lots of words describing family relationships. Put them into two word trees for male and female relations and add any other ones you know.

c Now form two groups to play the "Family Tree" game.
Group **A** look at **page 122** and Group **B** look at **page 127**.

10 Word bank

In **9b** you made two word trees for male and female relations. From some of the other exercises in this unit you could make other word trees for things like countries, nationalities, electronic equipment etc. If you think that this is a good way of remembering vocabulary, look at exercise **15e** in the back-up section of this unit.

> **Learning tip – Word trees and word bank**
> Learning words in word trees is – for some people – a good way of remembering vocabulary, but not everyone is interested in learning the same words.
> The names of different flowers may not be so important to you. Perhaps you're more interested in words or expressions which you can use for your job.
> In any case you should decide which words to put into your word bank and which words to leave out. It is not there for your teacher to check it; it's like your own bank account where you put as much into it as you want – or can! And it's not necessary to know every word in the English language. – Who does?!

(Back-up)

11 Filling in a form

Fill in this application form for a language school.

Application Form

Please write in CAPITAL LETTERS and in ink.

Mr /Ms Last name, surname _____ Christian names or forenames _____

Date of birth _____ Town/Country of birth _____

Present address _____ Post code _____

Daytime telephone number _____

Course of study _____

Occupation _____

How did you hear of the Course? _____

Date / Signature _____

Europe Summer School, 12 Bank Drive, Exeter CJ5 PE3

12 What's missing?

Use short forms where possible. In some examples there's more than one word missing.

1. Where _____ you live?
2. The express bus _____ stop here.
3. _____ you _____ a spare pen?
4. _____ "spare" mean?
5. _____ a phone in this building?
6. Sorry, I _____ know your name.
7. _____ your address?
8. I just _____ understand this exercise!

Unit 1

(Back-up)

13 Reading comprehension

a Look at this text about another commuter. There is coffee all over the page, and so you can't read some words, but can you answer these questions?

- How much does Mr Milbank's house cost?
- Is his wife a stockbroker too?
- What does he have for breakfast?
- Does he have breakfast with the children from Monday to Friday?

Daily Telegraph

Mr. Milbank, 32, commuter

peo. – Mr. Milbank, 32, commutes the 55 miles from Colchester to London where he works as a _____ stockbroker. He lives in a £185,000 _____ house. His wife, Caroline, works _____ as a vet, and they have two children of 5 and 8. Mr Milbank's _____ ticket costs him £2,454 a year. His journey takes an hour and a quarter. He gets up at around 6.20. He just has time for a _____ cup of coffee before he leaves at 6.50. He goes to the station by car rather than by bus because then he can have fifteen minutes longer in bed. "I'm not at my _____ best in the mornings," he admits! The car park costs him £380 a year, but it is worth it for those extra fifteen minutes! His _____ regret is that he only has time for breakfast with the children at the weekend. ∎

> **Learning Tip – Reading**
> Remember that in your language you don't read to answer questions on the text. You read to find information or just for fun. It is the same in English, and it isn't important if you don't understand every word.

Could you answer the questions? – So it's not so important to understand every word when you read English texts.

Here are the missing words.
Where do you think they go in the text?
Check your answers in the key.

1. four-bedroomed semi-detached
2. snatched
3. only
4. second class season
5. successful
6. locally
7. sparkling

Handy for commuters.

b Your life

Look back at the lives of the two commuters (in **6** and **13**) and write a few sentences about your daily life.

14 Angus' e-mail

a Angus, a young man from Haltwhistle near Newcastle, is coming to Prien on Chiemsee to improve his German at the Goethe-Institute there. All students stay with German families. Here is an e-mail that tells the Goethe-Institute something about him. With this information he hopes they can find a suitable guest family for him.

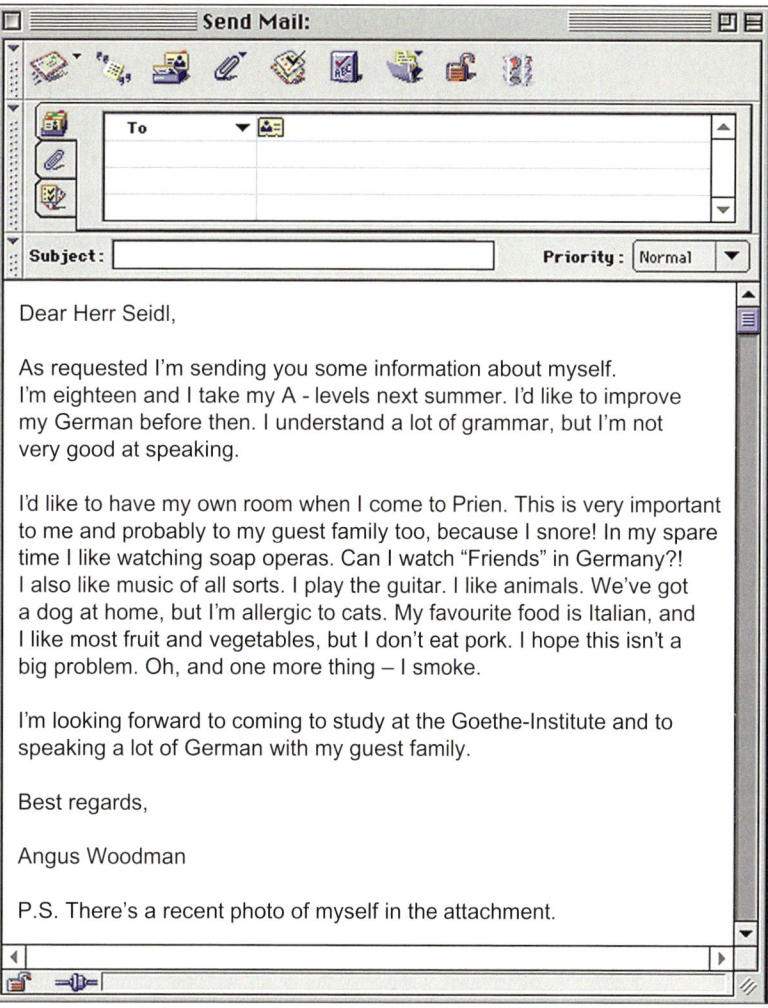

Dear Herr Seidl,

As requested I'm sending you some information about myself.
I'm eighteen and I take my A - levels next summer. I'd like to improve my German before then. I understand a lot of grammar, but I'm not very good at speaking.

I'd like to have my own room when I come to Prien. This is very important to me and probably to my guest family too, because I snore! In my spare time I like watching soap operas. Can I watch "Friends" in Germany?!
I also like music of all sorts. I play the guitar. I like animals. We've got a dog at home, but I'm allergic to cats. My favourite food is Italian, and I like most fruit and vegetables, but I don't eat pork. I hope this isn't a big problem. Oh, and one more thing – I smoke.

I'm looking forward to coming to study at the Goethe-Institute and to speaking a lot of German with my guest family.

Best regards,

Angus Woodman

P.S. There's a recent photo of myself in the attachment.

Could Angus stay with you? – Explain why or why not.

> No, he couldn't. We've got a cat.
> Yes, he could. We like soap operas, too.

b Now imagine you are going to study in Britain. Write an e-mail/letter to an English language school so that they can find a suitable guest family for you. In other units (e.g. in Revision Units 2 & 3) of this course there are more models of writing that will help you write your own version.

Learning Tip – Writing e-mails / letters
If you don't know the name of the person you are writing to, remember you should begin with "Dear Sir / Sirs / Sir or Madam" and end with "Yours sincerely".

Unit 1

(Back-up)

15 Vocabulary

a Riddles

What has got four legs but cannot run?

What has got a mouth but cannot speak?

What has got hands but cannot write?

What has got an eye but cannot see?

b This extract from a monolingual dictionary shows you how many interesting meanings the simple word "eye" has got.

Learning Tip – Dictionaries
When you see new words, be careful! Sometimes there is more than one translation of these words, so use a dictionary carefully. Try using a monolingual dictionary.

> **eye** [aɪ] **eyes, eyeing** or **eying, eyed**
> 1 Your **eyes** are the parts of your body with which you see. *I opened my eyes and looked… Maria's eyes filled with tears. …a tall, thin white-haired lady with piercing dark brown eyes… He is now blind in one eye.*
> 2 You use **eye** when you are talking about a person's ability to judge things or about the way in which they are considering or dealing with things. *William was a man of discernment, with an eye for quality… Their chief negotiator turned his critical eye on the United States… It did not take his practised eye long to notice that he was not the only one who was hanging about… He first learnt to fish under the watchful eye of his grandmother.*
> 3 An electric **eye** or infra-red **eye** is a device which can recognize the presence of people or objects by detecting the light or heat coming from them. *An infra-red eye is said to detect the movement of any animal within an angle of 110 degrees at up to 10 metres.*
> 4 An **eye** on a potato is one of the dark spots from which new stems grow.
> 5 An **eye** is a small metal loop which a hook fits into, as a fastening on a piece of clothing.
> 6 The **eye** of a needle is the small hole at one end which the thread passes through.
> 7 The **eye of** a storm, tornado, or hurricane is the centre of it. *The eye of the hurricane hit Florida just south of Miami.*

Using a good dictionary – it shouldn't be too small – look up one of the words from the riddles in **15a** – leg, mouth, hand – and see how many definitions you can find for this one word.

15a Answers
A chair.
A river.
A clock.
A needle.

18

c Listen and repeat these words from this unit.

commuter	○ com	● mut	○ er	
countryside	● coun	○ try	○ side	
facilities	○ fa	● cil	○ i	○ ties
attractions	○ at	● trac	○ tions	
application form	○ ap	○ pli	● ca	○ tion ● form
information	○ in	○ for	● ma	○ tion
relationship	○ re	● la	○ tion	○ ship
divorced	○ di	● vorced		

> **Learning tip – Word stress**
> When you write down new words, it is a good idea to show the stress so that you know how to SAY the words.

d Word-finding

There are thousands and thousands of words (around 750,000) in the English language, but even native speakers of English only use a small percentage of them.

How many other words can you find in the word "English"? You can use the letters as many times as you want but only once in each individual word.

You can try this game with other English words during the course to test your vocabulary.

E N G L I S H
line, gin, ...

If you're interested in doing the **European Language Certificate in English B1**, the word list at the back of the book will help you with the words you need to know in order to be successful in the exam. But you'll also hear words and expressions in your English course which are not in the word list. If you want to add them to your **word bank**, do so. However, don't just leave them there; use them as often as possible.

e To finish off make up a word tree about a topic which you are interested in. Keep adding any new words and expressions to it that you want to remember as you go through the course.

(Unit 2)

Sports and Hobbies

1 Sports and hobbies

a In groups make up word trees for sports and hobbies.

b Your hobbies

Talk to as many people as you can in the class. Ask questions and find out how many people:

like	golf
	skiing
	mountain biking
	football
	pottery
hate	sport
watch	sport on TV

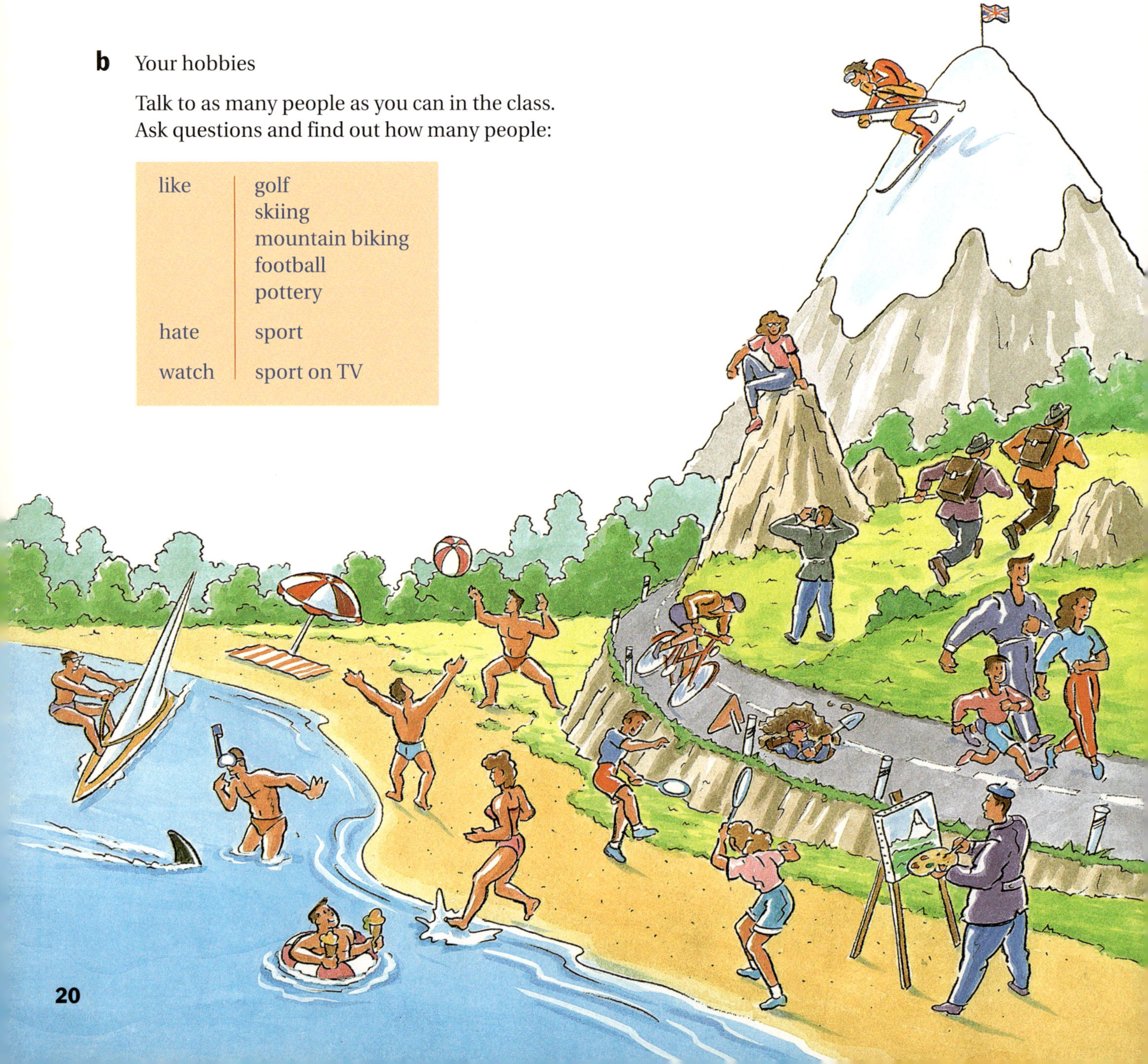

2 An unusual sport

a What do you think of when you think of racing?
What do you think of when you think of camels?
So what do you think of when you think of camel racing?

Read this text to find out more about this sport.

For my regular column about unusual sports I was in Virginia City, Nevada, USA, last week and talked to Jan Chirco. Jan's a member of the International Order of Camel Jockeys and rides camels just for fun. Some jockeys, in Australia, for example, catch, break in and train wild camels for racing, others at a farm in Stagecoach, Nevada, train camels for safari treks that are very popular with tourists. But Jan prefers the races.

Anyone over the age of 18 can take part, but this sport is not for the faint-hearted. As Jan explains: "When you are racing it feels like you are sitting on top of a badly-functioning washing machine. You have an accelerator, if you scream loud enough the camel will go faster, but you don't have any turning or braking equipment, when the camel is galloping at 35 mph you close your eyes and hang on. If a camel stops suddenly in a race there isn't really anything a jockey can do."

It sounds dangerous, so why do jockeys like Jan go to race meetings in Virginia City or fly half-way round the world to take part in the USA-Australia Cup that takes place every year in Alice Springs? "Because no sport in the world compares with camel racing for excitement. Sure you take some risks, but they are calculated risks – like most jockeys I wear a crash hat – and if there aren't any risks there isn't any fun. It really gives me a buzz if I stay in the saddle, and to win is way past cool."

At the Virginia City international camel races in September the buzz that Jan talks about is everywhere. Would you like to have some fun, kids? Come to the colourful parade that starts this three-day event.

Fun for adults? Join in the cheers of the crowd as the three or four jockeys race for a place in the final, or go down to the start and listen to the enthusiastic volunteers who help the jockeys onto the camels and tell stories about other races and explain to a complete amateur like me that a camel doesn't have any water in its hump but only fat.

At the end of it all there is fun for everyone at the camel hump ball that raises some money for local charities.

Complete these sentences in any way you like to make a summary of the text.

Camel racing is ...
When jockeys ride a camel they ...
At the Virginia City international camel races ...

b Some or any?

Look back at the text and find examples of sentences with "some" or "any" and then say whether these "rules" for "some" and "any" are true or false.

	True	False
'Some' means a certain number or amount of.		
'Any' is used only in negative sentences.		
'Some' is used only in positive sentences		

Look in the grammar reference section on **page 136** to check the uses of "some" and "any".
Look in the back-up section on **page 28** for some practice with "some" and "any".

(Unit 2)

3 The commentary

Listen to the sports commentaries and decide what's happening in each:

1.
2.
3.

Which words helped you decide?

> **Learning tip – Listening**
> When you're listening to English, listen for the important words (nouns and verbs). They help you decide what's happening.

4 What does he do?

a Look at this picture.

What does he do? What's he doing?

> Gerard Depardieu is an   .
> He's   a cigarette.

What's the difference between:

> What does she/he do?   What's she/he doing?

▷ Check the answers in the grammar reference section on **page 134–135**.

b Now you!

With a partner make up sentences in the simple present and present progressive using one of these pictures.

5 Four phone calls

a Listen to four phone calls. As you listen, fill in details of them:

	1	2	3	4
Number called				
Person calling				
Is the person called in?				
What is she/he doing?				

Fill in this grid for telephoning. What do you say when you answer the phone?
What expressions do you use when you make a phone call?

	answer the phone	make a phone call
say hello		
confirm who's speaking		
ask to speak to someone		
message		
call to the phone		
finish the call		

b 0181 345 4567. Hello.

Now find a partner. Make up telephone conversations with her/him. Use the following guidelines to help you. Remember this is a phone call, so don't have any eye contact.

Example 1

Student A	Student B
Answer the phone.	
	Say hello and ask to speak to X.
Say she/he is busy. She/he is •••ing. Message?	
	No. Ring back later.

Example 2

Student A	Student B
Answer the phone. (Give your number.)	
	Check who is speaking.
Confirm.	
	Say hello and ask to speak to X.
One moment. Call to the phone.	
	Say thanks.

Unit 2 23

(Unit 2)

6 Are you a big spender?

a   We asked some people some questions.
    Here are their answers.
    What do you think the questions were?

Peter Baron
26, student, single
Wallet: £5.37.
Extravagance: Football supporters' club. I travel to Europe with my team, Manchester United, as often as I can.
Meanness: Washing!
I take all my washing home to my Mum!

Teresa Evans
32, a bank clerk, single
Wallet: £22.62.
Extravagance: Food and drink.
Meanness: I don't spend much money on expensive cosmetics.

Robert Derbyshire
35, security guard, divorced, two sons
Wallet: £24.79.
Extravagance: My hobby. Photography.
Meanness: Shoes. I buy cheap shoes.

Bill Dixon
39, investment adviser, married with one son
Wallet: £75.
Extravagance: Cars. I drive a Corvette, which uses a lot of petrol around town.
Meanness: Wine.
I think wine in restaurants is very expensive.

Pat Smith
55, a teacher, married with one daughter
Wallet: £17.05.
Extravagance: Golf.
Meanness: Hairdressers. I go to the hairdresser's once a year!

Helen Wood
27, solicitor, single
Wallet: £30.
Extravagance: Expensive perfume.
I always buy a lot of it.
Meanness: Shoes.
I buy one pair and then wear them every day.

Christine Watson
37, advertising executive, married, two daughters
Wallet: £50.
Extravagance: Heating.
I have the central heating on 28° all winter.
Meanness: Hairdressers.
My sister cuts my hair.

b Look at the profiles and answer these questions:

1. What does Mrs Watson do?
2. What does Peter Baron do?
3. How much money has each person got in her/his wallet?
4. What does she/he spend a lot of money on?
5. What doesn't she/he spend much money on?

c Look again

Look at the profiles and decide:

How many people	are married?
	are _____ ?
	are _____ ?
	have got two children?
	_____ ?
	_____ ?
	_____ ?

Now add questions of your own and ask the person sitting next to you.

d How much or how many?

▷ Look at the grammar reference section on **page 137** to check the difference.

e Who's extravagant?

Talk to three people in the group.
Ask them some questions about what they spend their money on.

How much money do you spend on:	sport/your hobbies?	
	_____	
	_____	a week?
	_____	

Tell the class what you found out!

Unit 2

(Unit 2)

7 You are what you eat

a To be fit for your chosen sport you have to eat and drink the right things, but how do you buy them in the UK? You need to understand the difference between countable and uncountable nouns.
You can say, "I'd like two apples, please." But you can't say, "I'd like two milks, please." You say: "I'd like some milk, please." You can count apples, but you can't count milk.

Look at this list. Put the food and drinks into the columns "countable" or "uncountable".

bars of chocolate	wine
water	slices of toast
eggs	tea
bottles	tomatoes
beer	sugar
lemonade	biscuits
orange juice	butter
glasses	salad
cups	meat
coffee	chops

Countable	Uncountable
eggs	water

b So is what you eat and drink good for you and your fitness?

Here is a questionnaire. First fill in the blanks in the questionnaire with "much" or "many".
Now interview a partner and write down her/his answers.

1. How _____ chocolate do you eat a week?
2. How _____ eggs do you eat a week?
3. How _____ beer do you drink a week?
4. How _____ glasses of wine do you drink a day?
5. How _____ water do you drink a day?
6. How _____ oranges do you eat a day?
7. How _____ orange juice do you drink for breakfast?
8. How _____ sugar do you take in tea/coffee?
9. How _____ cups of coffee do you drink for breakfast?
10. How _____ slices of toast do you eat for breakfast?
11. How _____ butter do you (does your husband/wife) buy a week?
12. How _____ times a week do you eat salad?

Report your findings to the class.

> Simone drinks a lot of water.
> Gottfried doesn't drink much beer.
> Alice doesn't eat many oranges.
> Melanie doesn't drink any orange juice for breakfast.

(Back-up)

8 Words, words, words

You don't buy "a lemonade". You CAN'T count "lemonade". You buy it in a bottle.
You CAN count matches, but you don't buy just one match, you buy a box of matches.

A bar of …   chocolate.

A bottle of …   beer.

A box of …   matches.

A can of …   coke.

A carton of …   milk.

A crate of …   beer.

A glass of …   lemonade.

A jar of …   jam.

A litre of …   mineral water.

A packet of …   biscuits.

A slice of …   toast.

A tin of …   tomatoes.

A tube of …   toothpaste.

Now add these items to the list (some you can add to more than one list):

ham, wine, orange juice, cigarettes, beer, chocolates, sweets, soap, lemonade, washing powder, crisps, soup, peas, bread, tea, pineapple, tomato puree, rice, honey, bacon, 6 eggs / 12 (a dozen) eggs

▷ Check with the key that you are right.

Learning Tip – Vocabulary
DON'T try to learn all these words now. You are very busy, and you haven't got much time. OK, but you clean your teeth every morning. Put ten new words that you want to learn on the mirror in the bathroom and look at these words when you clean your teeth!

Unit 2 27

(Back-up)

9 Shopping

a Listen to these conversations and tick off what the people buy.

b Listen again and decide which of the following statements are true, false or possible.

1. Aspirins cost 35p for a packet of 16.
2. There are 16 capsules in a packet of paracetomol.
3. You can buy soap, shampoo, toothpaste and aspirin in the same shop in Britain.
4. It costs 37p to send a letter to Germany from Britain.
5. You can't always buy stamps where you buy postcards.
6. It isn't possible to get current German newspapers in Britain

KIOSK / POST OFFICE
- five postcards
- 37 stamps

NEWSAGENT
- copy of 'Hello' magazine
- a street map of London
- a map of the London tube
- a German newspaper

PHARMACY COUNTER
- a bar of soap, some shampoo and a tube of toothpaste
- some aspirins
- a packet of paracetomol

10 The party

Fill in the gaps in these sentences with "much" or "many" and "some" or "any".

- ☐ How _____ people are coming to the party?
- ○ That's a good question because _____ people we invited are spending New Year away I think, but I should say about 40.
- ☐ So how _____ wine do you think we need?
- ○ We don't need _____ more white, but we need _____ red. _____ Italian or South African will be OK, but don't buy _____ sweet stuff.
- ☐ And do we need _____ more beer?
- ○ How _____ have we got now?
- ☐ A barrel.
- ○ And how _____ litres does the barrel hold?
- ☐ About 50.
- ○ Well, that should be enough even if Jim comes. You know how _____ glasses of beer he drinks in an evening!
- ☐ Shall I get _____ mineral water and soft drinks for the people who are driving?
- ○ Yeah that's a good idea.
- ☐ How _____ shall I get?
- ○ Get two crates of mineral water and one of orange juice. If there's _____ left over we can always keep it in and drink it later.

11 What does he/she do or what is he/she doing?

In these short texts choose the correct answer.

▷ If you are not sure, check the rules in the grammar reference section on **pages 134** and **135**.

1. Peter's a student. He _____ (to study) German and French at Belfast university. At the weekend he _____ (to work) in a pub. He _____ (to enjoy) the work because he _____ (to meet) a lot of interesting people and because he can drink free Irish whiskey!

2. Pat's a teacher and she _____ (to teach) 11–18 year-olds in a London comprehensive school. She _____ (to teach) History and English, but this year she _____ (not/to teach) English, she _____ (to teach) History. She _____ (to enjoy) her weekends because she _____ (to play) golf. She _____ (to spend) a lot of money on this hobby! She isn't very good, but she _____ (to have) lessons for six weeks.

3. Teresa is a bank clerk, and she _____ (to work) for Lloyds Bank. At the moment she _____ (to work) in the branch in Hampstead. She _____ (to spend) a lot of money on food and drink because she _____ (to enjoy) inviting her friends to dinner. But at the moment she's on a diet, and so she _____ (not/to drink) any alcohol.

12 Do you like poetry?

I'm just going out for a moment

I'm just going out for a moment.
Why?
To make a cup of tea.
Why?
Because I'm thirsty.
Why?
Because it's hot.
Why?
Because the sun's shining.
Why?
Because it's summer.
Why?
Because that's when it is.
Why?
Why don't you stop saying why?
Why?
Tea-time why.
High-time-you-stopped-saying-why-time.

By Michael Rosen

Learning tip – Reading
You don't have to read a long novel or *The Times* to read English! Even little verses like this one can be fun to read.

(Unit 3)
Behaviour in Society

1 Time for tea?

a When do you think people in Britain:

go to bed?
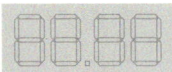

have tea?

have a coffee break?

start school?

have lunch?

Are these routines the same in your country or one that you know?

b Question time

Ask the person sitting next to you.

When do you get up	on weekdays? on Sundays? when you are on holiday?
When do you go to bed	in the summer? in the winter? on Saturdays?
When do you finish work	from Monday to Thursday? on Fridays?

2 Mrs Hatton's Saturday

Here is Mrs Hatton's routine on a Saturday.
Put the sentences in the correct order.
The first one has been done for you.

A ___ She parks the car near the bank. It's usually easy to park before 8.30.
B ___ She buys some fruit and vegetables at the market.
C _1_ She leaves the house at 7.40.
D ___ She hates crowds so she likes to be at the supermarket when it opens at 8.30.
E ___ She always takes the car to the supermarket car park.
F ___ She pays by credit card.
G ___ She gets some money from the cash machine at the bank.
H ___ She gets to Skipton town centre at 8.10.
I ___ She usually gets home at 10.45, but sometimes it is 11.15.
J ___ Here she pays cash, of course. They don't accept credit cards.
K ___ She puts the bags of groceries into the car. They're often heavy.
L ___ She goes to the library, which is next to the supermarket.
M ___ She buys all her groceries, meat and fish in the supermarket.
N ___ She seldom buys ice-cream, but, when she does, she buys that last at the freezer centre by the market.
O ___ Sometimes she meets friends in the library, and they go for coffee in a little restaurant opposite the department store.

3 Sometimes

a Use the diagram to help you try and fill in the correct word in the blanks in this text.

Mrs Hatton _____ goes shopping early on Saturday. She _____ buys her groceries at the supermarket, but she _____ buys her fruit and vegetables there. She seldom buys ice-cream. She _____ goes to the library, and she _____ has coffee with her friends.

always	usually	often	sometimes	seldom	never
100%	80%	60%	50%	25%	0%

Now look again at Mrs Hatton's Saturday in **2**.
Where do words like "sometimes" and "never" go in a sentence?

> She **always** takes the car to the supermarket car park.
> It is **usually** easy to park before 8.30.

▷ Check the rules in the grammar reference section on **page 137**.

3b How often?

You can answer the question "how often?" with "always", "never" or "sometimes", but you can also answer:

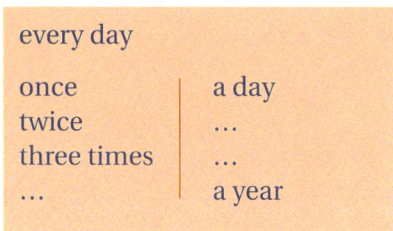

every day	
once	a day
twice	...
three times	...
...	a year

Interview a partner.

How often do you:
- clean your windows?
- invite friends to dinner?
- speak to strangers in the train or at the bus stop?
- talk to your neighbours?
- hear a different language spoken?
- phone friends?
- go to the cinema to watch a film in a foreign language?
- go shopping for groceries?

Tell the others in the group the things you found out about your partner.

c And you?

Tell us something about yourself.

> I never smoke.
> I seldom clean my windows.

4 Are you tolerant?

a How do you feel about a neighbour who:
- has got both ears pierced six times.
- can't speak any German.
- has got a tattoo.
- has got a ring in her / his nose.
- plays loud music after ten o'clock in the evening.
- has got green hair.
- cuts the grass in their garden twice a year.
- has got a dog that barks.
- eats curry every night.
- has got six children.

What other questions would you add to this list?

b I'm in love with a big blue frog.

How do you feel about a young girl who goes home and tells her parents: "I'm in love with a big blue frog"?

Look at the text of the song on page 33 and with a partner try to decide on the missing words.

I'm in love with a big blue frog
A big blue frog _____ me.
It's not as bad as it appears
He wears _____ and he's six foot three.

I'm not worried about our _____
I know they'll turn out neat.
They'll be great lookers cos they'll have my _____
Great swimmers cos they'll have his _____ .

I'm in love with a big blue frog
A big blue frog loves me.
He's not as bad as he appears
He's got rhythm and a PhD.

Well I know we can make things work
He's got good family since
His _____ was a frog from Philadelphia
His _____ an enchanted prince.

The neighbours are against it
And it's clear to me.
And it's probably clear to you
They think value on their property will go right _____
If the _____ next door is blue.

Well I'm in love with a big blue frog
A big blue frog loves me.
I've got it tattooed on my _____
It says P-h-r-o-g Phrog and me,
P-h-r-o-g.

By Peter, Paul and Mary (written by Leslie Braunstein)

 Now listen to the song and check your answers.

c Imagine you had lunch with Mr Phrog and his girlfriend last week. His girlfriend's mother is one of your school friends. She is worried about her daughter and asked you some questions.

Write an e-mail to answer her questions about Mr Phrog.

What was he like?
What did he look like?
Where was he born?
Do you know anything about his family?

You can take some information from the song and from the grammar box on this page and – from your own imagination.

When you describe someone in the past you can use the following:

> He **was** charming / intelligent.
> He **was** tall. / He **had** big feet.
> He **was wearing** glasses.

d Were your parents happy with your choice of boyfriends/girlfriends when you were young?
Are you happy with your daughter's/son's choice of friends?
Do your parents like your boyfriend/girlfriend/partner?
If you live in a small village, do any foreigners live there?

Unit 3

(Unit 3)

5 A citizen of the world?

a Where were you born?
Where do you live now?
When you think of "home", where do you think of?

Read this text about Ben Okech who was born in Uganda, but who is now a German citizen. What do you think his answer to the third question above would be?

> Ben Okech was born in Padibe, a small village in the north of Uganda in 1952. Life was hard for Ben. Every morning he walked barefoot the two miles to his church mission primary school. From 8.00-8.45 every morning the children had religious education and this was Ben's favourite subject and he got 100% in all his tests. He liked maths, too. When he was 7 years old one of his uncles helped him with his maths – every time Ben got his times tables right his uncle gave him some liver. Children often dislike liver, but Ben loved it. In 1971 while he was studying for his A-levels, he attended a gospel meeting and he became a born-again Christian. For years afterwards he travelled around Uganda and talked to thousands of people about Christianity.
>
> The nineteen seventies were troubled times for Uganda, and a lot of Idi Amin's opponents died, so in 1975 Ben accepted a scholarship and studied architecture in Thessaloniki. In 1982 he moved to Munich, where he hoped to study for his doctorate. This wasn't possible as he had a Ugandan passport. He waited 7 years for his German passport. For the first year he washed dishes at the old Munich airport – "I worked with my hands and so I had a lot of time to pray."
>
> Later he worked in an architect's office, and then he qualified as a draughtsman and worked on projects for many different companies. But jobs for architects were difficult to find in the nineties and so Ben re-trained as a computer programmer. When he finished his course, however, he was nearly 50 and a lot of job applicants were a lot younger than him so he didn't get a job in this field. He is married and he now takes any job he can, washing-up or cleaning in hotels and hospitals.
>
> Life in 2003 is hard again for Ben, but he is always cheerful. In 1997 he attended a peace conference where he explained the dangerous political situation in Uganda, and as a result human rights groups started campaigns to stop political corruption and violence. Work for peace is still the most important part of Ben's life.

b Ben remembered maths and religious education from his primary school. What do you remember?

c Odd one out

Look at these lists of words and say which one is the odd one out, which is different from the others for a certain reason.

- home, school, bus, work
- biology, English, mathematics, religious education
- dishes, clothes, windows, hands
- a museum, primary school, a meeting, a conference

(suggested answers)

bus: because you say "on the bus", but you say "at home", "at school", "at work"

English: because you can learn and speak English, but you learn all the other school subjects

windows: because you "clean windows", but "wash dishes, clothes and hands"

a museum: because you "visit a museum", but "attend primary school, a meeting or a conference"

d In the text in **5a** underline all the verbs in the past tense. Now write them in the correct box. 5 are irregular and 20 are regular.

regular	irregular
walked	was/were

How do we make the past tense of regular verbs?

> He work**ed** in an architect's office.

6 Your past

Look at these dates. Fill in the information about YOURSELF.

	lived	worked	was
1998			
1999			
2000			
2001			
2002			

Now tell a partner about your life in 1998, 1999, 2000, 2001, 2002.

Unit 3   35

(Back-up)

7 Me   Write sentences about yourself on a piece of paper. Bring this piece of paper with you to the next lesson.

I always ...
I usually ...
I am often ...
I sometimes ...
I seldom ...
I can never ...

8 Reading

This is from a play written about a black man in South Africa before the free elections. A black man could not love a white woman.
Can you guess what the missing words are? If you know what the missing words are in German but not in English, you can look them up in a dictionary.

▷ Check your answers in the key.

> **Learning tip – Reading**
> When you read English, you will not always understand every word. Sometimes you have to guess what the words mean.
> So let's start guessing!

If they take away your _____ you can't see.
If they take away your _____ you can't taste.
If they take away your hands you can't feel.
If they take away your nose you can't _____.
If they take away your _____ you can't hear.
I can see.
I can _____.
I can feel.
I can smell.
I can _____.
I can't love.

   I must understand it.
   If they take away your legs you can't _____.
   If they take away your arms you can't work.
   If they take away your _____ you can't think.
   I can walk.
   I can _____.
   I can _____.
   I can't love.

I must understand it.
When you are hungry you _____.
When you are _____ you drink.
When you are tired you _____.
I will _____.
I will _____.
I will sleep.
I won't love.

I must understand it again.
If they take away your soul* you can't go to heaven
I can go to heaven
I can't love.

* Seele

From: Statement after an arrest under the immorality act by Athol Fugard

9 Listening

Look at these two sentences:

☐ I want beer.
○ Excuse me, can I have a beer, please?

The second is more polite, of course, but the person you are talking to would understand the first sentence too because the verb (want) and the noun (beer) give us the important information. Good speakers of English put the stress on the important words in a sentence and not on the little 'grammar' words like "can" or "a".

Look at these dialogues. What is the important information in each sentence? Underline this.

1. ☐ Where were you on 29th June 1995?
   ○ I've no idea.

2. ☐ Where were you at ten o'clock yesterday?
   ○ In the morning or in the evening, officer?
   ☐ In the evening.
   ○ I was at the pub.
   ☐ Were you alone?
   ○ No, my mates were with me. We were playing darts.

3. ☐ Where were you between six o'clock and midnight on Saturday evening?
   ○ At a disco.
   ☐ What, the whole time?
   ○ Yeah, that's right.
   ☐ What were you doing there?
   ○ Playing the drums.

Now listen to the recording of these dialogues and see if you underlined the important words. The unimportant words often have the same sound. It's called "schwa" and is written like this [ə].

> **Learning tip – Listening**
> If you listen for the important words like nouns and verbs, you will find listening easier.

10 Dialogues

Where would you hear these dialogues?

1. _____
2. _____
3. _____
4. _____
5. _____
6. _____

Try to practise them with someone from your English course, or with someone English!

Unit 3 37

(Revision 1)

1 Gap-fill reading

Have a look at this introductory text on the Lakeland Leisure Centre web site and fill in the gaps with one of the options from the list below.

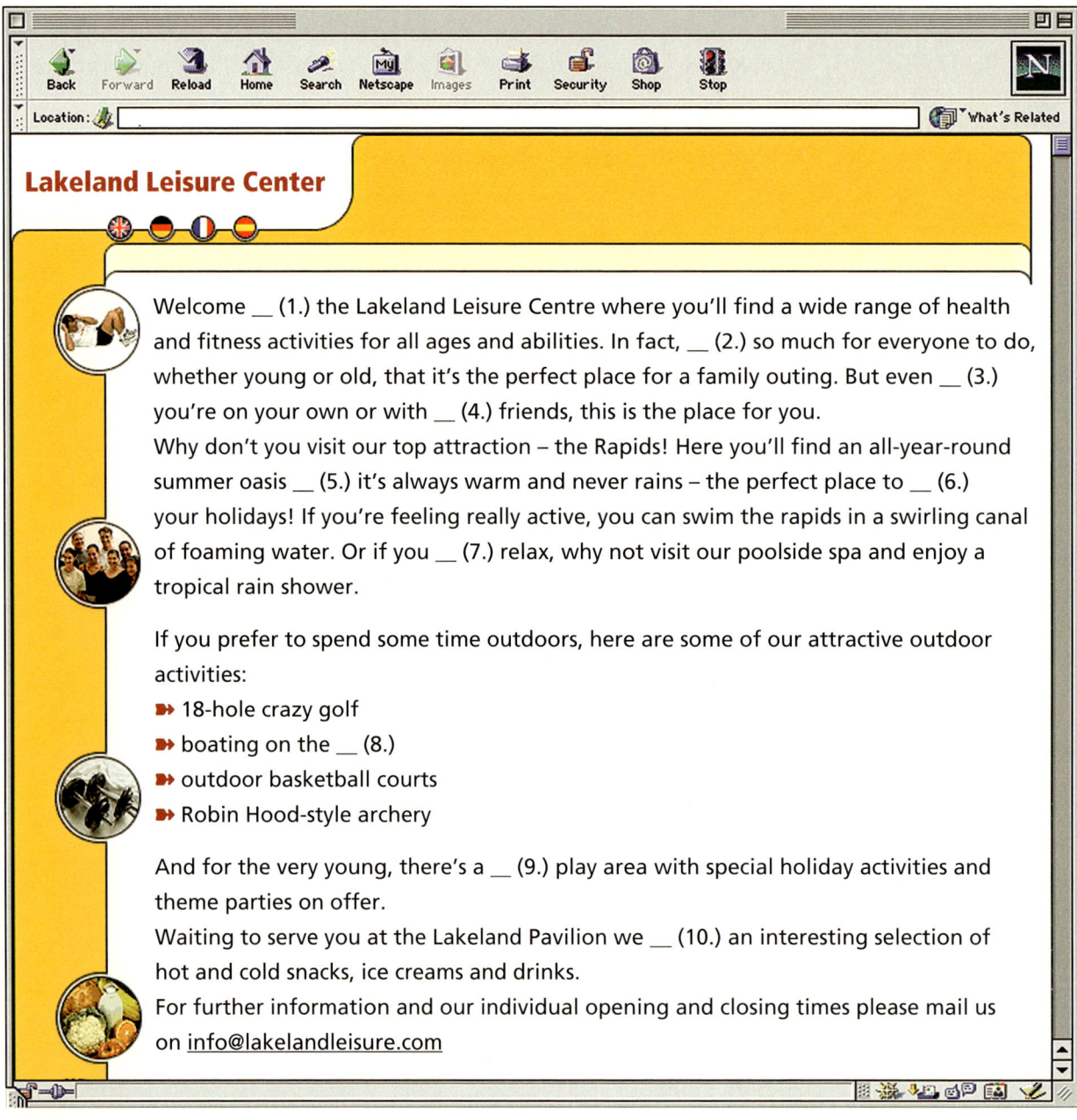

Lakeland Leisure Center

Welcome __ (1.) the Lakeland Leisure Centre where you'll find a wide range of health and fitness activities for all ages and abilities. In fact, __ (2.) so much for everyone to do, whether young or old, that it's the perfect place for a family outing. But even __ (3.) you're on your own or with __ (4.) friends, this is the place for you.

Why don't you visit our top attraction – the Rapids! Here you'll find an all-year-round summer oasis __ (5.) it's always warm and never rains – the perfect place to __ (6.) your holidays! If you're feeling really active, you can swim the rapids in a swirling canal of foaming water. Or if you __ (7.) relax, why not visit our poolside spa and enjoy a tropical rain shower.

If you prefer to spend some time outdoors, here are some of our attractive outdoor activities:
- 18-hole crazy golf
- boating on the __ (8.)
- outdoor basketball courts
- Robin Hood-style archery

And for the very young, there's a __ (9.) play area with special holiday activities and theme parties on offer.

Waiting to serve you at the Lakeland Pavilion we __ (10.) an interesting selection of hot and cold snacks, ice creams and drinks.

For further information and our individual opening and closing times please mail us on info@lakelandleisure.com

1. a. at   b. to   c. in   d. on
2. a. there is   b. it is   c. it gives   d. there are
3. a. if   b. when   c. so   d. that
4. a. a   b. any   c. some   d. their
5. a. who   b. what   c. that   d. where
6. a. bring   b. take   c. spend   d. give
7. a. will   b. enjoy   c. want to   d. would
8. a. sea   b. see   c. water   d. lake
9. a. children's b. childrens'   c. children   d. child
10. a. got   b. get   c. getting   d. 've got

2 Writing an e-mail

You have been asked to organise the office outing and think it would be nice to do something different. While browsing the Net you found the Lakeland Leisure Centre web site and decide to get some more information. Write an e-mail asking about the following points:

- the opening and closing times for the date of your office outing
- two additional outdoor and/or indoor activities you know some of your colleagues would be interested in
- the possibility of having a buffet / picnic / barbecue for your group (how many?)
- the costs (special group rates?)
- one other piece of information you would like to have

When you've written your mail, exchange it with someone else in your class. Write a reply, imagining you work for the Lakeland Leisure Centre, and hand it back.

3 Working with words: definitions

a Can you complete the missing words in each of theses sentences?

1. Something which costs a lot of money is e_____.
2. Someone who has a favourite football club is a s_____.
3. Someone who has a husband or wife is m_____.
4. Someone who gives medical treatment to animals is a v_____.
5. A house which is joined to another house is s_____.
6. A place where you can drink and chat with friends is a p_____.
7. Someone who cuts your hair is a h_____.
8. Something which is not sour is s_____.
9. Someone who is between 13 and 19 is a t_____.
10. Someone who travels to work and back home every day is a c_____.

b Now can you complete the definitions in each of these sentences?

1. Someone who _____ is single.
2. Something which _____ is a route-finder.
3. Someone _____ is a camel jockey.
4. Something _____ is a hobby.
5. Something _____ is cheap.
6. Someone _____ is a bank clerk.
7. Something _____ is a crate.
8. A place where _____ is a pharmacy.
9. Something where _____ is a cash machine.
10. Someone _____ is a stranger.

When you're finished, compare your ideas in small groups.
Then together, make up three sentences as in **a** and three sentences as in **b**. Use the first three units of the book to give you some ideas if you want. Pass your sentences on to another group in your class (you will also receive some sentences to complete) and then check the other group's suggestions when they are finished.

(Revision 1)

4 Speaking and writing

Carolyn and Robert are both looking for a partner and they write to a dating agency. The agency then sends Robert's profile to Carolyn and Carolyn's to Robert.

Profile 1

Name	Carolyn Robinson
Age	25
Occupation	bus driver
Hobbies	reading, swimming
Pets	two cats
TV	football, "Friends", holiday programmes
Favourite drink	Italian red wine
Favourite food	pasta
Dislikes	fish (allergic to it), mountain-biking
Holidays	by the sea
Languages	English and Italian

Profile 2

Name	Robert Linden
Age	28
Occupation	security guard
Hobbies	reading, mountain-biking
Pets	none (allergic to cats)
TV	football, holiday programmes, current affairs
Favourite drink	Coca Cola (never drinks alcohol)
Favourite food	fish
Dislikes	swimming
Holidays	in the mountains
Languages	German, English, Italian

Carolyn's talking to her friend about Robert's profile. She doesn't think he's her perfect partner, but her friend is always an optimist.

Carolyn: He's 28, that's a good age, but he doesn't like swimming.
Friend: Yes, but he likes reading.
Carolyn: But he doesn't drink alcohol.
Friend: Yes, but he _____.

Together with a partner, continue the conversation.

Then write a similar conversation that Robert could have with his friend about Carolyn's profile. Look in the key for some suggested answers.

5 Working with grammar: some and any

In the following sentences fill in the blanks with "some", "any" or "anything". Then order the sentences to make a short dialogue at a hotel. The first and the last sentences have been done for you.

__ **A** This is Mr Haberecht from room number 10. Er, there's a problem with my room.

9 **B** Not at all. Don't hesitate to ring again if we can be of assistance.

__ **C** Well, there aren't _____ towels and there isn't _____ soap.

__ **D** I'm very sorry about this Mr Haberecht. I'll ring the housekeeper right away. Is there _____ else you need?

1 **E** Reception. Can I help you?

__ **F** Er, yes. Could I have _____ ice for the mini bar, please.

__ **G** What seems to be the trouble exactly?

__ **H** Certainly. I'll send _____ up immediately.

__ **I** Thank you.

6 Pronunciation

How do you pronounce these words? Use the stress marks to help you.

chocolate	**choco**	late		different	**diffe**	rent		
usually	**u**	su	ally	favourite	**favou**	rite		
Wednesday	**Wednes**	day		business	**busi**	ness		
comfortable	**comfor**	ta	ble	anniversary	an	ni	**ver**	sary
commentary	**com**	men	tary	restaurant	**restau**	rant		
aspirin	**as**	pirin		vegetables	**vege**	ta	bles	
library	**li**	brary		evening	**eve**	ning		
interesting	**in**	terest	ing					

Listen to the CD and check that you were right.
No-one can hear you at home, so say the words after the recording!

Which letters do you not hear?
Listen again and cross them out.

7 Matching and listening

Do you remember the text about the camel racing in Unit 2? Here are some questions and answers taken from a radio interview with one of the jockeys. Match a question with an appropriate answer in the right-hand column.

1. What do you do?
2. What are you doing?
3. What else do you do?
4. Which do you prefer?
5. Who do you work for?
6. How old were you when you started racing?
7. Where was your last race?
8. How many races do you take part in each year?

a. I have my own company.
b. I train camels for Sahara treks.
c. The races.
d. Alice Springs.
e. I'm a camel jockey.
f. About 10-12.
g. I'm training for the next race.
h. 18.

Now listen to the radio interview and check your version.

Revision 1   41

(Unit 4)

Holidays

1 Every day

a How many sensible questions can you make out of this list of words?

for breakfast
your boss
does
have
finish work
what
when
your partner

Now fill in four more people in column 3 and four more verbs in column 4 in this table to make more questions.

1	2	3	4	5
			wear	at work
What				lunch?
When	does	your boss		for supper?
Where				work?
How		your partner		to work?
			spend	her/his holidays?

How many questions with "does" can you make from the table?

These questions all have the word "does" in them to ask questions about "every day". What little word do we use if we want to ask questions about "yesterday?"

> Where **did** your boss **spend** his holiday last year?

▷ Look at the grammar reference section on **page 139** to check how to make questions in the past.

b What did you do?

Think of all the verbs that describe holiday activities. Collect the verbs in groups. Your teacher will then write them on the board.

2 Holidays

a In groups fill in vocabulary on this word tree.

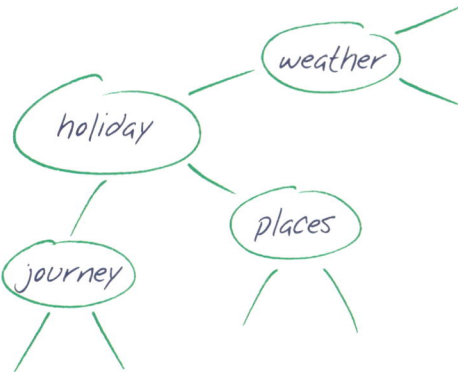

b The holiday

Find a partner. Partner **B** looks at this page and partner **A** looks at **page 123**. Ask your partner to give you the information that is missing and give her/him the information she/he asks for. Only give the information that is printed bold in your text. Partner **B** asks the first question and Partner **A** the second and so on. The first three questions have been done for you.

B Where did they go to? – Malaysia.
A How did they fly? – Singapore Airlines.
B Where did they fly to in Malaysia? – _____
A _____

etc.

Partner B

Last year it was Mr and Mrs Lang's 20th wedding anniversary, and they went on a wonderful holiday to _____ (where). They flew **Singapore Airlines** from London Heathrow to _____ (where). They flew first class. When they arrived, they spent **three** nights in the Federal Hotel in Kuala Lumpur and then _____ (how/get) to the new luxury resort on Pangkor Island. Their bedroom looked out over the sea, and it was air-conditioned. Temperatures in Malaysia rose to **35 degrees** during the day, and even in the evening it was 20 degrees. Every morning after a breakfast of _____ (what/eat) and **coffee** they relaxed _____ (where), drank **cold drinks** and wrote _____ (what) to their friends in England. In the afternoon they went **snorkelling** and saw _____ (what), and once they had a demonstration of how to fly a Malaysian kite. In the evenings they usually watched **Malaysian dancing**, but on their last evening they watched _____ (what). They only stayed for **two weeks**, and the holiday passed very quickly.

Unit 4 43

(Unit 4)

3 Sound interested

a In exercise **2b** one person asked a question and the other person answered it. When you are talking to a friend or business associate you sometimes ask questions, but you also want to sound interested! You can do this by using question tags.

Look at these short dialogues with question tags. When do you say "do you" and "did you"?

1. I always fly Lufthansa
   Do you? What's the service like?

2. I flew to Dubai last weekend.
   Did you? Did you stay in the world's only 7-star hotel?

3. I went to Edinburgh on business last year.
   Did you? Did you have good weather?

4. I love English beer.
   Do you? Most people prefer their beer cold.

5. I had an awful journey.
   Oh dear. Did you? What was the problem?

▷ Check your answers on **page 142** in the grammar reference section.

Now listen to the dialogues and notice the intonation of these tags. If you start with your voice too low, you won't sound interested.

b My enjoyable holiday / successful business trip

The Langs had a very enjoyable holiday. Work with a partner and tell her/him about one of your enjoyable holidays or successful business trips. If you are listening, try to sound interested! Remember regular and irregular verbs! Look at the list on **pages 162–163**.

> I **spent** a wonderful holiday in Kenya.
> I **enjoyed** my holiday in Kenya.

> **Learning Tip – Verb forms**
> When you learn new verbs, it's a good idea to learn the past tense, too!

4 Something different

The holiday in Malaysia was enjoyable for Mr and Mrs Lang because it was different. They usually go to France, go to art galleries and eat French food, but last year:

> They didn't go to France, they went to Malaysia.
> They didn't eat veal, they ate fresh pineapple.
> They didn't go to art galleries, they saw a puppet play.

Listen to the CD. On it you will hear about the Lang's holiday again, but this time there are mistakes in it. When you hear a mistake, ask the teacher to stop the CD and correct it.

5 The flight attendant

a Think of the things that a flight attendant does. Would you like to be a member of the cabin staff? Now you are going to hear about a flight attendant who had a very unusual job to do.

As you listen, cross out the words that you DON'T hear:

▷ betting / getting tired of my job
▷ delivered / delivering a baby
▷ worked / was working for Singapore Airlines
▷ flew / were flying between Abu Dhabi and Singapore
▷ watched / were watching the film
▷ the Indians attacked / were attacking the fort
▷ the soldiers were shouting / were shooting the Indians
▷ they heard / hurt the cry of a new-born baby
▷ she travelled to the airport / she was travelling to the airport
▷ her taxi collided / was colliding with a bus

> They **were flying** to Singapore when a passenger **complained** of pains.
> She **was travelling** to the airport when the taxi **collided** with a bus.

▷ Look at the grammar reference section on **page 141** to see how these two forms of the past go together.

b Talk to three people in the group and find out what they were doing / where they were working / where they were living when the following things happened:

| What were you doing
Where were you living
Where were you working | when | you started school?
you bought your first car?
your first child was born?
you met your wife / husband?
you met your present girlfriend / boyfriend?
Princess Diana died?
Germany was re-unified?
you got your first job?
the Euro became the new currency in the EU?
the new century began? |

> I'm not sure, I think I was …
> Let me see …
> I know exactly what I was doing because …
> No idea.

Now tell the group what you have found out.

(Back-up)

6 Just for fun

There are at least 20 irregular past tenses in this square arranged horizontally, vertically and diagonally. How many can you find? Write ten sentences using the verbs you found!

```
B S A W T O O K F B
E R O S A T E N O T
G N O T S P U E U P
A L O U T I H W N E
N H T H G U O B D L
S C A U G H T C E S
L T S P E N T U V S
L F H E A R D T A H
E E D A M A W S G U
F L E W F O R G O T
```

7 Holiday postcards

Imagine you're on holiday in one of the places shown on these postcards. Write a postcard to your English-speaking friends and tell them about your holiday. Use some irregular verbs in the past if you can!

8 The best weeks of the year?

Not for Mr and Mrs Windsor. They didn't enjoy their holiday at all. In the gaps in these sentences fill in the negatives of the following verbs: buy, hire, take, lie, enjoy, go. Make sense!

1. We _____ on the beach because it was so dirty.
2. We _____ to the market because of the pickpockets.
3. We _____ any souvenirs because they were so expensive.
4. We _____ a car because the drivers were so dangerous.
5. I _____ many photos because I broke my camera.
6. We _____ the food because it was so spicy.

I had a wonderful holiday. I stayed at home!

9 History?

What special events in history or in your own life do you remember? What were you doing / where were you living at the time? Write some sentences using the two forms of the past on a piece of paper and bring them to the next lesson.

10 Be an interested listener

You are talking to a friend, and she or he says the following things. What would you say to sound interested? Check your answers with the recording.

1. I met Claudia Schiffer last year.
   _____ ? What was she wearing?

2. We always go wind-surfing when we go on holiday.
   _____ ? Where do you go?

3. We spent Christmas in Florida last year.
   _____ ? What was the weather like?

4. We went to Berlin for the millennium celebrations.
   _____ ? Did you take any photographs?

5. I lost my passport when I was on holiday in Spain last year.
   _____ ? Did you go to the police station?

6. I had a car accident last week.
   Oh dear. _____ ? Not serious, I hope.

7. Our daughter got a divorce last year.
   Oh, _____ ? I'm sorry. Has she got any children?

Learning Tip – Intonation
Remember, if you want to sound sympathetic, your voice starts lower.

Now listen again. Notice how you sound interested. What is different about sentences 5., 6. and 7.? How is the intonation different?

(Unit 5)

Law and Order

1 Questions! Questions!

When did you last ride a bicycle?

When did you last kiss your partner?

When did you last take bottles to a container?

When did you last visit your parents/children?

Think of some of your own ideas and ask the questions.

When did you last punch a police officer?

Me? Never!

He's never punched a police officer.

> When did you last punch a police officer? – I've (have) never **punched** a police officer.
> And you? **Have** you ever **punched** a police officer? – No, never.
> **Have** you ever **parked** illegally? – Yes, I have.

▷ The form of the verb we are using here is called the present perfect. You use it in different ways. The first way is to talk about an indefinite time in the past. Look at the grammar reference section on **page 143** to check the form.

2 Contact with the police

a Go round and ask as many people as possible the following questions to find someone who has …

driven more than 60 km/h in a town.
travelled on the underground without a ticket.
parked illegally.
taken home stationery from the office.
taken part in a protest march.
mowed the lawn on a Sunday.
washed their car in the street in front of their house.
played loud music after 12 o'clock at night.
found something valuable in the street and taken it to the police.
had a car accident.

If someone says "YES", write down her/his name.

b Now tell the rest of the group what you have found out.

> Karl **has** never **taken** part in a protest march,
> but he **has played** music after twelve o'clock at night.

3 On a Sunday!

a Listen to this little conversation. In it someone says what happened when he mowed the lawn on a Sunday. As you listen fill in the verb forms.

☐ _____ you ever _____ the lawn on a Sunday?
○ Yes, I _____.
☐ When was that?
○ Last year. We _____ back after three weeks' holiday, and the lawn _____ very long, so we _____ it.
☐ And _____ anything _____?
○ Yes. One of our neighbours, we don't know which, _____ the police.

> ☐ **Have** you ever **mowed** the lawn on a Sunday?
> ○ Yes, I have. I **mowed** it when I came back from holiday.

▷ When do we use the simple past and when do we use the present perfect? Look at the grammar reference section on **page 143** to check your answers.

b Pairwork

Now talk to a person who answered "Yes" to two of your questions in **2a** and ask them to tell you more about it. When? Why? Did anything happen?

(Unit 5)

4 Crime stopper

a Have you ever witnessed a crime? Have you ever witnessed an accident? What did you do? Here is a true story of someone who prevented a serious crime.
Look at the title. – An 'eavesdropper' is someone who hears something that was not for them to hear. – What do you think the story will be about?

Saved by an Eavesdropper

■ Last year Gary McGee gave his wife, Donna, a police scanner for Christmas. "They are popular in Memphis," says the 40-year-old kindergarten teacher. "People like to listen to police calls. Sometimes a scanner will even pick up the President talking from Air Force One."

A couple of days later Donna learned she could also listen to conversations from cordless phones. She was listening to messages on her scanner when she heard a conversation between a man and a woman. The man asked: "Are you sure you want to do this?" McGee remembers. The woman said, "Yes. Do you love me enough to kill for me?" The man answered, "Yes." The conversation lasted about 45 minutes.

Horrified, McGee listened while the two people planned to murder Kenny, the woman's husband, for his insurance money, make the killing look like a break-in and use a green van to escape. As she was listening, McGee's daughter Stefanie joined her. It was like a soap opera. The date set for the crime was December 30.

Then as they were listening, they heard a young girl's voice. The woman shouted: "Get out of the room, Angela."

Stefanie said she knew a girl named Angela, and she lived four houses away. "And they have a green van," she told her mother. The McGees realized the woman on the phone was their neighbour Jacqueline Greene and the person she wanted killed was her husband Kenny.

McGee drove with her husband to the sheriff's office, where they gave a statement on tape. The police investigated, and later that day they arrested Jacqueline and her boyfriend Christopher Scott Davis and charged them with attempted murder.

On December 30 Kenny Greene visited McGee and hugged and thanked her. Mrs McGee hasn't got her scanner now. "It brought too much excitement," she says. ■

(adapted from a true story in Good Housekeeping)

b Look at the following sentences and put them in the correct order to give a summary of the story.

   a. On it she heard a conversation between a man and a woman planning a murder.
   b. They arrested Jacqueline Greene and her boyfriend and charged them.
   c. Donna McGee had a scanner for Christmas.
   d. Her daughter listened to the conversation with her and recognised the name Angela and the reference to a green van.
   e. Mrs McGee sold her scanner.
   f. They realised that one of the people on the phone was their neighbour Jacqueline Greene.
   g. Mr and Mrs McGee went to the police and gave a statement.

How do you feel about the story?

Which of the "crime words" from this unit do you want to put into your word bank?

> **Learning Tip – Word stress**
> Remember to mark the stress for new words. How can you find the stress from looking up the word in a dictionary? Ask your teacher if you can't find the answer.

5 The Presentation

The Managing Director of this ice-cream company is giving a presentation. He has also had problems with crime.

"Welcome to Mr Frosty Ice-cream Company ladies and gentlemen. As you know we have invested a lot of money in the company this year and I would like to talk to you about this. We've bought twenty robots that now do a lot of work in our factory in Bath and we've introduced a computerized ordering and delivery service that has also reduced costs. As you can see from these graphs our profit's increased this year by 15%. We've sold 20,000 tonnes more ice-cream this year than we sold in 2003. This is the good news.

Unfortunately 2000 people in the Bath factory have lost their jobs. We've also had three break-ins recently and so we've installed a new alarm system and employed one extra security guard. If there's a break-in, the alarm rings at the local police station. The police suspect that one of the men who lost their jobs last September is responsible."

a Underline the examples of the present perfect in this text. How is this form of the verb used here?

▷ Look at the grammar reference section on **page 143** to find out.

b Choose one of these jobs, or one of your own, and working in pairs write some sentences that this person might use in a presentation about their work this year.

- an investment adviser
- a writer
- the manager of an airline

6 The news

a You are going to listen to the news. The three stories are about fires, a robbery and drugs. Before you listen, try to decide some sentences you will hear. Choose one element from each of the three columns below: e.g. The police have taken the lorry driver to the police station.

The police (2x)	have stolen	large areas of a national park.
Art thieves	have seized	the firemen's jobs very difficult.
Fires	have destroyed	a reward.
Strong winds	have left	the lorry driver to the police station.
The art gallery	have taken	10 kilos of heroin.
Many families	has offered	their homes.
	have made	two paintings.

b Listen again and in groups see how much of each news story you can remember. Think again of why we use the present perfect so much in news bulletins. Has anything exciting (or dangerous?) happened in your area recently?

Unit 5 | 51

(Unit 5)

7 Wednesday Morning 3 am

a In this song you will hear these words:

breathing, asleep, hair, pillow, moonlight, heavy heart, recall (remember), crime, liquor store, unreal, morning, leaving.

What do you think the song is about?

Here are the four verses of the song, but the lines are in the wrong order. In groups try to sort them out. Then listen to the song and see if you were right.

- [ ] Reflecting the glow of the winter moonlight.
- [ ] As she lies here beside me asleep with the night
- [ ] I can hear the soft breathing of the girl that I love
- [ ] And her hair in a fine mist floats on my pillow

- [ ] And I watch as her breasts gently rise gently fall
- [ ] For I know at the first light of dawn I'll be leaving
- [ ] She is soft, she is warm, but my heart remains heavy
- [ ] And tonight will be all I have left to recall.

- [ ] I held up and robbed a hard liquor store.
- [ ] Oh, what have I done? Why have I done it?
- [ ] For twenty-five dollars and pieces of silver
- [ ] I've committed a crime. I've broken the law.

- [ ] The morning is just a few hours away.
- [ ] My life seems unreal, my crime an illusion
- [ ] A scene badly written in which I must play.
- [ ] Yet I know as I gaze at my young love beside me

By Simon & Garfunkel

b What do you think?

The man in the song "held up and robbed a hard liquor store".
Why do you think he did this?

a. He was an alcoholic?
b. He was unemployed and he wanted to get some money to buy a present for his girlfriend?
c. He had a lot of debts?
d. His friends persuaded him to go with them to hold up the liquor store?
e. Another reason?

Do you think his "young love" knew anything about the crime?
How old do you think the man is?

8 The lost property office

a Have you ever lost anything? Where did you go to find it? Listen to the following conversations in a lost property office and write down what the people have lost, a description of the lost item and where and when they lost it.

Dialogue	1	2
Item		
Description		
Where/when		

> Is this umbrella **yours**? No, that's not **mine**. **Mine's** dark blue. **My** bag's black, and **his** is blue.

▷ Look at the grammar reference section on **page 144** to check the difference between "my" and "mine".

b Working in pairs make up similar dialogues using the prompts given.

- umbrella / brown and white / on the bus
- wallet / driving licence / £50 in notes and some change / 2 photographs / on the train
- 2 tennis rackets / one in a blue case, one in a red one / in McDonald's
- red mountain bike / outside the swimming pool

Unit 5

(Back-up)

9 Simple past or present perfect?

Fill in the gaps in the following text with the simple past or the present perfect.
Be careful with the questions!

1. ○ Why isn't Henry playing squash this evening?
   □ Oh, didn't you know, he _____ (break) his leg.
   ○ Oh dear, how?
   □ He _____ (break) it while he was skiing in Austria. Some idiot who was skiing very fast _____ (hit) him from behind.
2. △ Right, madam. You _____ (lose) your purse. Where do you think you _____ (drop) it?
   ○ In the supermarket car park, I think. I _____ (have) it when I paid for my groceries.
   △ _____ (you talk) to the supermarket manager at the time?
   ○ Yes, I _____ (do).
   △ Well I'm afraid no-one _____ (hand it in) here, but we'll ring you if someone does.
3. □ Emergency. Which service do you require?
   △ Police and ambulance. It's very icy and a bus _____ (fall) on its side on the motorway.
   □ Can you give me your name, sir, and tell me exactly where you are.
4. △ Someone _____ (steal) my car from the station car park.
   ○ When _____ (you park) it there, sir?
   △ This morning at 7.45.
   ○ _____ (you lock) it?
   △ Of course, I _____ (do).

10 Where is it?

Match these sentences with the place where you would hear them.
The first one has been done for you.

1. He's scored two goals this season.
2. I've checked your luggage through to Bangkok, madam.
3. You've missed the connection, I'm afraid.
4. I've lost a green umbrella.
5. I think you've charged me for champagne from the mini-bar by mistake.
6. I think I've broken my finger.
7. Someone has stolen my passport.
8. You haven't countersigned this last traveller's cheque, sir.
9. I've checked the oil.
10. I've booked the tickets for Saturday.

○ hotel
○ airport
○ at home
① football stadium
○ station
○ bank
○ garage
○ hospital
○ lost property office
○ police station

Now, choose one of the sentences above, and make up a short dialogue you would hear in that situation and bring it with you to the next lesson.

> □ I've booked the tickets for Saturday.
> △ Great. It starts at 8, doesn't it?
> □ Yes. We should leave here about seven.
> △ That's fine. Any idea where the opera glasses are?

11 What is it?

a Read these sentences and decide what the people are talking about.

Mine eats a lot.
His is dangerous.
Hers has got long ears.
Theirs barks a lot.
Ours goes for a walk in the park twice a day.
Has yours got long legs?

Mine has got a stereo cassette player.
His is very old.
Hers is blue.
Theirs has got four-wheel drive.
Ours has got a sun-roof.
What's yours like?

Write some similar sentences using an idea of your own and give them to a partner to guess in the next lesson.

b ▷ Now check your possessive pronouns and adjectives in the grammar reference section on **page 144** and fill in the missing words in the following sentences.

1. Is that man over there _____ brother? He looks like you.
2. I don't like my boss, but _____ secretary likes him.
3. We're a two-car family. My husband's car is a Rover, and _____'s a Ford Fiesta.
4. My parents' neighbours have got a wonderful garden. It's not like _____; that's always untidy.
5. "_____ house is near the station, isn't it, Mrs Hut?" – "It isn't very convenient for the centre, but it's near the station as _____ husband commutes."

▷ Check your answers in the key.

> **Learning Tip – Listening**
> Note that "he's" can be short for "he is" or "he has"! If you understand short forms, you will find listening to spoken English easier!

12 Short forms

22

In spoken English we often use short forms. We say: "I've never punched a police officer" and not "I have never punched a police officer". Sometimes, however, we have to use the full form as in: "Have you ever lost your purse?" – "Yes, I have."

Look at this little text and put in short forms. Check your answers with the recording.

- ○ Where is Phillip?
- □ He has gone to the police station.
- ○ Why? What has happened? Is he OK?
- □ Do not panic, he is fine, but he has lost his driving licence. He thinks he dropped it in the post office yesterday because he used it then as a form of identification.
- ○ Has he asked there?
- □ Yes, he has, but no luck.
- ○ I have never lost mine, touch wood. I hope he is lucky, and someone has handed it in.
- □ Yeah. Let us hope so.

(Unit 6) Ecology Down Under

1 Questions! Questions!

Look at these pictures. Which country's this?

2 Green Olympics?

a Did you watch the Sydney Olympics? What will you remember about them? In the planning stages of the Sydney Olympics the organising committee considered very carefully the impact that such a big project would have on the environment and they tried to make the impact as small as possible. Make a list of what you think the committee considered.

Example: – save water

_____
_____
_____
_____
_____
_____
_____
_____

Now listen to the recording. How many of your suggestions did the committee consider? You too can help protect the environment. Look at the next page and decide what you are going to do.

b Save our planet

Have you decided to do anything about saving the planet? Work in groups and decide which of the following you're going to do and what you're not going to do. Why? Why not?

How many ideas can you add to the list?

We're going to / we're not going to	Yes	No	Why?
buy only returnable bottles.	☐	☐	
use recycled writing paper at home and in the office.	☐	☐	
cycle to the container with newspapers.	☐	☐	
have a shower once a week.	☐	☐	
buy only biodegradable cleaning products.	☐	☐	
have the central heating at 15 degrees in winter.	☐	☐	
buy plastic bags at the supermarket.	☐	☐	
water the garden in the summer.	☐	☐	
go skiing.	☐	☐	
play golf.	☐	☐	
buy only free-range eggs.	☐	☐	

▷ Why do we use the 'going to-form' in the sentences in **2b**?

3 The future

There are many ways of expressing the future in English.

> We**'re going to** recycle all our rubbish.
> I think the hole in the ozone layer **will get** worse.
> The opening ceremony of the next summer Olympics **will take place** in August.

▷ Look at the grammar reference section on **pages 144–146** to see how we use "will" and "going to" for the future.

4 An optimist or a pessimist?

Work in pairs. Partner **A** looks at **page 123** and partner **B** at **page 127**. What did you decide? Are you optimists or pessimists?

Examples: I think a lot of people will only buy recycled products in 2050.
More and more people will avoid sunbathing.

(Unit 6)

5 The trip to Australia

Mr and Mrs Robertson have won some money on the national lottery, so they're going to fly to Australia to visit their daughter who lives in Sydney with her husband and two young children. When they've organized everything, Mrs Robertson writes to her daughter to tell her all about it.

Read her letter and find out how many different places they are going to visit.

Dear Sarah,

Well, we've done it. We've organized the holiday, booked everything. I can't wait to see you all.

We're arriving in Sydney on April 6th. We're coming Qantas and having a stop over for two nights in Bangkok. The flight arrives in Sydney rather late, I'm afraid, 10.30 your time, so I hope you can still meet us.

Dad has planned all sorts of tours for us, so we won't be under your feet for too long! We've booked one of those round-Australia flights that you can get from Ansett, or is it Australian Airlines? Anyway, one of those tickets where you can stay as long as you like in one place and then fly on.

When we leave you on April 27, we're flying to Cairns and from there we're going on a cruise round the Barrier Reef for a week. Then we're flying on to Darwin, and from there we're going out to Kakadu National Park. We're staying in a place called Jabiru, you know, the place with the hotel shaped like a crocodile! I want to see the Aboriginal Art sites there and the bird life, of course.

After that we're flying on to Alice Springs on 12th. Your Dad wants to see the Flying Doctor service headquarters there. We're not staying in Alice itself very long. Only three nights, and then we're flying out in one of those little light aircraft to Ayers Rock. It isn't called that anymore though, is it? Well, you know what I mean. I'm not going to climb it, but your Dad might have a go! What do you think?

From there we're flying on to Adelaide on 17th. Your Dad's old friend James Hughes is still professor of geology at the university there, and he's invited us to stay with him and his wife Jean until 24th. Dad wants to drink some good wine from the Barossa Valley, but I'm more interested in buying myself an opal. They come down direct from Coober Pedy and are cheap in Adelaide, aren't they?

Well, from Adelaide it's back to Sydney. Our flight arrives on Saturday evening, late again, I'm afraid, but then we can have a few relaxing days with you before we fly home on June 1st.

I hope your cold's better. I'll phone you as usual on Saturday. Give our love to Kevin and the children.

Lots of love, Mum

a You've read the letter and a friend asks you about what you can do on a holiday in Australia. What do you tell her/him?

> What's there to do in Australia?
> – Well, you could go diving.
> – There are lots of national parks.

b The visit

Now read the letter again and fill in Mrs Robertson's diary for the trip.

April
5 Good Friday
6 Arrive Sydney
7 Easter Sunday
27
28 cruise

May
4 cruise
12
15 Ayers Rock
24
26 Pentecost Sunday

March
1 2 3
4 5 6 7 8 9 10
11 12 13 14 15 16 17
18 19 20 21 22 23 24
25 26 27 28 29 30 31

June
Leave Sydney 1 2
3 4 5 6 7 8 9
10 11 12 13 14 15 16
17 18 19 20 21 22 23
24 25 26 27 28 29 30

Monday | You | Partner
Tuesday
Wednesday
Thursday
Friday
Saturday
Sunday

c It's all arranged

In this letter we have examples of another way of talking about the future in English.

> We're coming Qantas.

How's this different from "will" and "going to"? You'll often hear it in English, so it's a good idea to understand it.

▷ Look at the grammar reference section on **page 146**.

d Your diary

Fill in your arrangements for next week in this diary. Then talk to a partner and ask what she/he's doing next week.

Share some things you found out with the rest of the group.

> _____ and I are both _____-ing _____ .

Unit 6

(Unit 6)

6 Welcome!

a You work for a wine company in your area that specialises in the import of Australian wines and the export of German wines.
Your partner in Sydney has run a competition to promote the sale of German wines and the prize for four lucky winners is a free flight to Germany and a one-week holiday in October. All the prize winners will stay together for a week. On **page 124** there is some information about the visitors. You work in the PR department of the wine company. Work in groups and decide where you are going to take the winners.

Note how to make suggestions:

> How about going to a museum?
> Shall we take them to a lake somewhere?

> **Agreeing**
> Yes. That's a good idea.
> Yes. I agree with that.

If you disagree with suggestions remember to do so politely!

> **Disagreeing**
> Well, yes, but couldn't we …
> Well, maybe, but I think it would be better to …

b Now let's hear the groups' suggestions. Which trip would people in the class vote for and why?

c Are you a "comper"? – A "comper" is a new word in the English language. What do you think it means?

"A comper is a person who spends a lot of time entering competitions, because she/he wants to win good prizes (like the trip to Germany for the Australians)."

Have you ever entered a competition? Have you ever won anything? What did you win?

7 A good holiday?

a You're going to listen to a man who works for the Great Barrier Reef Marine Park talking about his job. Do you know anything about the Great Barrier Reef?

As you listen, answer the questions. Use the answer lines to make a note of the key words. Then put these into full sentences after you have finished listening.

1. When and why was the Great Barrier Reef Marine Park founded?
   _____
   _____

2. The reef's divided into zones. What three does he mention?
   _____
   _____

3. How does tourism damage the reef?
   _____
   _____

4. Is it only tourists who damage the area?
   _____
   _____

b Harmful sports?

Alistair Grant doesn't say that diving is harmful to the reef. What do you think? Which of these sports do YOU think is the most harmful to the environment? For example, if you think wind-surfing damages the environment the most, write number 1 next to it.

golf	
downhill skiing	
cross-country skiing	
mountain biking	
wind-surfing	
hang-gliding	

Now talk to a partner.
Has she/he got the same numbers as you? Explain your opinion.
See if she/he agrees with you. If you disagree, remember to disagree politely!

What does the whole group think?

Unit 6

(Back-up)

8 On the phone

Here are two phone conversations, but they've got very mixed up. Can you sort them out? Here is some information to help you.

- Brian's telephone number is Hemel Hempstead 58023, and Jane's phone number is 0171 242 1437.
- Alice is Jane's flatmate.
- Roy is Jane's boyfriend.
- Brian is a friend of Peter's.

Try to collect the sentences for one dialogue and then sort them out.

A Hemel Hempstead 58023.
B Jane?
C No, this is Alice.
D Is that Brian?
E Yes.
F Well, the film finishes at 8.30, I think, so she should be back at about 9.
G Hi, this is Peter.
H Oh, hello, Peter. How are you?
I Fine. Look Brian, Kate, Jean and I are going to a pop concert near Avesbury next week. Would you like to come?
J No, she's not, I'm afraid. She's gone to the cinema with Pam.
K Yes, I'd love to. How are you getting there? Are you driving down?
L Oh, Alice, I didn't recognize your voice. This is Roy. Is Jane there, please?
M Yes, we're leaving at about 4 on Friday.
N Fine.
O I'll pick you up just before 4 then. OK?
P Great. See you then. Bye.
Q Bye.
R Yes, I'll tell her. Bye.
S Thanks. Bye.
T 0171 242 1437
U Any idea when she'll be back?
V OK. Can you tell her I phoned, and I'll phone again about 9.15?

Dialogue 1

1 ☐
2 ☐
3 ☐
4 ☐
5 ☐
6 ☐
7 ☐
8 ☐
9 ☐
10 ☐
11 ☐
12 ☐

Dialogue 2

1 ☐
2 ☐
3 ☐
4 ☐
5 ☐
6 ☐
7 ☐
8 ☐
9 ☐
10 ☐

9 Everyday English

Read the following sentences and choose the best reaction from the list on the right.

1. We're getting married next Saturday.
2. I'm playing tennis with the club champion tomorrow.
3. I'm going to the doctor's at two o'clock.
4. The boss is flying to the Bahamas next Wednesday for a four week holiday.
5. I'm catching the ten o'clock train from the main station.
6. I won't be able to come to the party on Saturday, I'm afraid.
7. Are you going to the David Copperfield show on Friday?
8. I'll phone you again when I get back from Tuscany.
9. I'm going to the launderette after work. My washing machine's broken down.
10. We're inviting some friends for dinner on Saturday. Would you and Charles like to come, too?

___ Congratulations.
___ The lucky man!
___ Good luck.
___ Yes. We'd love to.
___ Oh, that's a nuisance.
___ Nothing serious, I hope.
___ Have a good journey.
___ What a shame.
___ OK. Have a good holiday.
___ No, I didn't get a ticket, unfortunately.

10 The pessimist

Here people are talking about their holiday plans. Their friend is a pessimist. What does he predict will happen on their holiday? Choose his answers.

1. ☐ We're going to fly British Airways.
2. ☐ We're going to have a diving holiday.
3. ☐ We're going to spend three weeks in a luxury resort in Morocco.
4. ☐ We're going to climb Ayers Rock.
5. ☐ My son's going to have a wind-surfing holiday in Fuerteventura.

A You'll never get to the top at your age!
B You won't like the food.
C There'll be a strike of air traffic controllers. They always go on strike in the summer.
D There won't be enough wind at this time of year.
E You'll frighten the fish.

11 Running together of sounds

a Where are these people going? Match the places they are going with the names as you listen.

Gill	Antalya
Charles	Melbourne
Mike	Edinburgh
Mrs Hatton	Rome
Sheila	Ottawa
Walter	Athens
Carolyn	Alice Springs
David Quarrie	Garmisch
Bruce Foster	Istanbul
Helen	Aspen

b The little word "to" in these sentences is not important, so it is unstressed, but it has two different sounds. Listen again and decide if the sound is [ə] or [uː].

> **Learning Tip – Unstressed sounds**
> Notice the running together of sounds when you listen to the dialogues in this course. We don't have the stop in English, and we run sounds together if there's a consonant at the end of one word and a vowel at the beginning of the next one. "He's‿an‿actor."
>
> If you make the stop, you can sound unfriendly, so try to run the words together.
>
> If there's a vowel at the end of one word (to) and a vowel at the beginning of the next one (Edinburgh) then we still run the sounds together because we add the sound [w]
>
> Gill's going to   Edinburgh.
> [tuː‿w‿e]
>
> You'll find listening easier if you understand this running together of sounds.

c Now listen again. How many other examples of the unstressed sound [ə] can you hear in these sentences? We talked about this sound in **Unit 3**.

(Revision 2)

1 Working with grammar: simple past

The letters of these past tense forms have got jumbled up. Can you put them in the correct order?

newt   went
solt   _____
tea   _____
trowe   _____
rahed   _____
gans   _____
hoghutt   _____
lotes   _____
apid   _____

Now put each simple past tense form together with its infinitive and past participle.

go	went	gone
___	___	___
___	___	___
___	___	___
___	___	___
___	___	___
___	___	___
___	___	___
___	___	___

How many of these verbs have three different forms and how many have only two?

2 Working with grammar: present perfect and simple past

a Put a suitable verb in the following chart:

Have you ever

_____	your leg?	**(a)**
_____	octopus?	**(b)**
_____	a tractor?	**(c)**
_____	a famous person?	**(d)**
_____	champagne for breakfast?	**(e)**
_____	a high mountain?	**(f)**
_____	a car accident?	**(g)**
_____	a protest march?	**(h)**

b We asked some people the questions in **2a**. Here are their answers. Put the correct form of the verb in the blanks below and decide which answer fits which question.

___ 1. Yes, I have. I _____ (get) to the top of the Eiger when I was on holiday in Switzerland last year.

___ 2. Yes, I have. I _____ (have) a bad accident when I was skiing in Colorado two years ago.

___ 3. No, I haven't, but my husband has. He _____ (grow up) on a farm.

___ 4. Yes, I have. I _____ (shake) hands with Prince Charles when he came to Munich in October 1995.

___ 5. Yes, I have. We _____ (celebrate) with it on our first wedding anniversary.

___ 6. No, I haven't. I'm allergic to seafood.

___ 7. Yes, I have, unfortunately. I _____ (drive) into the back of the car in front of me when the road was very icy in the winter of 1996.

___ 8. Yes, I have. When I was a student, the South African rugby team _____ (come) to our university town and a lot of students _____ (march) through the streets then.

3 Working with grammar: simple past and past progressive

Choosing one item from each column make up some sentences using the simple past and the past progressive:

I	drive	to Florida		his lover	run out of	an accident
he	fly	a newspaper		he	meet	his passport
she	travel	a bath	when	the postman	have	a parcel
we	read	to work		a mugger	steal	his wife
they	have	abroad		she	bring	petrol

> He **was driving** to work when he **ran** out of petrol.

4 Working with grammar: future forms

Have a look at this pair of sentences. What is the difference in meaning between them?

1. I'll get some petrol on the way to work.
2. I'm going to get some petrol on the way to work.

Could you also say 'I'm getting some petrol on the way to work'?

▷ Check up on the use of the different future forms on **pages 144–146** in the grammar reference section if you're unsure.

Now have a look at the following text and decide which future form would be best in each case. Think about the speech intention you want to express.

I'm seeing / will see / am going to see my dentist tomorrow at eleven o'clock. After the appointment at the dentist's I'm going to meet / I'm meeting / I'll meet a friend for lunch.

She'll probably be late / is probably going to be late. I have known her for ten years and she's never been on time! We're going to have lunch / are having lunch in a beer garden if the weather is hot.

It's going to be / it'll be nice to see her but I can't stay long because I'm taking / I'm going to take / I'll take the children swimming at three o'clock. They always go swimming on Thursdays. My youngest daughter's a very good swimmer.

She'll be / is going to be seven in two weeks and she has been able to swim since she was three! We are having / we'll have a birthday party for her but she hasn't decided how many people she's inviting / is going to invite. All I know is that I'll be exhausted / I'm going to be exhausted after the party.

(Revision 2)

TAKE A BREAK WITH ACORN

Bonfire Dance Weekend
Murder Mystery Weekends
Bridge & Scrabble Weekends
Over 50 Arts & Craft Courses
Walking • Wildlife • Golf
Gourmet Cooking
Cider & Wine Tasting
Festive Decorating Course
Learn to Drive • Learn to Swim

For your free brochure
with over 100 activities

ACORN ACTIVITIES
7 East Street, Hereford HR1 4RY
Tel: 01432 357335

"akes" selected inspected in Lakeland. For 4 32321.

COAST & COUNTRYSIDE Colour brochure of 500 farmhouses /cottages throughout Wales. All tourist board inspected/graded. WALES HOLIDAYS 01686 625267.

Small, friendly, private, ETB 3 Crown. All en-suite, backing onto National Trust, overlooking sea. NON-SMOKING, PARKING, SPECIAL OFFER 5 Course DB&B £26 p.n. or £169 p.w. Summer 4 night specials DB&B from £115 inc. cost of car ferry. Sorry no children or pets.
Tel: 01983 853109

CHILDREN WELCOME

A PARADISE for parents perfect for children. Facilities inc. playgroup, entertainment, indoor heated pools, games room, eve baby listening. All rooms ensuite. Superb cuisine.
♛♛ Commended

Radfords Country Hotel, Dawlish, Devon. EX7 0QN
Tel: 01626 863322
VERY SPECIAL OFFERS AVAILABLE IN JUNE

BRECON BEACONS. Over 100 s/c cottages some sleep to 30. Many less than £250 pw high season. Tel: 01874 676446.

EDINBURGH FESTIVAL Central 1st floor flat, clean, comfortable, 2 twins, all mod cons. £250 pw. Avail 10th-31st Aug. 01890 840633

ESCAPE THE Crowds.Guided & Independent. Hillwalking & Trekking with Irish Ways. Broch. Tel/Fax 003535527479.

A BIG BARGAIN BREAK. Enjoy your Autumn break in Ireland in one of our approved cotts. From mid-September your second week is rent free. Also 5 & 7 day bargain farmhouse holidays. Phone Irish Country Holidays nNow on 01 502 560 688 (24hrs)

N.WALES 1,000 cottages, etc. Free brochures 01758 701 702.

ST DAVIDS Coastal studio, slps 2, gdn, Sept/Oct. 01437 720001

NORTHUMBRIA BYWAYS. S/c cotts. Unspoilt locs.01228 573337.

HISTORIC COUNTRY HOUSE. 4 nights DB&B from £140 pp. Glen Rothay Hotel, Rydal Water. Tel: 0500-657-847.

PEMBS. Best selection of quality, sensibly priced cottages. Col. Broch. 01239 881297, Pembs Coast & Country Cottages.

Master Builder's Hotel

The Master Builder's Hotel at Bucklers Hard in Hampshire is proud of its link with British history. Henry Adams, who built ships for Lord Nelson, lived and worked in the house. The hotel serves good traditional English ales and offers accommodation to suit all tastes and budgets.

Master Builder's Hotel
Bucklers Hard, Hampshire
Tel. 01590-616253

PORT ISAAC Selection of S/C cottages in fishing village, personally chosen for position and comfort. Vacancies September onwards. Brochure 01208 880302.

FOWEY/POLRUAN. Charming Waterside cottages with CH & CTV. Superb views. Dinghies available. Pets welc 01726 870406

LUXURY farm cottages, indoor swimming pool Brch 01726 75174.

CORNWALL & DEVON.300 cottages throughout.01752 260711.

CONNEMARA: Co Galway Cashel House Hotel- Gardens Restaurant and Riding Stables-Tel:00 353 95 31001.Fax 31077.

HILLTHWAITE HOUSE,Windermere Thornbarrow Road, overlooking lake. All rooms ensuite (some with Jacuzzi baths) Satellite TV, teamaking, Sauna, Tylo Steam Room & heated indoor pool solely for our guests' use. 2 nights, 5 course Dinner Bed & Breakfast incl.VAT only £99. 3 nights only £130. 015394 43636.

A free-house pub in peaceful Dorset offering comfortable family accommodation. Garden with two slides and swimming pool. Small portions of food for the children.
Fox Inn
Wood Lane, Dorset
Tel: 01282 33278

YORKSHIRE DALES

Total comfort & relaxation.
Wonderful fresh food. Home baked bread.
No smoking. No tv. Bliss! Colour brochure:

SCARR HOUSE,
Thoralby, Bishopdale, DL8 3SU
Tel: 01969 663654

DEVON CONNECTIONS Luxury thatched cottage, barns & hses. Also Dartmoor. 01548 560964.

SHAMROCK COTTAGES. 50 High St. Wellington, Somerset. 01823 681060. Col Broch of 280 Select Houses. Disc Fares AITO.

LAKELANDS best cottages and apartments around Windemere. FREE Leisure club facs. Some lake views. 01564 771150.

COSY WASDALE Cottages in 7 riverside acres. Slps 2/4 & 5/7 GCH, avail fr Sept.01946 726233.

INVENT your own Multi Activity Break. Over 80 activities avail incl 4x4 Driving, Quad Biking, Karting, Sailing, Riding, Gliding, Painting & Crafts. Come for a weekend or stay a week and choose something different every day! Accomm arranged from £20 per night. Groups and singles welcome.
ANGLIAN ACTIVITY BREAKS 01508 492132

Bovey Tracay, S.Devon TQ13 9EY
Beautiful Country House hotel with spectacular views of Dartmoor. 24 bedrooms with all facilities. Good walking, riding and golf nearby or relax in our new indoor swimming pool, sauna & solarium. For a special offer with excellent cuisine, DB&B £38 pppn for 3 nts or more
AA ★★ **Tel 01626 832476** RAC ★★★

HISTORIC COUNTRY HOUSE. 4 nights DB&B from £140 pp. Glen Rothay Hotel, Rydal Water. Tel: 0500-657-847.

LAKELOVERS. The cream of Lake District self catering holiday homes at value for money prices. Freephone 0500 131227

COTTAGES, caravans & campsite holidays. Last min vacancy service/broch. 017687 75500

LAKE DISTRICT Specialists Choose from 375 cottages. 01282 445726 (LOA105)

NORFOLK Beautiful Collection of Holiday Homes. Brochure Norfolk Country Cottages 01603 871872

ST NON'S HOTEL, St David's. It's a great place to stay following a change of ownership and extensive refurbishment. Good food and reasonable prices too. It's a myth that there is oil around St David's peninsula which is as beautiful as ever. B&B from £32 per person. TEL: 01437-720239

HARRIER TRAILS. Norfolk guided walks thru intimate Broadland landscapes,relaxed stay at superbly located riverside home. Tel/fax 01692 630792.

ACTION HOLIDAYS, 5 to 15 yr olds. Superb centres. 1 to 4 staff ratio. Tel: 01706 814554.

AMAZING Colourful canal boats. Chug thru' the Chilterns. Bridgewater Boats 01442 863615.

CANALBOAT HOLIDAYS Free brochure. Route planner & Vacancy chart. Tel 01327 340739

CRUISE THE CANALS - Hire a narrowboat fr Claymoore Navigation, Cheshire. 01928 717273

GOWER. Idyllic 3 crown 17thC Farmhouse. Ensuite B&B & EM £25.50. Lic bar. Log fires, fishing AA/RAC. Broch 01269 595640

DOWLISH WAKE Quality village 1-8 June 01460-54128 anytime

ISLE OF IONA. St Columba Hotel next to Abbey offers peaceful Hebridean holiday on this tiny Island with superb views and lovely beaches; home cooking. Children welcome. Brochure: Angus Johnston, Argyll, PA76 6SL. 01681 700 304/700 335

COSY COTTAGES IN far N.West. Choice of remote sandy bay or quiet costal Village.Lochs, Mountains,Beaches.01732 882320

LITTLE HAVEN Pembs National Park. Stone cotts close to safe beaches.Stephens (01291)623337

PEMBS Large s/c house, Sleeps 10. (Discount for fewer people) Available Sept. Tel 01437 710324.

SCOTLANDS WELCOME Cottages. Pets, linen, fuel inc. Many less than £300 p/w May-September. Brochure. 01756 702213.

THE CREAM OF COTTAGES. 400 in all loveliest parts of the UK. Phone 01305 268988.

HAMSTER COTTAGES Throughout Scotland. Brochure 01899 308543 or 308775.

LAKELANDS best cottages and apartments around Windemere. FREE Leisure club facs. Some lake views. 01564 771150.

Coastal Cottages
of North Devon

A superb selection of cottages near sandy beaches & unspoilt coast.
Colour brochure
Caen Street, Braunton,
N.Devon EX33 1AA
01271 814984/816448

Old Manor Estate

Come and be spoilt at this superbly positioned hotel.
Relax in style and enjoy our Health and Fitness Spa,
Beauty Programme, Fine Golf Course and Tennis Court,
Sheltered Gardens, Fine Food and Friendly Service.

Prices start from £160 per person per night.

You'll never want to leave.

South Sands, Salcombe, South Devon
Tel: 01548-925634   Fax: 01548-925635

AA Rosette and Courtesy Award ♛♛♛♛♛ ETB Highly Commended

LAKE DISTRICT. Over 200 self catering cottages, flats & houses. Great value holidays. Free use of leisure facilities. Free colour brochure. HOLIDAYS IN LAKELAND. Tel 015395 31549.

DEVON CONNECTIONS Luxury thatched cottage, barns & hses. Also Dartmoor. 01548 560964.

CUMBRIA/LAKE District We've got it all! Free 1996 official 120 pg colour guide phone 0191 518 3933

BEST IN WALES 400 luxury cotts in beachside locations. Unbeatable prices. Coastal Cottages of Pembrokeshire. Tel 01437 765765

LYME REGIS and Seaton cottages, 01297 33078/0181 904 4581

WEST DORSET v. comf. cottage, gardens, 1m sea, sips 6, free 25th August on: 0171 9784705

HILLTHWAITE HOUSE,Windermere Thornbarrow Road, overlooking lake. 015394 43636.

586,000 Observer readers have taken a holiday in the UK in the past year. They are more likely to have taken a British holiday than readers of any other quality Sunday title. Source: TGI 1995

5 Reading and writing

a Look at the advertisements on p. 66 for places to stay in Britain.
Decide which hotel or pub would be good for which people.

1 Angela and Alan have a small baby and two children aged 6 and 10. They want to have a holiday where there are a lot of activities for the children, but where they themselves can relax and have good food. They would also like to go out and enjoy themselves in the evening without the children.

2 Rod and his family want to stay in a pub. Rosemary likes the atmosphere in pubs. "The people are friendly, and I feel I can really make myself at home. And Rod likes warm English beer!" They want to have good food, and they have one daughter and hope that children can stay in pubs!

3 George and his wife Sandra usually rent a cottage for their summer holiday. "That way we can completely please ourselves," says Sandra. Cooking is one of George's hobbies, but he doesn't have much time to cook when he's not on holiday. They want peace on their holiday, and they would like to be by the sea.

4 Jim and Mieke want to stay in a pub when they tour the southern part of Britain. "We don't book our holiday in advance because then we can always be flexible, but it's sometimes expensive. We usually stay in pubs and then we treat ourselves to a good hotel in London at the end of the holiday," Mieke explains. They're particularly interested in British history.

5 Sarah, Andrew, David and Ruth are students, and so they haven't got much money. They want to go away for the weekend to celebrate. They took their exams last week. They love sports of all kinds but want to try something different.

6 Marjorie and Robert Stevens and Vanessa and Brian Thomas want to go away together for a long weekend. The two husbands are top directors of an electronics company and have very stressful jobs. They want to relax and play golf while their wives spoil themselves with a weekend of beauty treatment.

b And you?

Which sort of hotel accommodation would the members of the group choose. Money is not a problem, of course!

c Here's an e-mail written to one of the places advertised to ask for a colour brochure and more details. There's something very wrong with the word-processor, and all the words in the sentences are mixed up. Can you sort them out?
Now choose one of the places advertised on page 66 and write an e-mail asking for details.

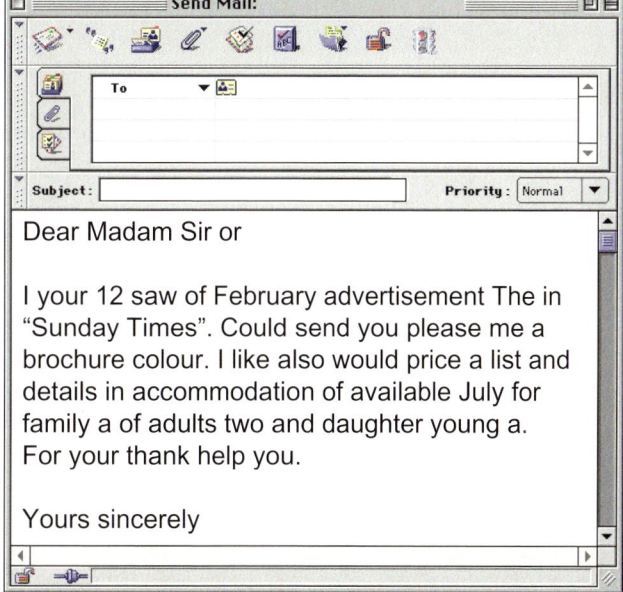

Dear Madam Sir or

I your 12 saw of February advertisement The in "Sunday Times". Could send you please me a brochure colour. I like also would price a list and details in accommodation of available July for family a of adults two and daughter young a.
For your thank help you.

Yours sincerely

(Unit 7)

A Question of Luck

1 What's the weather like?

a How many words do you know to describe the weather? (adjectives and nouns) Arrange them in good and bad weather trees.

b Compare your weather trees with a partner and add any words you want to remember. Use the words in your trees to make up four new weather trees, this time for the four seasons of the year: spring, summer, autumn and winter. You'll probably use some words more than once.

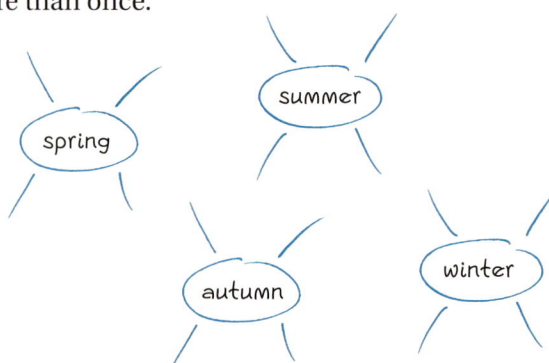

c Talk to your partner about your favourite time of year. What kind of weather do you love/hate? Which season of the year do you prefer? Are you a summer or winter person, spring or autumn type?

2 Weather forecasts

a Listen to the following forecast and decide which of the two weather charts it fits.

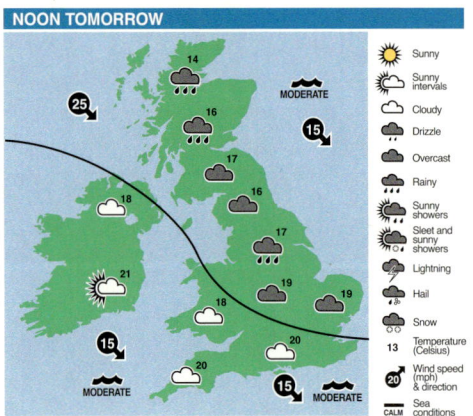 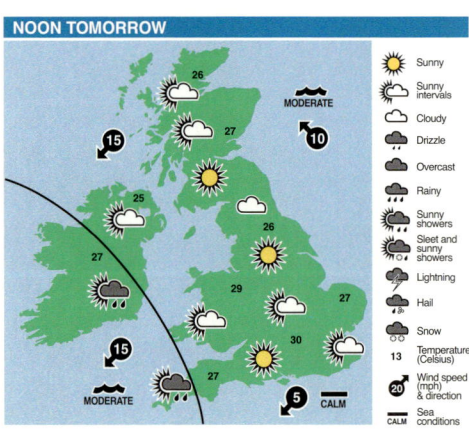

b Your partner has just missed the weather forecast. Tell him/her what the weather will be like if you live in Belfast, Manchester, Cornwall, Aberdeen, North Wales, Dublin.

Look at this example. They live in London.

> ☐ Have you heard tomorrow's weather forecast?
> ○ Yes, it'll be another dry, hot day.

c Together with a partner try to make up a forecast for the other weather chart.

3 If only it snows!

a When did you last experience a white Christmas? Where was that? Does it usually snow at Xmas where you live? Would you ever bet money on the possibility of a white Xmas? Have a look at the following newspaper article. Do you think you could ever find an article like this about the country you live in?

If only it snows!

THAT'S what thousands of people around the country are wishing as Xmas draws near. The chances of a white Xmas are not bad. Biting winds, falling temperatures and grey skies were a sure sign yesterday that winter had taken its grip on Britain. Freezing north-easterly winds from Scandinavia reached most of the UK over the weekend with temperatures dropping to near freezing-point last night. Reports from the met office warned that the cold snap was likely to keep the country shivering for at least four more days.

In most areas, however, there was still no sign of snow. Dartmoor was the

only exception, with reports that some light snow had fallen in the afternoon. Good news for snow lovers came from the met office with the prediction of some snow in the middle of the week. There was, however, a question mark over where that might be and whether temperatures would be low enough.

It's not only snow lovers who are keeping their fingers crossed. For some people a white Xmas could mean an extra Xmas present as bookmakers continue to report good business with bets on the chance of snow for Xmas. The bookies, who are offering odds of 4-1 have taken more than £25,000 worth of bets since last Boxing Day. According to a William Hill spokesman, punters will win their bets even if only a single snowflake falls on Christmas Day.

(adapted from a text in The Guardian)

b Here are some words and expressions from the article. Work with a partner and decide which of the following explanations is correct in each case.

1. A cold snap is
   - ☐ an ice-cold drink.
   - ☐ a sudden period of very cold weather.
   - ☐ a way to get rid of a cold.

2. Bookmakers
   - ☐ take bets.
   - ☐ make books.
   - ☐ look after finances.

3. A punter is someone who
   - ☐ places a bet.
   - ☐ likes to take a boat out on the river.
   - ☐ likes to play putting.

c Have another look at the article and decide whether these statements are true, false or possible.

	True	False	Possible
1. It doesn't always snow in Britain at Xmas.	☐	☐	☐
2. The weather in Britain yesterday was quite winter-like.	☐	☐	☐
3. The weather forecast is for better weather in the next few days.	☐	☐	☐
4. There was no snow at all in the UK yesterday.	☐	☐	☐
5. There will be snow during the week.	☐	☐	☐
6. In Britain you can bet money that there will be a white Xmas.	☐	☐	☐
7. People started to place their bets on 26 December last year.	☐	☐	☐
8. Bookmakers will lose at least £100,000 on these bets.	☐	☐	☐

Discuss your choices with a partner.

Unit 7

(Unit 7)

3d What do you think is the best ending for this sentence?

If it snows on Christmas Day, some people will be very
- ☐ happy.
- ☐ disappointed.
- ☐ rich.

4 Conditions

a Take another look at the sentence in **3d** with your chosen ending. Divide the sentence into two parts and enter them in the following table.

if-clause	main clause

▷ Compare with the grammar reference section on **page 146**. This is what we call a real condition because there is a good chance that it will happen and we are sure of what will happen if the condition is fulfilled.

b Put together an if-clause and a main clause to make sensible statements.

1. I'll call you tomorrow
2. We'll take the train
3. You'll get sunburnt
4. I'll be late for work
5. The hole in the ozone layer will get bigger
6. They'll go on a world trip
7. She'll do well in the exam
8. The milk will go sour

A if you stay in the sun too long.
B if she studies hard.
C if they win the lottery.
D if I can't come.
E if you don't put it in the fridge.
F if I miss the bus.
G if the weather is bad.
H if we don't stop using CFC's.

c Complete the following if-sentences with your own endings. Think about the verb forms!

1. I'll send you an e-mail if _____.
2. I'll take a taxi if _____.
3. I'll be rather disappointed if _____.
4. You'll get there in time if _____.
5. There will be chaos on the roads if _____.
6. I'll come to the conference if _____.

5 Money isn't everything!

a As you saw in the newspaper article in **3a**, people in Britain like to bet, and they do this in different ways. One of the most popular ways is by playing in the weekly lottery.

Since the National Lottery was introduced in Britain in 1994, millions of pounds have been won, people's lives have been changed and headlines have been made. As you can see from the above headlines, it hasn't always been good news. However, it hasn't stopped people trying their luck week after week, just like the person who filled in this lottery coupon.

1. How much did the person spend on the lottery?
2. How much does each board cost?
3. Which date was it for?
4. What was the most you could win that week?
5. What's the maximum you can win in your country?
6. Would you choose these numbers?

b Like many other families in Britain, the Burton family has formed a syndicate to play in the National Lottery every week. Listen to this interview with Irene and Ted Burton, their children Alison and Andrew and Irene's mother Sally. Make a note of how they would divide the money if they won and what they would do with it.

	How would she/he divide the money?	What would she/he do with the money?
Ted would		
Irene would		
Alison		
Andrew		
Sally		

(Unit 7)

6 More conditions

a The Burton family say what they **would** do if they won the National Lottery. Which two tenses are used in this type of if-sentence (if-sentence type 2)?

if-clause	main clause

▷ Compare with the grammar reference section on **page 147**.
When you use an if-sentence type 2, you imagine what you would do in certain situations. Some of these situations you would like to happen and others not. Some are more likely than others.

b What would you do if …

	You	Your Partner
you won the lottery jackpot?		
you found a spider in your bed?		
your car broke down on the motorway?		
you couldn't find your keys?		
you heard strange noises in the night?		
you smelt gas in your house?		
you got stuck in a snow drift?		
you lost your way in New York?		
you met your favourite film star?		

Write down your own reactions to these situations and then interview your partner for his/her reactions. You may agree or disagree about what you would both do. Here are some useful expressions for agreeing and for disagreeing:

Agreeing

Yes, I think that's what I would do, too.
Yes, I'd probably do the same.
That's just what I would do.

Disagreeing

Well, I'm not so sure about that. I think I would …
I wouldn't do that if I were you.
Well, if I were you, I would …
Oh, no. I certainly wouldn't do that. I'd …

(Back-up)

7 Tomorrow's weather

a Have another look at the weather charts on **page 68** and then fill in the missing weather words in this forecast. Use a different word in each gap.

England and Wales will be mostly c_____ with some scattered s_____ in places, although southern parts of England may start fairly b_____. Later in the day, a few s_____ intervals may also develop in other parts of the country.
Scotland and Northern Ireland will be m_____ with occasional r_____ or d_____, but parts of Northern Ireland may stay d_____. During the afternoon, some t_____ may develop over western coasts and hills. It will be less w_____ than today.

b There are only three things which the weatherman is certain about. What are they? Which verb form is used? Which verb form is used for the other parts of the forecast? What does that tell us?

c Think of five things that will happen in the coming year and five things you may do.

8 If I were you

When we give advice in English, or when we think we know better, we often begin our sentence with "If I were you, I'd / I wouldn't …". – What advice would you give to the following people?

Someone who …

- is sunbathing in the midday sun.
- is hosepiping his car in a drought.
- can't decide which dress to buy.
- is trying to start his car, but with no success.
- has burnt a cake.
- has lost all his money on holiday.
- wants to drive home after drinking too much.
- wants to learn English.

9 Mixed conditionals

Fill in the verbs in the following sentences. Think about the tenses! Your choice of if-sentence type 1 or 2 depends on whether you find each condition real or more unlikely, so also think about a reason for your choice.

1. If the weather _____ (stay) like this, we _____ (have) a barbecue at the weekend.
2. She _____ (come) back home if she _____ (find) a job.
3. There _____ (be) fewer road accidents if everyone _____ (drive) more carefully.
4. If you _____ (follow) the signs, you _____ (not lose) your way.
5. We _____ (buy) a new car if prices _____ (fall) by the end of the year.
6. The Prime Minister _____ (resign) if he _____ (not get) a clear majority in the next election.
7. I _____ (die) if I _____ (get stuck) in a lift!
8. If you _____ (give) me your number, Ms Henderson _____ (call) you back as soon as possible.
9. The milk _____ (boil over) if you _____ (not turn down) the gas!
10. I _____ (write) more often if only I _____ (have) more time.

Unit 7 **73**

(Unit 8)

Childhood

1 He used to be a dock worker

a Can you decide which jobs these well-known people had before they suddenly had the spotlight focused on them?

Sting	unemployed
Sabine Christiansen	a Maths teacher
Sean Connery	a flight attendant
J.K. Rowling	an English teacher
Queen Sylvia	a dock worker
Reinhold Messner	a hostess

Sabine Christiansen used to be a flight attendant.

What about the others?

Now that the person is famous her routine has changed. She doesn't do the same things every day as she did in the past.

> She **used to** go on holiday in Europe, and now she goes to the Bahamas.

b Changes

Make up sentences as above and say what is different about two of these people's lives.

2 Saturdays

a Listen to this person talking about her Saturday routine as a child. She used to go to Watford with her sister and her father, and they all used to go to the library and get back home at about one o'clock. As you listen, fill in what else the family used to do.

She	sister	father	mother

> **Did** she **use to** read historical novels? Yes, she did.
> Her father **didn't use to** read novels, he **used to** read biographies.

▷ When do we say "used to"? Look at the grammar reference section on **page 148**.

b Has your life changed?

What was your routine when you were a child and what's your routine now?
What did you use to do when you were little? Did you use to go to ballet classes?
Did you use to support a different football team?
Work with a partner, interview each other and find out!
Then report back to the class.

3 School!

This little boy didn't enjoy his first day at school. Can you remember your first day at school or the first day for one of your children? Tell the group about it. Has the school routine changed for the better or the worse, do you think?

(Unit 8)

4 Rules and Regulations

a Notices

Private
No entry

You are kindly requested to refrain from smoking

Passengers must show a valid ticket on demand

Visitors are advised to beware of pickpockets

Please do not obstruct this entrance

No buskers in this station

Visitors are requested not to touch the exhibits

What do you think these notices mean?

> You **mustn't** / you **are not allowed to** play music in the station.
> You **mustn't** smoke.

Where could you see these notices?
Where else do you see notices about rules and regulations?

b Using the rules on the notices above write some more sentences using "must" and "mustn't". Then in pairs think of a place where there are a lot of rules: in a hospital or an aeroplane, for example. Think of six notices you would see in this place. Then explain them to the rest of the group using "must" and "mustn't" or "not allowed to", and they have to guess where the place is.

5 Uniforms

a Children in England often don't like school because they have to wear a uniform. Parents have to spend a lot of money when their children go to a new school. Look at this picture of some schoolchildren in their new school uniforms. What do their parents have to buy?

▷ What do you think the difference is between "have to" and "must"? Look at the grammar reference section on **page 148** to find out.

b In Germany children don't have to wear school uniform. What do their parents have to buy at the beginning of a new school year?

> Parents **have to** buy books for their children.
> Parents **don't have to** buy school uniform.

Do you know any other differences between the English school system and the system in your country?

76

6 Now we have left school

At school there are a lot of rules and regulations, but is life easy when you've left school? Go round the class and ask questions.

Find someone who or whose partner has to / doesn't have to

- wear a tie in the office.
- get up before six o'clock in the morning.
- pay for coffee in the office.
- wear a uniform for their job.
- travel abroad for their job.
- clock in and out of work.

Find someone who or whose partner isn't allowed to

- wear trousers / jeans in the office.
- smoke in the office.
- use the office phone for private calls.
- eat in the manager's canteen.

Share the information with the group.

7 Are you a good detective?

a Look at this picture and think about these questions.

Mr. A. Phillips

- Is his first name Anthony?
- Is his first name Alois?
- Is his first name Alexandra?
- Is he retired?

His first name | **may** be Anthony.
might be Alois.
can't be Alexandra.

He **must** be retired because he's in his eighties.

▷ Look at the grammar reference section on **page 150** to see how we use "may", "might", "can't" and "must".

Unit 8

(Unit 8)

7b Now look at these people and answer the questions about them using the modal verbs "may", "might" or "can't".

Miss P. Sutton

- Is Miss Sutton's first name Pamela?
- Is her first name Paul?
- Is she a good swimmer?
- Do you think she is still at school, a policewoman or a dentist?

Ms J. Allmark

- Is Ms Allmark married?
- Is Ms Allmark divorced?
- Do you think she's a flight attendant, a bus driver or the manageress of a supermarket?

8 When I was young

Think back to when you were young. What did you have to do? What were you not allowed to do?

> I **had to** get home at ten o'clock.
> I **wasn't allowed to** eat ice-cream in the street.

▷ Check the use of the past of "have to" and "mustn't" in the grammar reference section on **page 149**.

Write down some sentences using "I had to" and "I wasn't allowed to" on a piece of paper and give it to your teacher.

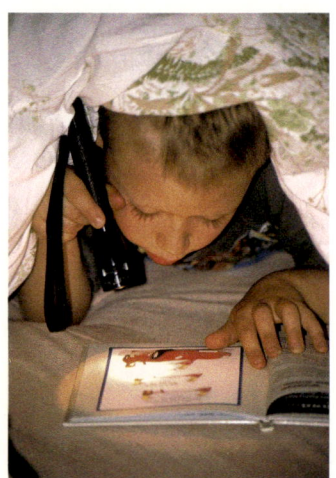

She/he will give the paper to another person in class and they have to guess who wrote the sentences.

> This may be Andrea because …
> This can't be Helen because …

9 Childhood toys

Did you have a favourite toy as a child? Why did you like it?
Have you still got it?
If not, can you tell us what happened to it? Would your favourite toy still be popular with young children today? Why? Why not?

As a child I had ...   When they were young my children had ...

You are going to read a short text about toys. As you read, make some notes of the toys mentioned.

Throwing your childhood away

It was a double whammy! First my best friend Nancy announced she was going back to Canada and then my daughter Paula told us she had accepted a job in Calcutta for two years. "Will you help me clear out the attic?" "Can I leave some of my stuff with you, Mum?" Of course, I said yes to both these requests, so I spent two weekends remembering my childhood and that of my children.

"Gosh, look at this," said Nancy opening a large trunk. "This is my first Barbie doll. I used to spend hours dressing and undressing her. Does anyone in the world really have a figure like that?" That was only the beginning. On that Saturday we found, laughed over and finally threw away as well as Barbie her friend Midge and boyfriend Ken, a hula hoop, a skipping rope, a spinning top, a doll's house and a nurse's uniform. The only thing that Nancy refused to throw away was her teddy bear Edward.

The following weekend when Paula and I were clearing the attic to make room for her trunks, I found my teddy bear called Boris. I really couldn't remember why that was his name. No, I couldn't throw him away. "Old softie, Mum," was Paula's reaction. Is the younger generation so much less sentimental than I am? I wasn't surprised when Paula sent a quick e-mail to brother Miles to ask if we could give away his action man, gameboy, Rubik's cube and scalextrix racing track complete with Mini-Cooper and he agreed without really thinking about it. But there was, to my surprise, soon a large black plastic bag full of Paula's childhood treasures: Duplo, Lego, a Playmobil farmyard, two 'My Little Ponies' and a grooming parlour and her 'Furby'. The only thing she rescued was 'Frederic the Frog', a soft toy in hideous green now with both eyes missing, that she chose on her third birthday and who used to go everywhere with her until she was 6.

What will grandchildren of mine play with I wondered as I loaded everything into the car boot and set off for the flea market. Will they still treasure teddy bears but throw away all the other childhood memories?

How would you answer the last question in the text?

How many of the toys mentioned in the text did you know about? Work with a partner and compare notes. Tell your partner about toys that he or she didn't recognise.

(Back-up)

10 Berlin then and now

Berlin has changed dramatically over the past few years. Using these photographs tell a visitor how things have changed. Try to use the grammar from this unit.

▷ Look at the grammar reference section on **pages 148–150** before you begin.

> British people **didn't use to** walk under the Brandenburg gate, they **had to** cross to East Berlin at Checkpoint Charlie.

11 Read the notice

a You can read a lot of English from the words on notices. Where would you read these words?

	On the bus / At the bus stop	In the supermarket	In the park
Queue here	■	■	■
Express checkout five items or less	■	■	■
Dogs must be kept on a lead	■	■	■
Please give up this seat if an elderly person needs it	■	■	■
No ball games	■	■	■
Do not drop litter – Penalty £25	■	■	■
No credit cards at this checkout	■	■	■
Do not talk to the driver	■	■	■
Please pay here	■	■	■
Cash only at this checkout	■	■	■
Please tender exact fare	■	■	■
Do not feed the ducks	■	■	■

b True or false?

Are the following sentences about the words on notices in **11a** true or false:

		True	False
1.	You don't have to pay cash at the supermarket.	☐	☐
2.	You mustn't talk to the bus driver.	☐	☐
3.	You mustn't play football in the park.	☐	☐
4.	You mustn't take your dog for a walk in the park.	☐	☐
5.	You must have small change for your bus fare.	☐	☐
6.	You are not allowed to use the express checkout if you have bought a lot of groceries.	☐	☐

> **Learning Tip – Modal verbs**
> You can practise these modal verbs in English without leaving your country! Every time you see a sign think of what it means in English! On a train for example: "Passengers mustn't throw anything out of the window! Passengers mustn't drink the water." Then think of how you follow rules and regulations in that situation: "I had to buy a ticket, I had to reserve a seat, I had to change trains in Bochum."

12 Make your choice

Fill in the gaps in the following sentences with "must", "mustn't", "has to", "have to", "don't have to", "had to", "was not allowed to".

1. The patient has got food poisoning and _____ have anything to eat.
2. You _____ touch that. It's the alarm button.
3. When I was a teenager, I _____ be home by ten o'clock.
4. Passengers with goods to declare _____ go through the red channel.
5. When she was at school in England she _____ wear a uniform.
6. You _____ worry about the tickets. I have already bought them.
7. Barbara's mother was very strict, and Barbara _____ eat in public when she was a child.
8. My son goes to secondary school, and he _____ be in school by 8.45.
9. We missed the last bus home yesterday evening and we _____ call a taxi.
10. As a German citizen he _____ have a visa for entry to the United States when he went there in 1993, but people from England _____ have a visa.
11. I love holidays because I _____ get up early.
12. In my job I _____ wear a suit, but I'd prefer to wear jeans.

Unit 8

(Unit 9)

The World of Work

1 A job for a man?

a In groups think of as many jobs as you can. Which of these jobs used to be jobs for women and which used to be only for men?
Is this still true in the 21st century? What can a man do that a woman can't? Has this changed over the last few years?

b A journalist and then an opera singer

What are the advantages and disadvantages of being a journalist? What are the advantages and disadvantages of being an opera singer? Do some of the disadvantages make either of these jobs not very suitable for a woman?

Listen to the story of someone who changed their job, and, as you listen, fill in the information on the chart.

She used to …		Now she …	
be		is	
be		is	
live in		lives in	
drive		drives	
sing		sings	
speak		speaks	

82

c Listen again and answer the following questions.

- How long was she a journalist?
- How long has she been an opera singer?
- How long did she live in New York?
- How long has she been living in Berlin?
- How long did she drive a Lincoln Continental?
- How long has she been driving a Golf?

Why do we have some questions with "did" or "was" and some with "has / have"? The "has / have" questions have got two parts. What are they?

▷ Look at the grammar reference section on **page 151** to help with the answers.

2 Listen again

a Listen again (text **1b**) and remember. In pairs ask and answer questions with "How long did …" or "How long was …" and "How long has …". **A** asks the first two questions and **B** answers, and then **B** asks the second two questions and **A** answers.

A	She used to be a journalist.	Now she is an opera singer.
B	She used to be married.	Now she is divorced.
A	She used to live on East River Drive.	Now she lives in Grazer Straße.
B	She used to drive a Lincoln Continental.	Now she drives a Golf.
A	She used to sing at the theatre in Leeds.	Now she sings at the Deutsche Oper.
B	She used to speak English all day.	Now she speaks German.

What about the answer to the questions "How long has she …?". When do you say "for" and when do you say "since"?

> She has been living in Grazer Straße **for 10 months**.
> She has been living in Grazer Straße **since 2003**.

▷ Look again at the grammar reference section on **page 152**.

b And you?

Write six sentences on a piece of paper about yourself. Three sentences that are true today and three sentences that used to be true. For example:

> I wear contact lenses.   I used to wear glasses.
> I work in St. Gallen.   I used to work in Baden.
> I drive a Fiesta.   I used to drive a Honda.

Give your piece of paper to a partner.
Your partner will ask you questions with "How long …"

(Unit 9)

3 Take two careers

a Work with a partner. Partner **A** reads the profile on this page. Partner **B** reads the profile on **page 126**.

Name Barbara Barsa Jamison
Age 38
Occupation Vice-President of Membership Rewards, American Express Europe Ltd, London SW1
Route to the job Barbara left university in 1989 with a BA in economics and French and an MBA in marketing and finance and went to work at the General Food Corporation in New York as an assistant product manager. After three years she became product manager of seven dog-food lines. Two years later she moved to American Express as Director of Airline Marketing. In 1997 she spent two years as Vice-President of Small Business Services in New York, then in 1999 she moved to Rome as Vice President General Manager of Corporate Card and Travel. In 2000 she came to the UK as Vice-President of Customer Development, becoming Vice-President of Membership Rewards Europe in 2002.
Dress Smart business suits.
Salary £85,000 a year
Monthly spending £1,750 mortgage and utilities (shared with husband); £750 American express card: £250 on clothes and £500 on eating out and food.

Now ask your partner for information about Jenny Dickson. First make the questions.

Name Jenny Dickson
Age
Occupation

Route to the job

?
When / leave school?

First job?

How long / stay / first job?

What / next?

How long / present job?

How many different jobs / since she left school?

How much / earn?

How much / spend / clothes a month?

b Your first job

What was your first job?
How long did you stay in your first job?
Where do you work now?
How long have you been working there?

4 What's the job?

Match a verb from column A with a word or phrase from column B.
The first one has been done for you.

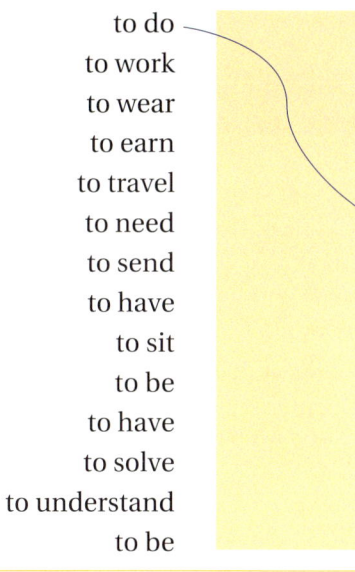

A	B
to do	problems
to work	a degree
to wear	a lot of responsibility
to earn	creative
to travel	technology
to need	shift work
to send	computer literate
to have	to foreign countries
to sit	at the weekend
to be	e-mails
to have	a competitive salary
to solve	at a desk
to understand	a uniform
to be	good communication skills

Learning tip – Word partnerships
Learning vocabulary in word partnerships helps when you want to express this idea later. Then you don't have to search for individual words to put together.

Use these word partnerships to make up questions about a job.

> Do you send a lot of e-mails in this job?
> Do you have to be computer literate for this job?

Your teacher will put a piece of paper with a 'job' on your back. Get up and move around the classroom and ask the other members of the group questions so you can guess what the job is.

5 Office life

a When you want to contact a colleague at work which of the following do you do?

- pick up the phone
- shout across the open plan office to him or her
- send her/him an e-mail
- walk to her/his office
- do something else

b Could you live without e-mail?

Work in two groups. Group A lists the good things about having e-mail at work. Group B lists the bad things about having e-mail at work.
Then compile a class list.

Unit 9

(Unit 9)

5c Here is the headline of a newspaper article:

> **Office workers told to take an e-mail holiday**

What do you think it will be about?
Now read the first paragraph to see if you were right.

> You've got e-mail, but you mustn't open it until first thing on Monday morning.
> Companies are telling their staff not to use electronic communication on Fridays.

Why do you think companies are doing this? Think of your ideas from **5b**.
Read the next part of the text to see if you were right.

> Managers are banning the click of the mouse as an experiment to see if staff are more creative when they have to talk to one another face to face. E-mail experts can't agree on whether the ideas will benefit businesses and their employees. Some scientists have warned of information overload as office workers live virtual existences, sending and receiving up to 150 e-mail messages a day.
> Nestle Rowntree, the confectioner, is the first to say goodbye to Friday e-mails. The idea grew out of the introduction of 'casual Friday' when employees leave their suits and ties in the wardrobe and come to work in casual clothes.
> Alan Henderson of Rowntree said "A no e-mail Friday does two things. It removes unimportant information flow across the organisation and it forces people to talk face to face and agree plans together. An e-mail ban begins to build a culture of designing and delivering ideas together."
> He added, "Some people use e-mail to protect themselves, as proof that they have thought about a problem. Often all that they do is send a quick e-mail and hope it will get lost among all the others instead of actually achieving a solution to a problem. You can't get away with that in a face-to-face meeting."
> Diane Whitfield, chief executive of a leading UK company, said "Often e-mail is sent between people who sit quite close to each other. Some of the best ideas come from brainstorming sessions when colleagues throw ideas at each other, which does not happen when you use e-mail. It can stifle creativity."

What might be the arguments for the use of more e-mail and no Friday ban?
Think of your arguments from **5b**.
Read the last part of the article to find out.

> But Dr Billy Jensen of the Open University published research that suggested that the use of e-mail can increase creativity. As he explains, "In an exercise such as brainstorming, people often come up with more ideas when using e-mail than when sitting face to face with their colleagues. There is less social pressure to conform or to worry about making a fool of yourself."
>
> Dr Jeremy Jones a psychologist at Nottingham Trent University in UK sees arguments on both sides. "Companies should be congratulated for giving no e-mail Fridays a go. It is bizarre to get an e-mail from a colleague in the next office when they could pop their head round the door. We have definitely come to overuse e-mails, but it could be counter-productive if you tell staff they cannot send an e-mail on a Friday and you have to wait till Monday."
>
> *(adapted from an article in The Sunday Times)*

d What do you think of the ideas?

Do you get 150 e-mails a day as the article suggests?
If not, how many do you get either at work or at home?
Do you answer all the e-mails you get every day?

(Back-up)

6 For or since

a Decide whether "for" or "since" is correct.

_____ the spring election of 2003
_____ she left school
_____ the beginning of the winter term
_____ they won a million Euro in a TV quiz show
_____ over three years
_____ the cat ran away
_____ two weeks
_____ an hour

b Now complete the following sentences using phrases with "for" or "since" from the list above.

1. They have been living in a villa with a swimming pool _____.
2. She has been a bank clerk _____.
3. He has been talking to his girlfriend on the phone _____.
4. They have been on holiday in Portugal _____.
5. The president has been in power _____.
6. The family has had a dog _____.
7. He has been studying English in Linz _____.
8. He has been working for the same company _____.

c Now you

Write some sentences about yourself that you have practised in this unit using the present perfect simple or continuous.

> I **have been living** in Kiel for fifteen years.
> I **have been** an engineer since September 2000.

Learning Tip – Grammar
When you are doing something that is boring but has to be done, make it more exciting by thinking of how many sentences using the grammar from this unit you can think of in English. For example when you are mowing the lawn in your garden:
"I have been cutting the grass for twenty minutes."
"I have had the lawn mower since last year."
"We have been living in this house for ten years."
"My children have been playing in the garden for over two hours."

(Back-up)

7 The job

a Put the following in the correct order.

- [ ] a. She accepted it.
- [1] b. She found an advertisement for the job of investment adviser online more than four years ago.
- [ ] c. She filled it in and e-mailed it to the company immediately together with her CV as an attachment.
- [ ] d. The Personnel Manager rang her a week later and offered her the job.
- [ ] e. Ten days later the company invited her for an interview.
- [ ] f. Now she has been working for the company for four years.
- [ ] g. After two years she got a pay rise.
- [ ] h. She would like promotion.
- [ ] i. She was very nervous at the interview.
- [ ] j. If she doesn't get it, she'll look for another job and leave the company.
- [ ] k. She downloaded an application form.

b Look again at exercises **4** and **7a** and decide which words for jobs you want to put into your word bank.

8 Help, I don't understand!

A friend of yours knows you're desperately looking for a job, finds this advertisement online and phones you to tell you about it. He or she dictates it to you over the phone.

Sales Assistants

From foodhall to fashion in Hippers

We are looking for motivated Sales Staff with the right personal manner and presentation to work in Hippers. Successful candidates must have six months' retail background, excellent interpersonal skills, enthusiasm and a flexible and positive approach.
If you are interested and wish to find out more, please telephone 020 921 3355 extension 2200 or 2201 or e-mail a CV and covering letter to:

Jennie.Lotts@hippers.co.uk

Job advertisements are often full of quite complicated language, so you may have to stop and ask for help. How can you do this?

You ask your friend to spell difficult words:	Sorry, can you spell that?
You show that you didn't understand:	Sorry? *(rising intonation)*
	Sorry, what does ... mean?
You repeat information to check that you have got it right:	So that's ...

Where do you think you would have to stop and ask for help if this advertisement were read to you over the phone? In the next lesson you can practise asking for this help with a partner. This is a useful exercise if you often take telephone messages in your job.

9 Word stress

Remember how you can mark word stress.

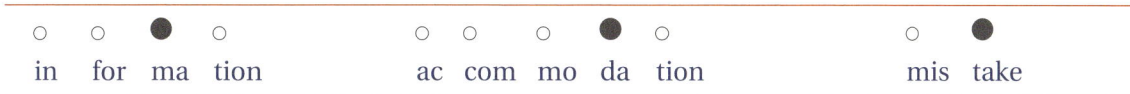

Put these words into the correct box. There are five words for each box.

personnel, personal, photographer, promotion, impossible, invitation, organizer, advertising, optimist, programmer, heroin, lemonade, election, sentimental, interviewer, competitive, committee, questionnaire, emergency, conversation, presentation, journalism, tolerant, develop, ceremony, cigarette.

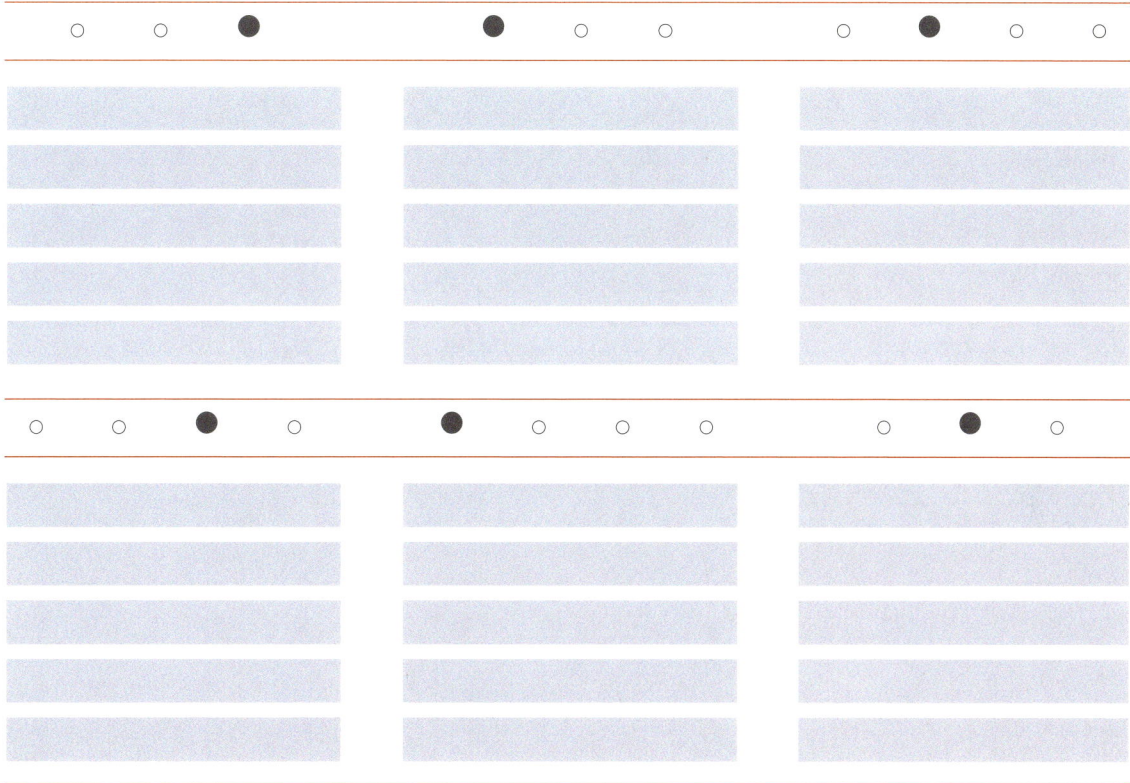

 Now listen to the recording to check your pronunciation.

(Revision 3)

1 Gap-filling and listening

How would you fill these gaps to make sensible sentences about the weather?

1. What _____ we're having!
2. It's _____ for the time of year.
3. It _____ all day yesterday. Wasn't it _____ ?!
4. I hope there won't be any _____ tomorrow. I have to drive up north.
5. Oh no, that sounds like _____ I'm afraid of _____ .
6. What a _____ there was last night. I couldn't get to sleep all night.
7. We got stuck in a _____ coming back from our skiing trip.
8. It's so _____ today! If only there were a nice _____ .

Now listen to the CD and see how close you were.

2 Working with grammar: if-sentences type 1+2

Think about whether it would be better to use an if-sentence type 1 or 2 in each sentence. Remember the sequence of tenses in each case!

1. Your son/daughter is ill but doesn't want to take his/her medicine.
   If _____.
2. A friend has bought a new armchair, but you don't think it's in the right place.
   The room _____.
3. Your partner has just reminded you of a dinner invitation for that evening.
   You hope to be home in time, but you're very busy at work.
   I _____ if _____.
4. It's 8.15, and your son's/daughter's bus leaves at 8.19.
   You _____ if _____.
5. Your next-door neighbours are having a very loud party, and you have already asked them twice to turn down the music.
   If _____.
6. A colleague can't decide whether to accept a new job offer or not.
   If _____.

3 Working with grammar: present perfect simple and progressive

Put the pairs of sentences on page 91 together.

Be careful!
Which sentences can't you use in the progressive form and which sentences do you have to use in the progressive form?

He has got a dog. He bought the dog in 1995.
He has had a dog since 1995.

He works for AEG. He started his job ten years ago.
He has been working for AEG for ten years.

1. He lives in Erfurt. He bought his house there in 1994.
2. He drives a Mercedes. He bought it three years ago.
3. She's the Personnel Manager. She got promotion to this job two years ago.
4. He's married. He got married in 1986.
5. He has got a DVD player. He bought it a year ago.
6. He plays tennis in the village club. He started playing tennis five years ago.
7. She works as an editor for a local newspaper. She started work for the paper in January 1993.
8. They're fishing. They got to the river three hours ago.
9. She wears glasses. She started wearing glasses when she was at university.
10. She's studying engineering. She started studying in October 2000.
11. They're divorced. They got their divorce six months ago.
12. He's digging his garden. He started digging at three o'clock.

4 Working with grammar: modals of obligation

a Look at the following signs. Under each sign fill in the gaps with 'don't have to' or 'mustn't' + the verb which is given.

1. `Keep off the grass` (walk)

   Example: You <u>mustn't walk</u> on the grass.

2. `NO SMOKING` (smoke)

   You _____ here.

3. `Do not walk` (cross)

   You _____ the road now.

4. `Entrance free of charge` (pay)

   You _____ to go in.

5. `No photos` (take)

   You _____ photos here.

6. `Bar open to non-residents` (be)

   You _____ a resident of the hotel.

b Now look at the following company regulations. Use 'have to', 'don't have to' or 'mustn't' to re-write the rules and regulations

Example: 2nd class rail travel not essential. – Company employees don't have to travel 2nd class by train.

1. No smoking at the workplace.
   Company employees _____
2. No parking at the front of the building.
   Company employees _____
3. In the back office, shirt and tie are optional.
   Company employees _____
4. It is necessary to hand in a timesheet each week.
   Company employees _____
5. Do not use recycled paper in the photocopier.
   Company employees _____
6. Important: 2 weeks' holiday at Christmas is not optional.
   Company employees _____
7. Wine at the Christmas party is free.
   Company employees _____

(Revision 3)

5 Reading

MMC

As part of our plans for expansion we are looking for talented, creative and experienced computer programmers to work on a range of exciting multi-media projects.

We need:
Macintosh programmers who understand Macintosh Toolbox
Windows programmers for MPC products (experience of Visual Basic an advantage)
CD-i programmers for consumer and games titles

We offer: Flexible working hours or teleworking plus a company car.

Send your CV to: John Wells, General Manager, The Multimedia Corporation, 192 Maple Park Road, London NW3 7EJ
E-mail: UK0034@applelink.com

The Multimedia Corporation

KingstonSmith

We are a firm of accountants, and we are looking for an **Assistant Personnel Officer** to join our busy Personnel and Training Department. The successful applicant will ideally have a degree, be a member of the Institute of Personnel Management, and he or she must have good organizational and communication skills, be able to work well under pressure and be under 30.
Your responsibilities will include recruitment and the organisation of training courses.
We offer a competitive salary, good career prospects and an informal but professional working environment.

If you are interested, please write with CV to:
Carol Canon,
Kingston Smith, Park House,
195 Dale Avenue, London EC1J 9AB
The closing date for applications is September 4.

FOR women

Please send CV and covering letter to: Michele Lavery, Features Editor, For Women, 3 Sommerfields, London EC3 8EU Closing date for applications is 31 August.

We require a **Deputy Features Editor**.

The ideal applicant will have a degree in journalism and three years experience.

Responsibilities will be to edit and do research for articles for our monthly magazine.

We offer an attractive salary plus additional expenses budget.

We are an Equal Opportunities employer.

Sales Assistants

From foodhall to fashion in Hippers

We are looking for motivated Sales Staff with the right personal manner and presentation to work in Hippers. Successful candidates must have six months' retail background, excellent interpersonal skills, enthusiasm and a flexible and positive approach.

If you are interested and wish to find out more, please telephone 0181 921 3355 extension 2200 or 2201 or send a CV and covering letter to:

Miss Jennie Lotts, Recruitment Department, Hippers Ltd, 91–101 Cross Street, Queensbridge, London SE9C 4EA

---

a The right applicant?

Decide which jobs would be suitable or not suitable for the following people.

1. Harald has got a degree in computer science.
2. John has worked in a shop for a year.
3. Alex got her degree in journalism a year ago.
4. Barbara has been a journalist for five years.
5. Jane has got a qualification in Personnel Management.
6. Angela has run training courses for three years.
7. Joanna's a bit shy but would like to work in a shop.
8. Mike wants a job that will give him a good career.
9. Frank has worked in a large department store for two years, but he lives a long way from London.
10. Pat likes working with people and can work on Saturdays.
11. Peter's very creative with computers, but he can't use Windows.

b Would you like any of these jobs?

What is important for you in a job? Look at this list and then add ideas of your own or ideas from the ads.
- long holidays
- responsibility
- money
- ...
- ...
- ...

Would any of the jobs on page 92 interest you? Why/why not?

```
                                    19 Meadow Gardens
                                    Staines
                                    TW18 3HE
Ms Carol Canon
Kingston Smith
Park House
195 Dale Avenue
London EC1J 9AB

                                    6 August 2003
Dear Ms Canon

Your Advertisement for an Assistant Personnel Officer.

I am very interested in the post of Assistant Personnel
Officer as advertised in The Times of August 4.

As you can see from my CV, I have been working in the
Personnel Department of Debenhams since September 2000
and have been responsible for organizing training
courses for the sales staff.

I enjoy working with people and would like to expand
my experience in Personnel work. Although I do not have
a formal qualification in Personnel Management, I am
willing to work for this in my own time, and I feel that
with my background and experience I am a suitable
candidate for the post advertised. Mr Henderson, the
Personnel Manager, has agreed to act as my referee,
and he can be contacted at any time on 01784 465809
extension 237.

As requested I enclose a full CV. I am available for
interview any day except Tuesdays. I look forward to
hearing from you.

Yours sincerely

Rosemary Brown
Rosemary Brown
```

c Now look at this letter of application for one of the jobs on the left. What differences do you notice between this letter and the informal/personal letter on page 58? Then answer the following:

1. If you begin a personal letter with 'Dear ...' and a first name you don't finish it with 'Yours sincerely'. – True or false?
2. You have a lot of contractions in formal letters. – True or false?
3. If you write a letter to a friend, you add his/her complete address at the top. – True or false?
4. Which of the following could you also use to finish a personal letter?
   'Love from'
   'Best wishes'
   'Yours'
5. The letter and three of the job advertisements mention a CV. Which of the following information would you put in your CV?
   - date of birth
   - place of birth
   - family status
   - religion
   - names and occupations of parents
   - names and dates of schools attended
   - formal qualifications
   - previous job experience
   - hobbies and interests

Revision 3

(Unit 10)

Transport and Technology

1 Transport

a What kinds of transport are there in your area? Make a list.
Then enter the items in the following grid according to how often you use them.

usually	sometimes	hardly ever	never

Compare your grid with a partner.

b Can you think of any other forms of transport, which are not to be found in your area but which you know? Enter them in the grid in **1a**, too. Then go round the class and ask other students questions like:

> How often do you travel/go by _____ ?
> Do you ever take/use _____ ?

c How do your fellow students get to the English class? –
By car, by bike, on foot, …? Make a quick survey.
What are the results?

```
_____ %   come   by car
_____              by bus
_____             _____
_____             _____
_____             _____
```

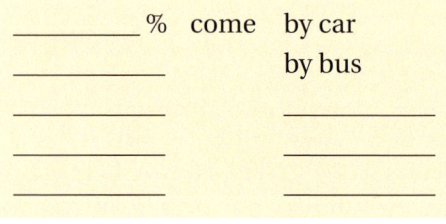

d Now listen to five people talking about how they travel to work or school and fill in the missing details in the grid below.

name	place	method of transport	reason
1.			
2.			
3.			
4.			
5.			

Compare your entries with a partner and then listen again, this time listening very carefully for any information that is still missing.

2 Likes and dislikes

> **Learning tip – Listening**
> Having an idea of what you want to listen for beforehand helps you to concentrate on specific details when listening.

a Are the following statements about the five people in **1d** – Ronnie, Sharon, Michael, Christine and Sally – true or false?

		True	False
1.	Ronnie prefers taking the underground to work because it's faster.	☐	☐
2.	Sharon hates going anywhere by car.	☐	☐
3.	Michael hates using public transport because it's so uncomfortable.	☐	☐
4.	Christine doesn't mind travelling in crowded trains since they're cheap and fast.	☐	☐
5.	For Sally it would be a lot easier to use public transport.	☐	☐

Compare your answers with a partner and then listen to **1d** again to check.

b Can you add any others to this list of comparative adjectives to use when talking about transport?

– cheaper
– more comfortable
– ...

Try to use some of them as appropriate in the next exercise.

> Michael travels by car to work because it's **more comfortable**, not because it's **faster**.
>
> 'Faster' and 'more comfortable' are called the **comparative forms of adjectives**.

▷ What are the rules about forming the comparative forms of adjectives? Check with the grammar reference section on **page 153**.

c Look back at your list of different kinds of transport in **1a** and then complete these sentences about yourself.

1. I prefer travelling by _____ because _____
2. I hate going anywhere by _____ because _____
3. I don't mind taking _____ since _____
4. I love travelling by _____ because _____
5. For me it would be a lot easier / more difficult to _____
6. I would love to _____ but _____

> Sharon loves **taking** the ferry to work because it's so relaxing.
> I would love **to take** a ferry to work, but I don't live near the sea or a river.
>
> In the first sentence 'taking' is the **gerund** form of the verb.
> In the second sentence 'to take' is the **infinitive** form of the verb.

▷ Check with the grammar reference section on **pages 154–155**.

Unit 10

(Unit 10)

2d In some of the following sentences it's possible to use the gerund or the infinitive form. Tick those sentences where both forms are possible.
Score out the wrong form in those sentences where only one form is possible.

1. I enjoy going / to go by bike in good weather.
2. Do you prefer travelling / to travel by bus or train?
3. Would you like flying / to fly round the world?
4. I don't mind walking / to walk when I'm not in a hurry.
5. Some people like driving / to drive their car even in the rush-hour.
6. My neighbour hates travelling / to travel long distances.

3 Taking a cab

a Have a look at this text about using taxi-cabs in the US. Some words are missing in the text. Can you fill them in?

In American towns there are no taxi _____ (1), and taxis do not stand at the _____ (2). However, there is a separate taxi line _____ (3) airports and railway stations. You can also _____ (4) a list of cab companies in the _____ (5) pages of the local telephone book. When you _____ (6) to order a cab, remember to give _____ (7) of where you are and where you _____ (8) to go. Don't forget to give your telephone _____ (9) so that the cab driver can call you _____ (10) he has a problem trying to locate you. You can also _____ (11) for a wake-up call when you book a cab for the early morning.
Always ask for the estimated _____ (12) of the ride beforehand. Try to have _____ (13) change ($1, $5, $10) as sometimes taxi drivers don't have change, and you might end up _____ (14) a bit extra. You can also ask for a _____ (15) from the driver if you want, especially if you want to reimburse the fare from your company.

1 a. stands
   b. stalls
   c. seats
   d. rows
	4 a. find
	   b. search
	   c. look
	   d. seek
		7 a. ideas
		   b. details
		   c. description
		   d. address
			10 a. that
			    b. when
			    c. while
			    d. if
				13 a. any
				    b. much
				    c. many
				    d. some

2 a. road
   b. street
   c. roadside
   d. pavement
	5 a. blue
	   b. yellow
	   c. red
	   d. white
		8 a. like
		   b. enjoy
		   c. love
		   d. want
			11 a. look
			    b. ask
			    c. request
			    d. demand
				14 a. saving
				    b. giving
				    c. paying
				    d. keeping

3 a. on
   b. in
   c. for
   d. at
	6 a. cry
	   b. shout
	   c. call
	   d. speak
		9 a. number
		   b. call
		   c. book
		   d. line
			12 a. fare
			    b. tax
			    c. money
			    d. rate
				15 a. recipe
				    b. receipt
				    c. prescription
				    d. description

Compare your version with a partner.

b Did you find any differences in the text between taking a cab in the US and taking a taxi in your country? Do you know any other differences? Have you had any unusual taxi experiences in any other countries?

c What has been your longest taxiride?

What has been your	longest shortest most expensive cheapest most exciting	taxiride?

Fill in the table for yourself and then interview your partner.

	me	my partner
longest taxiride		
shortest taxiride		
most expensive taxiride		
cheapest taxiride		
most exciting taxiride		

Can you enter all three forms for each of these adjectives in this grid?

basic	comparative	superlative
_____	_____	_____
_____	_____	_____
_____	_____	_____
_____	_____	_____
_____	_____	_____

> The **cheapest** and the **most exciting** taxiride I've ever had was in Hong Kong.
>
> 'Cheapest' and 'most expensive' are called the **superlative forms of adjectives**.

▷ What are the rules about forming the superlative forms of adjectives?
Check with the grammar reference section on **page 153**.

d Some adjectives have special comparative and superlative forms.
Do you know them?

basic	comparative	superlative
good		
bad		
far		
much / many / a lot		
little / not much		
little / small		

▷ Check with the grammar reference section on **page 153**.

(Unit 10)

4 Technological developments

a For some people the invention of the motor car was the best development of the 20th century. What about you? Look at the following list and choose four items that you consider to be the most important technological developments in everyday life.

- ☐ aeroplane
- ☐ answering machine
- ☐ burglar alarm
- ☐ car
- ☐ dishwasher
- ☐ electric iron
- ☐ fax machine
- ☐ hairdryer
- ☐ radio
- ☐ telephone
- ☐ television
- ☐ toaster
- ☐ video recorder
- ☐ washing machine
- ☐ ...

Add another item of your own choice to your personal list. Compare your list with a partner and find out why your partner has chosen her/ his five items.

b Did you choose a burglar alarm in **4a**? Why/why not?

You're now going to hear a dialogue between a homeowner and a sales assistant at Holmes Security Services. The homeowner is interested in a new home defence system. Have a look at the following statements and then listen carefully to decide whether they are true or false.

	True	False
1. The man went to Holmes Security Services because he had seen their advert on TV.	☐	☐
2. There is another house attached to his house.	☐	☐
3. There are two ways to get into the house.	☐	☐
4. There's a road at the bottom of his back garden.	☐	☐
5. His house has been broken into twice.	☐	☐
6. He already has a burglar alarm.	☐	☐
7. The shop assistant offers him four different burglar alarm systems.	☐	☐
8. All of these systems are popular with the police and neighbours.	☐	☐
9. He decides to buy the last home defence system.	☐	☐
10. His wife wants to buy a guard dog.	☐	☐

Compare with a partner and correct the statements which are false.

c Would you choose any of the systems offered by the sales assistant? Why? Why not?

5 The passive voice

a Look at this sentence from the dialogue between the homeowner and the sales assistant in **4b**:

'Our house has just been broken into for the third time.'

In the active voice it would be something like this:

'They have / Someone has just broken into our house for the third time.'

Why do you think the passive voice is preferred here?
Here are some more sentences from the dialogue in **4b**. Highlight the passive verb forms in each one.

1. The police have been called.
2. As soon as a burglar enters your home, the room is filled with high-density smoke.
3. It's an electric wire system which is hidden behind the walls of your house.
4. When the system is set, any intruders who touch the wall are shocked or burnt.

The **passive voice** is made up of two parts. What are they?

▷ Check with the grammar reference section on **page 156**.

b Fill in the missing passive verb forms in these sentences. – Remember to think about the tenses!

1. Do you have a car which _____ (fit) with a route-finder?
2. I felt really excited when I _____ (tell) that I _____ (give) the job.
3. Our local supermarket _____ (break into) again last week.
4. I think it's a pity that fewer letters _____ (write) by hand these days. What about you?
5. Have you heard? Jan Scott _____ (make) head of personnel.
6. If you order the book today, it _____ (deliver) to your address within a week.
7. I hate it when mobile phones _____ (use) in restaurants.
8. Sorry, I'm going to be late. My flight _____ (cancel).

c Look at these pairs of sentences. What is the difference between the active and the passive sentence in each pair?

1. a. Did you know that 'Frankenstein' was written by Mary Shelley?
   b. Did you know that Mary Shelley wrote 'Frankenstein'?
2. a. Sweeter milk is produced by happy cows?
   b. Happy cows produce sweeter milk.

▷ Check with the grammar reference section on **page 156**.
Which version do you prefer? The active or the passive?

(Back-up)

6 Comparisons

a Matthew and Mark are twins, but they are not completely alike. Use the following information to make comparisons about them.

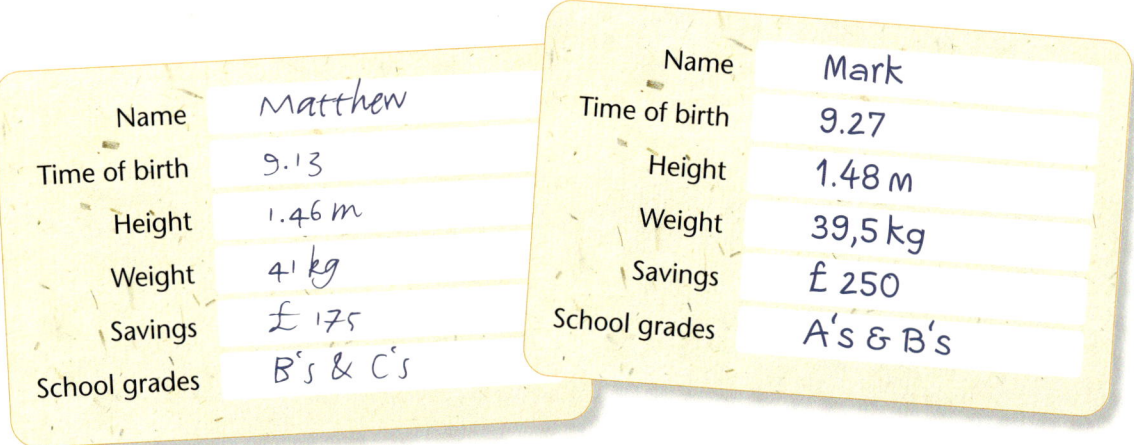

Matthew _____ than Mark.
Mark _____ than Matthew.

b And you? Can you make some comparisons about you and other members of your family, your friends, your colleagues, your fellow-students?

> **Learning tip – Personalisation**
> When practising structures, try to make up sentences that refer to you personally. Since they are true for you, you'll want to use them regularly. That way you'll become more confident and will use the structures naturally.

7 Superlatives

Complete the following sentences using your own choice of adjectives in the superlative form.

1. It was the _____ holiday I've ever had!
2. What's the _____ book you've ever read?
3. Do you know what the _____ country in the world is?
4. That's the _____ thing I've ever heard!
5. My father had ten brothers and sisters, and he was the _____.
6. Last year we had the _____ rainfall on record.
7. The _____ item on the agenda for today's meeting is the election of the chairperson for the coming year.
8. I think he's the _____ president the country has ever had.

8 Gerund or infinitive?

a Certain verbal expressions are always followed by a gerund, others by an infinitive and a third group by a gerund or an infinitive. Put the following verbal expressions into the correct column.

enjoy • like • begin • hope • don't mind • would like • promise • prefer • look forward to • give up • hate • want

gerund	infinitive	gerund or infinitive
_____	_____	_____
_____	_____	_____
_____	_____	_____
_____	_____	_____
_____	_____	_____

Can you add any other verbal expressions to the table?

▷ Check with the grammar reference section on **page 154**.

b Complete the following sentences with your choice of verbs in the gerund or infinitive form.

1. We're really looking forward to _____ you at the weekend.
2. Would you mind _____ that window, please?
3. What does your daughter want _____ after she leaves school?
4. Oh, yes, I stopped _____ years ago.
5. What about _____ this evening?
6. Where have you been? I've been trying _____ you all morning.
7. We're having problems with our neighbours. Our dog is very fond of _____ their cat.
8. If all goes well, we hope _____ to a bigger house in two years.

9 Be careful with the tenses!

Rewrite the following sentences using passive structures where possible.

1. They called the fire brigade as soon as the fire broke out.
2. Someone has stolen my car!
3. They gave me the painting when I retired.
4. Someone will deliver the dishwasher on Wednesday.
5. They send the exam results straight to the candidates.
6. They have arrested a man in connection with the Baker Street bank robbery.
7. In hospital they always waken you so early.
8. This is the worst meal anyone has ever served me!

Then add two more passive sentences of your own.
9. ...
10. ...

(Unit 11)
Health and Environment

1 How healthy are you?

*An apple a day
keeps the doctor away.*

*Early to bed, early to rise,
Makes a man healthy, wealthy and wise.*

a These two popular English sayings tell us something about a healthy lifestyle.
Test how healthy your lifestyle is with the following quiz.

		Yes	No
1.	Do you get eight hours' sleep a day?	☐	☐
2.	Do you eat fresh fruit and vegetables daily?	☐	☐
3.	Do you get regular exercise?	☐	☐
4.	Do you smoke?	☐	☐
5.	Do you have regular medical check-ups?	☐	☐
6.	Do you go to the dentist's at least once a year?	☐	☐
7.	Do you work very long hours?	☐	☐
8.	Do you take time to relax with your family and friends?	☐	☐
9.	Do you drink more than two cups of coffee a day?	☐	☐
10.	Do you worry a lot?	☐	☐

You can check your score on **page 108**.

Score 1 point for each "Yes" in nos. 1, 2, 3, 5, 6, 8.
Score 1 point for each "No" in nos. 4, 7, 9, 10.

b Now test your partner. You may agree on some things and disagree on others. Here are some useful expressions:

When you want to agree

> So do I.   (I usually go to bed by eleven o'clock. – So do I.)
> Neither do I. (I don't smoke. – Neither do I.)

When you want to disagree

> Oh, do you? I don't.
> Oh, don't you? I do.

And when you want to give some well-meant advice

> Perhaps you should …
> Don't you think it would be better to …
> It might be a good idea if you …

▷ Mind the tense in the last sentence!

c Use the last expression in **1b** to practise giving advice on all the points in the healthy lifestyle quiz (in **1a**).

1. It might be a good idea if you got more sleep.
2. It might be a good idea if you _____.
3. It _____.
4. _____.
5. _____.
6. _____.
7. _____.
8. _____.
9. _____.
10. _____.

Make two sentences each for nos. 4, 7, 9 and 10 (**1a** on **page 102**) with a positive and a negative verb form in the if-clause!

(Unit 11)

2 Safety first

a Too many accidents happen in the home, and most of them can be avoided. How safe are you at home? Answer these ten questions and find out.

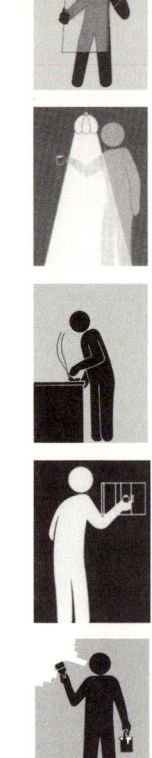

Do you …	Yes	No
keep matches where children can't see or reach them?		
stay by the pan when frying chips?		
have chimneys swept at least once a year?		
know what to do when you suspect a gas leak?		
have enough electrical sockets to avoid overloading?		
know how to wire a plug correctly?		
keep entranceways, stairs and passageways well lit?		
replace worn carpets, mats and floor tiles?		
clean up at once anything spilt on the floor?		
keep all medicines in a lockable cabinet?		

For each "Yes" score 1 point. Check your score on **page 108**.

b Accidents have happened again and again because people have not thought about these safety points. Afterwards it's always easy to say how accidents would not have happened.

> The fire **would not have happened** if they **had kept** the matches away from the children.
> The explosion **would not have happened** if they **had known** what to do about gas leaks.
> The accident **wouldn't have happened** if they**'d cleaned up** the spilt milk immediately.

▷ Look at the tenses of the verbs in the two parts of these sentences. What are they?

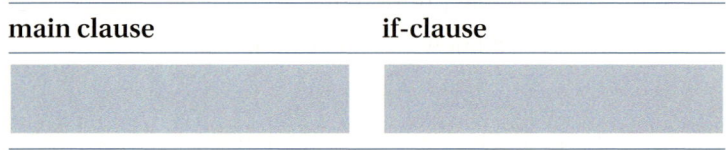

main clause	if-clause

What does this type of if-sentence (if-sentence type 3) describe? Do you use it often in your own language?

▷ Compare with the grammar reference section on **page 157**.

104

c Now write sentences for the other safety points in the list in **2a** to say

| The | accident
explosion
fire | wouldn't have happened | if | |

> **Learning tip – Sounding natural**
> Remember that short verb forms help you to sound natural in spoken English and in informal written English.

d When we use "would" or "wouldn't have", we are absolutely sure.

➤ The fire **wouldn't have** happened if they had kept the matches away from the children.

They are quite certain about this.

When we use "might" or "mightn't have", we are not so sure.

➤ The fire **mightn't have** happened if they had kept the matches away from the children.

They're not absolutely sure; something else might have started the fire or the children might have found some matches, anyway.

Use one of these forms to complete the following sentences in a realistic way:

1. If the ambulance hadn't arrived so quickly, _____.
2. If she hadn't gone to the dance, _____.
3. If they hadn't lost their way, _____.
4. If you hadn't overspent on holiday, _____.
5. If we hadn't left our luggage in the car, _____.
6. If last summer hadn't been so hot, _____.
7. If you had phoned first, _____.
8. If I had known you were coming, _____.
9. If there hadn't been a delay with our flight, _____.
10. If you had only taken my advice, _____.
11. If we hadn't gone for that walk, _____.

(Unit 11)

3 How green is your home?

a Nowadays we are very much aware of the close connection between the environment and our health. Here, too, safety begins in the home.

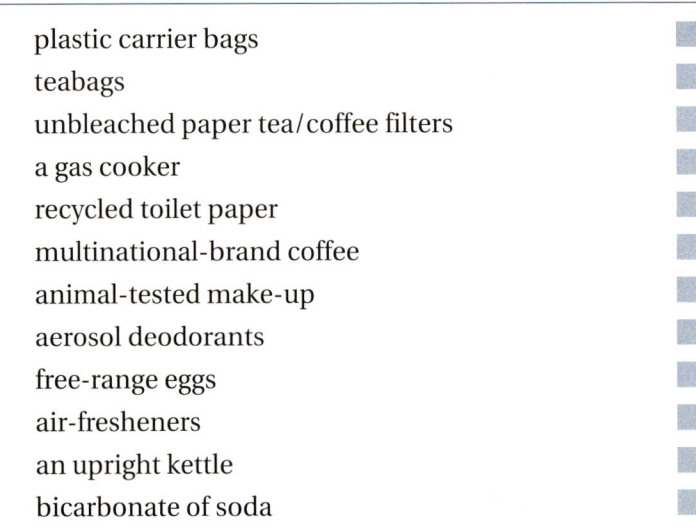

How many of these things do you have in your home?

plastic carrier bags	▪
teabags	▪
unbleached paper tea/coffee filters	▪
a gas cooker	▪
recycled toilet paper	▪
multinational-brand coffee	▪
animal-tested make-up	▪
aerosol deodorants	▪
free-range eggs	▪
air-fresheners	▪
an upright kettle	▪
bicarbonate of soda	▪

b Test your partner to see how green her/his home is and use the expressions from **exercise 1b** to agree, disagree and make polite suggestions.

Now enter the items in the following grid and add any more you can think of.

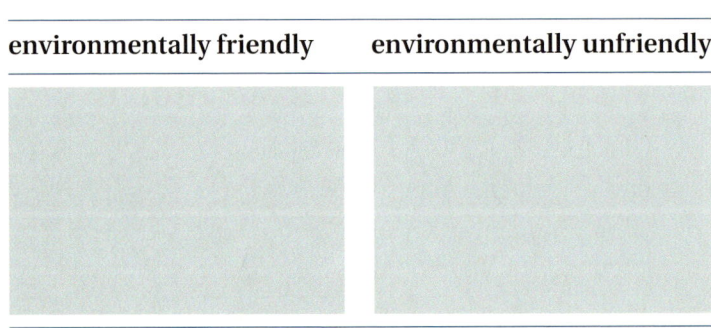

environmentally friendly	environmentally unfriendly

c Listen to this extract from the radio programme "Green or Greenish?" with the candidates Sue and Martin. For each answer put a tick in one of the boxes "Green" or "Greenish" and add up the candidates' score at the end.

	Green	Greenish
1.		
2.		
3.		
4.		
5.		
6.		
7.		
8.		
9.		
10.		
Score		

d Listen to the radio programme again, this time making a note of the ten questions. Then interview your partner and see how "Green" or "Greenish" he or she is.

1.
2.
3.
4.
5.
6.
7.
8.
9.
10.

Your partner's score

e Sue and Martin heat only two rooms at a time, and they use public transport and Martin's bike most of the time. In groups of three or four discuss the following points:

- What do you do to conserve energy?
- What else could you do?
- Why don't you do it?

Unit 11 **107**

(Back-up)

4 It's the same with me

Give short responses of agreement to the following statements using "So …" or "Neither …". Be careful with the tenses!

1. I never use plastic carrier bags.
2. I wash my hair every other day.
3. I'll never understand this grammar!
4. I've always wanted to be an opera singer.
5. I really enjoyed that film.
6. I certainly wouldn't wash cotton hankies on 40°!
7. I could do with a cup of tea.
8. I'm going to stop buying multinational-brands.

5 That little word "If"

Many things might / could / would never have happened if …
Fill in the missing if-clauses.

1. If _____, I wouldn't have been able to study.
2. If _____, they might never have met.
3. If _____, the fire could have caused serious damage.
4. If _____, we might not have had food poisoning.
5. If _____, many more people would still be employed in factories.
6. If _____, the Berlin Wall might never have come down.
7. If _____, the Pilgrim Fathers wouldn't have left England.
8. If _____, the party could have gone on for much longer.
9. If _____, the cat might have stayed up in the tree all night.
10. If _____, the government would have built more nuclear power stations.

Your score for 2a

10:	Excellent!
8–9:	Not bad, but take another look around.
6–7:	When did you have your last accident?
5 and under:	Does your insurance company still want to know you?

Your score for 1a

9–10:	Aren't you good!
7–8:	Welcome to the club!
5–6:	Perhaps you should have another look at your New Year resolutions.
under 5:	Oh dear! Urgent action needed!

6 Another sleepless night

a Where would you read this?
What would you have done to get some sleep?

Wed. 26th July

Hardly slept a wink last night! Couldn't get to sleep because Mike was snoring. Then upstairs switched on their vacuum cleaner at midnight. That woke the baby. Took her into bed with us, but that did no good. She slept, I didn't! Next door's burglar alarm went off next. I tried phoning them, no reply. It went off eventually. Great! I thought, now for some sleep. What a hope! The cats started next, five of them all along the car park wall. Got up, made a cup of tea. Didn't help. Tried sleeping on the couch. No good, the dog wanted to sleep there too. Going to take sleeping pills tonight!

Learning tip – Diary writing
Sentences in a diary are often shortened because you want to focus on the main points.

b Write a diary entry about what you did yesterday.

7 Do's and Don'ts for a quiet life

The Environmental Health Departments of British local councils have been receiving an increasing number of complaints about neighbourhood noise over the past five years. Like many others, the borough of Chesterfield set down some guidelines about reducing noise levels which it sent to all households. Enter each guideline in the correct column.

	do's	don'ts
1. use domestic appliances late at night	☐	☐
2. turn the hi-fi level down after 11 pm	☐	☐
3. think about your neighbours when you are doing something noisy	☐	☐
4. have frequent late parties in the same house or flat	☐	☐
5. leave a dog alone for long periods	☐	☐
6. sound car horns, rev engines and slam doors late at night	☐	☐
7. leave a key with someone who can be called to deal with false operation of alarms	☐	☐
8. carry out noisy DIY after 9 pm on any day and before 10.30 am on weekends	☐	☐

Add any more guidelines you can think of.

Unit 11

(Unit 12)

Entertainment

1 Saturday night at the movies?

How do you spend Saturday evening?
Do you always have a night out?
Or do you take the opportunity to relax
because you have a hard working week?
Have your habits changed over the years?

Interview the other members of your group
by asking them the following questions:

Do you spend Saturday evening	watching TV? at the pub? at the cinema? eating out with friends? doing something else?

What are the results of your survey?

Most people Some people Hardly anyone	in the class		on Saturday evening.

110

2 The Picturegoers

In the 1950's and 1960's one of the most popular forms of entertainment on a Saturday evening was going to the cinema or, to use a popular expression, to the pictures. While people were queuing up to get in, they were very often approached by unaccompanied children just as in this extract from "The Picturegoers" by David Lodge.

'Take us in, Mister?'
The question startled him.
'I beg your pardon?' he said politely and peered down through his spectacles at the group of rough dirty children who surrounded him.
'G'orn, Guv, take's in.'
Father Kipling smiled uncertainly and decided on an I'm-in-the-same-boat-as-you-fellows approach.
'Well, really, you know, I don't think I can afford it.' Things had come to a pretty bad pass when children begged unashamedly on the streets for money to indulge in luxuries such as the cinema. He began to feel quite indignant.
The ring-leader scrutinized him as if he could scarcely credit the evidence of his ears. He glanced meaningfully at his companions and began to explain.
'We don't want you to pay for us, Mister. We just want you to take us in.'
'Jus' say we're with yer,' backed up another.
''Ere's the money, Guv.' A grimy, shrivelled paw held up some silver coins.
'But why?' asked Father Kipling bewildered.
The leader took a deep breath.
'Well, yer see, Mister, it's an "A" and you can't get into an "A" …
Father Kipling listened carfully to the explanation. At the end of it he said, 'Then really, you're not allowed to see this film unless accompanied by a parent or guardian?'
'That's right, Mister.'
'Well, then, I'm afraid I can't help you because I'm certainly not your parent, and I can't honestly say I'm your guardian. Can I now?' He smiled nervously at the chief urchin, who turned away in disgust, and formed up his entourage to petition another cinema-goer. Father Kipling stared after them for a moment, then hurriedly made good his escape.

28

Learning tip – Reading for pleasure
When reading a novel in the original English version, don't look up every word that looks unfamiliar at first sight. Try to get a feeling for the scenario the writer is creating. Just sit back, relax and enjoy it!

G'orn, Guv (Cockney slang) = Come on, sir

(Unit 12)

2a Find the words or expressions in the text with these meanings:

- things were in a bad condition
- to satisfy a desire for
- very angry
- to examine carefully
- very dirty
- dried up
- confused
- s.one with the legal right to look after a person
- a dirty, untidy child
- strong dislike

- What's the meaning of the opening question of the text "Take us in, Mister?"
- How does Father Kipling react to the situation?
- Would this situation still be possible today? If not, could you think of a similar situation which would apply today? – Explain it to the group.

b The next morning at breakfast Father Kipling's housekeeper asked him about his visit to the cinema.

> 'Well then, Father, and how did you enjoy the film?'
>
> 'Not at all,' said Father Kipling. 'It was a big mistake. Not only was it the wrong film, but a group of young children asked me if I would take them into the cinema with me. I told them I couldn't afford it. You know, it really made me quite angry. But then they told me they didn't want me to pay for them; they just wanted me to take them in with me. Have you ever heard of such a thing? Anyhow, when they explained to me that they couldn't get into an 'A' film unless accompanied by a parent or guardian, I replied that I couldn't help them. Well, I'm neither their parent or their guardian, am I, Mrs O'Hare? Do you think I could have some more toast?'

Highlight the examples of reported speech in this passage and compare them with the direct speech used in the text on page 111. What are the differences in the tenses?

What are some of the rules about changing from direct speech to reported speech?

Father Kipling uses different verbs to introduce his reported speech. What are they? Which other verbs do you know which you could add to this list?

Compare with the grammar reference section on **pages 158–159**.

Think of some situations in which you would use reported speech. Compare with a partner.

112

c Put the following sentences into reported speech using an appropriate introductory verb.

1. "The car won't start because there's no petrol in the tank."
2. "Have you seen the latest Kevin Costner film?"
3. "Why don't you have a rest?"
4. "I'm going into hospital next week."
5. "I'll call you as soon as I get there."
6. "What's the problem?"
7. "You can borrow my car if you want to."
8. "Sorry, we can't come. We're having visitors on Saturday."

3 What's it about?

a Have you seen these films | in the cinema?
on DVD or video?
on TV?

Braveheart

Four Weddings and a Funeral

Goldfinger

Bridget Jones's Diary

The Lord of the Rings

If you don't know all the films which are presented here, then try to find someone else in the class who can give you some information.

> **Learning Tip – Exchanging information**
> You can't be expected to know everything. For example, there will be some films you have seen, some books you have read, some places you have visited that others don't know, and vice versa. Communication is also a means of getting and passing on information. So don't be afraid to ask others.

b Listen to five people talking about their favourite films and match each description with a title.

- [ ] The Lord of the Rings
- [ ] Four Weddings and a Funeral
- [ ] Bridget Jones's Diary
- [ ] Goldfinger
- [ ] Braveheart

c Think of a film that you really like. Make some notes, describing the film in a similar way to the descriptions on the recording in **3b**. Then read it out to the others in the class and let them guess which film it is.

Unit 12

(Unit 12)

4 Making a booking

Work together with a partner.
Student **A** look at **page 124**,
Student **B** at **page 128**.
When you have completed the
role play once, switch roles.

5 I couldn't live without it

a Imagine you're going on a camping holiday some distance from the nearest town. Which of the following items would you take with you for entertainment?

- ☐ playing cards
- ☐ a discman
- ☐ a portable TV
- ☐ a set of dice
- ☐ a set of boules
- ☐ a football
- ☐ a book or books
- ☐ a travel chess-set
- ☐ a laptop with DVD-player
- ☐ …
- ☐ …

Which other item(s) would you add to the list? Go around the class and try to find some other people who would take the same items as you.

b Now think of an eleven-year-old boy going on a school trip for a week. What do you think he would want to take with him for entertainment? You're going to hear a radio report about Charlie Dukes, who set off on a school trip to the small Scottish island of Iona and left something behind at home. What do you think it was? Listen and find out.

c Listen again and decide whether the following statements are true, false or possible.

	True	False	Possible
1. Charlie is an only child.	☐	☐	☐
2. Charlie and his classmates were travelling by train.	☐	☐	☐
3. Mrs Dukes spent £115 to catch up with her son.	☐	☐	☐
4. The school party was going to stay at a campsite on Iona.	☐	☐	☐
5. Charlie was very pleased to see his mother.	☐	☐	☐
6. It was his fault that he had left the toy at home.	☐	☐	☐

d How would you react to this story?

'Poor boy!'

'What a waste of money!'

'What a stupid thing to do!'

'That's just what I would have done.'

Discuss your reactions in groups of four.

Learning tip – Writing stories
When writing a story, remember the five W's – <u>W</u>ho did <u>w</u>hat <u>w</u>hen, <u>w</u>here and <u>w</u>hy? Of course, don't try to put all this information into one sentence!

e For some people the ending to Charlie's story might be 'All's well that ends well'. Do you know a true story that could end with those words? Write it down and tell the others about it in the next lesson.

6 Talking about the past

Mrs Dukes made a 900-mile dash across the country after her son had left on a school-trip without his favourite toy.

I was surprised when I heard that they had chosen an American actress for the leading role.

Highlight the verb forms in these two sentences and identify the tenses.
Why are two different forms of the past used?

▷ Check with the grammar reference section on **page 159**.

Unit 12 **115**

(Back-up)

7 Past tenses

Fill in the gaps in the following sentences using the simple past or the past perfect tense of the verbs in brackets as appropriate.

1. I just _____ (get) into the bath when the phone _____ (ring).
2. By the time he _____ (arrive) home, his wife _____ (give) his dinner to the dog.
3. Our next-door neighbour _____ (not be) very happy about last summer's hosepipe-ban since he _____ (sow) new grass in the spring.
4. No sooner they _____ (they/unpack) the picnic things than the rain _____ (come) on.
5. As a boy he _____ (always/want) to join the Navy, but a car accident at the age of 15 _____ (ruin) his hopes.
6. As soon as they _____ (have) breakfast, they _____ (go) down to the beach for a swim.
7. Val and Greg _____ (open) a small guesthouse after Greg _____ (take) early retirement.
8. They _____ (live) in different parts of the world before they _____ (decide) to settle in the Lake District.
9. I _____ (know) I _____ (dial) the wrong number when I _____ (hear) the voice at the other end.
10. Terry _____ (wake) up with a hangover because he _____ (have) too much to drink the night before.

8 Beginnings and endings

Match a beginning with an ending to make sensible sentences.
Sometimes there is more than one possibility.

1. He asked her	that they would be sent home for bad behaviour.
2. He admitted	that there were still some charts to complete.
3. She wondered	that the heating had been turned off.
4. The teacher warned them	where she came from.
5. The children said	that the investment fund was two million in the red.
6. I told him	where the strange smell was coming from.
7. John reminded me	that it was too early to tell.
8. We complained	that they didn't need any money.

9 What did they say?

Look at your sentences in **8** again. Write down what you think the persons actually said in each case.

1. _____
2. _____
3. _____
4. _____
5. _____
6. _____
7. _____
8. _____

10 What's it all about?

Choose four of the examples of direct speech from **9** and describe a little scenario for each one. Begin with the statement or question in direct speech. Think about who was involved, where and when it took place, why the statement was made.

For example: 'The heating's been turned off!' – We had just returned from a long day at work, my partner and I. It was the middle of December, and temperatures in Wisconsin are never much above freezing at that time of the year. I knew I had paid the last heating bill, at least I thought I had.

11 Watching films and reading for pleasure

Have you ever seen a film that was based on a novel, for example, 'Sense and Sensibility' by Jane Austen, 'Bridget Jones's Diary' by Helen Fielding or 'Chocolat' by Joanne Harris? Had you read the book before watching the film or did you decide to read the book after watching the film? How did the book and the film compare?

Talk to two or three other students about your experiences.

In most cases the book has been written before the film is made, but sometimes the book is not written until after the film has been produced and proved a success. Do you know any?

This was the case with the film 'Billy Elliot', the story of a young boy from the north of England whose great dream it is to become a ballet dancer. However, neither Billy's background nor his family's financial situation can support him in realising this dream. It's the time of the miners' strikes of the mid-1980's, and Billy's father is forced to break up the family piano for firewood. Billy, a half-orphan who also has to take care of his grandmother before and after school, would prefer to take ballet lessons than go to the weekly boxing class his father sends him to.

In his book based on the film the successful author of books for young people, Melvin Burgess, focuses on the father-son relationship in a man's world and shows that despite poverty and social misery dreams can come true.

(Revision 4)

1 Reading for understanding

Some taxi-drivers only work part-time as a taxi-driver and have another full-time job. What other jobs do you think some taxi-drivers do?
In the following extract from 'Father Frank' by Paul Burke the taxi-driver has a rather unusual full-time job? What do you think it is?

a The five paragraphs of the extract have got into the wrong order. Can you number them in the right order?

☐ 'Because your donation is strictly voluntary,' he told her, 'you are fully insured, but if you want to get out and hail a proper taxi, I quite understand.' Sarah didn't get out. Nobody ever did. It crossed her mind that 'Father Dempsey' might be a serial rapist but, then, so might anyone. 'No,' she said. 'If you can get me to Farringdon Road in ten minutes, I don't care if you're the Archbishop of Canterbury.'

☐ 'The taxi was left to me by a parishioner. I couldn't bear to sell it so I thought I'd put it to good use. I have to come down to Westminster two or three times a week on diocesan business, so on my way home I do a little bit of fund-raising.' 'Only when you come down to Westminster?' 'Depends. Sometimes on my day off, or if I'm a bit quiet, I just get in the cab and come into the West End. It's a fantastic way of raising money.' 'What do you do with it?'

☐ 'Well, the church and the parish cost an awful lot to maintain, and rather than organise endless coffee mornings and bring and buy sales, it's quicker and easier to go out cabbing.' Frank had given this schtick hundreds of times before, often to beautiful female passengers, literally without turning a hair, but this time was different.

☐ Frank smiled at her and headed out on to Regent Street. Sarah simply stared at him. People always did. A priest driving a taxi – well, you would stare, wouldn't you? But Sarah was staring for a different reason. God, what a handsome man, she was thinking. And what a terrible waste. Why the hell is he a priest? Look at him – tall, square-shouldered, short dark hair, navy blue eyes. God, what a waste. He reminded her of pictures she'd seen of Dean Martin in his Rat Pack heyday, standing outside the Sands Hotel in Las Vegas. She angled her head to get a better view of his face. 'Look, I know everyone must ask you this but, well, this taxi ... er ... why' How come?'

☐ Sarah Marshall clambered into the back of the taxi on the west side of Golden Square. 'Farringdon Road, please.' Instead of setting off, the driver turned round. 'Before I take you,' he said, as he had said a hundred times before, 'you ought to know I'm not a licensed taxi driver. I'm Father Frank Dempsey, parish priest of St Thomas's in Wealdstone. I'm happy to take you to Farringdon Road, if you wouldn't mind leaving a small donation in the box there.' Sarah then noticed that there was no meter. The driver was gesturing instead towards a collection box, where the meter would normally have been. It was bolted securely to the floor.

b Are the following statements about the text true, false or possible?
Make a reference to the text to prove your point.

	True	False	Possible
1. This was the first time that Father Frank had driven a taxi.	☐	☐	☐
2. Sarah didn't have to pay for the taxi ride.	☐	☐	☐
3. Some of Father Frank's taxi money had been stolen before.	☐	☐	☐
4. 'Father Dempsey' was really the Archbishop of Canterbury.	☐	☐	☐
5. Sarah thought Father Frank would make a good film star.	☐	☐	☐
6. Father Frank hates driving the taxi.	☐	☐	☐
7. He's very fond of organising coffee mornings.	☐	☐	☐
8. Sarah was the most beautiful passenger he had ever driven.	☐	☐	☐

c Can you find the words in the text which match these meanings?

1. to climb something with difficulty
2. money or goods that you give to an organisation
3. to make a movement with your hands or head
4. fixed
5. to signal a bus or taxi so that it stops for you
6. the time when a person is most successful or most popular
7. to make something point in a particular direction
8. someone who lives in a particular church district and regularly goes to church
9. concerning a district that a bishop is in charge of
10. an attention-getting or theatrical routine

Which of these words were really important for you to understand the text?

d Sarah describes Father Frank as tall, square-shouldered and handsome.
These words all describe his appearance.
Which adjectives would you use to describe his personality?
Why do you think he became a priest? And how do you think the story
will develop after this extract?
Discuss your ideas in small groups. Of course, if you want to find out
how close you were, you could always read the whole book!

(Revision 4)

2 Working with grammar: gerunds and infinitives

In the text in **1** Father Frank said to Sarah '… if you wouldn't mind leaving a small donation …'. 'Wouldn't mind' and 'leaving' are closely linked. The form 'leav**ing**' is determined by 'wouldn't mind'. At the same time the speech intention of asking someone politely to do something determines the use of the verbal expression 'wouldn't mind'.

Now take a close look at the form of the verb after the gap in the following sentences. That will help you with your choice of a suitable verb or verbal expression to fill the gap in each sentence. But think, too, of the speech intention behind each sentence.

1. We _____ to see you at the party on Saturday.
2. We _____ seeing you at the wedding.
3. Sharon _____ watching the skyline of the city from the bay.
4. _____ you _____ to have something to drink?
5. _____ you _____ eating outdoors in the summer?
6. When did you _____ smoking?
7. Christine _____ travelling on the MTR's crowded trains because they have air-conditioning.
8. I absolutely _____ getting stuck in a traffic jam.
9. I know I _____ to help you with those copies, but I'm pretty busy at the moment.
10. Could you drive a bit faster? I don't _____ to be late.

3 Working with grammar: if-sentences type 3

a Look at this chain of events where one thing leads to another.

1. Tony didn't hear the alarm.
2. He was late for work.
3. He rushed out of the house.
4. He slipped on the icy pavement.
5. He fell and broke his arm.
6. He cried for help.
7. The young nurse two doors along heard him.
8. She called an ambulance and went out to help him.
9. They talked all the way to the hospital.
10. They made a date for the following week.

Some months later at Angela's and Tony's wedding you are telling a friend the following story:

"If only Tony had heard the alarm that morning, he and Angela might never have met. You see, it all started like this … If …"

Complete the story with the information given above.

b Take another look at the extract from 'Father Frank' and imagine a chain of events which begins with

◦ Sarah was late for a job interview that day.

Add five or six sentences and exchange your paper with a partner. Now make an 'if-story' as in **3a** starting with 'If only Sarah ...' and using your partner's sentences.
When you're finished, read your story to the rest of the class.

4 Reading for pleasure

Perhaps now that you've completed the course, you'd like to take some time to read a novel like "The Picturegoers" or "Father Frank". If, however, you don't feel like reading a complete book in the original version, why not try one of these Macmillan Guided Readers? The books in the Intermediate Level have a vocabulary of about 1600 basic words.

Sue Grafton,
A is for Alibi

Thomas Hardy,
The Woodlanders

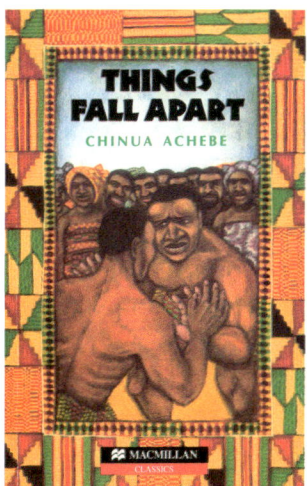

Chinua Achebe,
Things Fall Apart

Jane Austen,
Pride and Prejudice

File Section • (Unit 1)

5 BMW world-wide
(page 11, Partner B)

Read this short text about Betsy Chan, a line worker from BMW in South Carolina. Be ready to answer your partner's questions about Betsy.

Betsy Chan is **33** years old and works for **BMW**. She is **married** and lives with her husband **Joe** and their **son** Robert in a **three-bedroom house** in **Spartanburg, South Carolina**. She pays **$600 a month** for the mortgage on the house. She drives **a small BMW** that she leases from the company and she **drives** the **20 kilometres** to work every day. There are **two** shifts at the factory, a day shift and a night shift and each shift lasts **10 hours**. Betsy works **40 hours** a week, but she often works overtime. This is her 3rd year at BMW so she has **10 days'** holiday a year and the company pays a maximum of 7 extra days when the factory closes for maintenance. Betsy works on the night shift and so she earns **$23.75 an hour**. ❑

There is some information printed in bold in this text. Ask questions to find out similar information from your partner about Oscar Sigasa who works for BMW in Rosslyn, South Africa.

9c Family relationships
(page 14, Group A)

Your teacher will give you a name card. Study your family tree carefully and check your relationship to the other members of your "family".

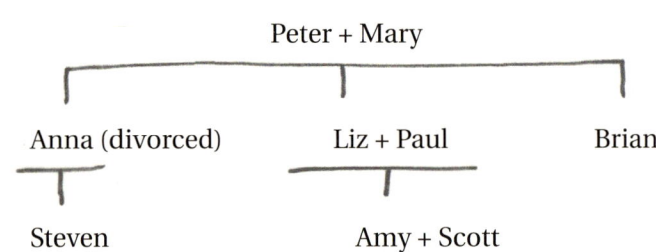

The other group will ask you "yes/no" questions about the relationships in your "family". Remember you can only answer with:

Yes, I am.
No, I'm not.
Yes, he/she is.
No, he/she isn't.
Yes, they are.
No, they aren't.

File Section • (Unit 4)

2b The holiday
(page 43, Partner A)

Last year it was Mr and Mrs Lang's 20th wedding anniversary, and they went on a wonderful holiday to **Malaysia**. They flew _____ (how) from London Heathrow to **Kuala Lumpur**. They flew first class. When they arrived, they spent _____ (how many) nights in the Federal Hotel in Kuala Lumpur and then **took a taxi** to the new luxury resort on Pangkor Island. Their bedroom looked out over the sea, and it was air-conditioned. The Temperatures in Malaysia rose to _____ (how high) during the day, and even in the evening it was 20 degrees. Every morning after a breakfast of **fresh pineapple rolls and butter** and _____ (what/drink), they relaxed **by the pool**, drank their _____ (what) and wrote **postcards** to their friends in England. In the afternoon they _____ (what/do) and saw **lots of beautiful coloured fish**, and once they had a demonstration of how to fly a Malaysian kite.

In the evenings they usually watched _____ (what), but on their last evening they watched **a Chinese puppet play**. They only stayed for _____ (how long), and the holiday passed very quickly.

File Section • (Unit 6)

4 An optimist or a pessimist?
(page 57, Partner A)

Ask your partner the following questions:

- Do you like sunbathing?
- Do you think we'll be able to lie in the sun in 2050?
- Do you think we'll use only solar and wind energy in 2050?
- Do you think we'll use a lot of recycled products in 2050?

File Section • (Unit 6)

6 Welcome!
(page 60)

Here are your visitors. They all want to have some time to just relax, but they want to see a lot of things on their visit because it's a long way to Europe from Australia and this may be their first and only visit. Money is no problem for the visitors.

David Quarrie's a doctor and worked for a long time as a flying doctor based in Alice Springs. He would like to do some sightseeing from the air, but otherwise he's only here for the beer!

James Hughes is professor of geology at the university in Adelaide. He's very interested in anything to do with geology!

Helen Meere's an artist who lives and works in the outback. She wants to visit a lot of museums and galleries on her stay. She also wants to drink some good German beer because all her male Australian friends say that Australian beer is best!

Bruce Foster's a teacher who works in a school in Melbourne. He's particularly interested in modern history.

File Section • (Unit 12)

4 Making a booking
(page 114, Student A)

You are going to call the Citizens' Theatre Box Office to make a theatre booking.

Look at the summer theatre programme on **page 125** and decide
- which play you want to book tickets for
- the date and time
- the number of tickets

Also ask about
- car parking
- reductions for senior citizens/unemployed persons/students

When you have completed the role play once, switch roles.

File Section • (Unit 12)

CITIZENS THEATRE.

25 July – 5 August

Arsenic and Old Lace

By Joseph Kesselrig
Directed by Andy Arnold
Arches Theatre Co

Following their recent sell-out success with *Accidental Death of an Anarchist* and *The Hostage* over the last two years, the Arches Theatre Company once again visits the Citizens' with a comedy classic. *Arsenic and Old Lace* is the famous and most hilarious play about multiple murder, telling the story of two charming and gentle old ladies who poison their poor orphan lodgers in order to save them from the sorrows of this world.

Free matinees: 26 July, 2 August 2.30pm

1 – 23 September

Don Carlos

By Friedrich von Schiller
Directed and Designed by Phillip Prowse
Translated by Robert David Macdonald
The Citizens' Company

Schiller's sweeping romantic drama is both a passionate love story – the forbidden love of Carlos for his father's second wife Elizabeth and the betrayal of that love by the Princess Eboli – and a great hymn to freedom as Carlos and his companion champion the cause of Liberty in a small country trying to break free of a colonising world power.

Free previews: 18, 31 August 7.30pm
Free matinee: 6 September 2.30pm

18 July – 12 August

Quelques Fleurs

By Liz Lochhead
Directed by Joyce Deans
Nippy Sweeties Theatre Co

In her house like a palace, Verena the oil-widow waits. On the train from the rigs, Derek (two weeks on, two weeks off) journeys towards a Christmas he'll never forget.

Free matinees: 26 July, 9 Aug 2.30pm

31 August – 23 September

Ebb Tide

By Robert Louis Stevenson
Adapted and Directed by
Robert David Macdonald
Designed by Kenny Miller
The Citizens' Company

In *Ebb Tide*, Stevenson takes a sensational plot involving smuggling and murder in the South Sea Islands and finds in it a powerful story of man's quest for self-knowledge.

Free preview: 30 Aug 7.30pm
Free matinee: 13 Sept 2.30pm

Circle Studio
AT THE CITIZENS THEATRE

File Section **125**

File Section • (Unit 9)

3 Take two careers
(page 84, Partner B)

Read this profile.

- **Name** Jenny Dickson
- **Age** 26
- **Occupation** Coach driver for Western Coach Travel Ltd.
- **Route to the job** Jenny left school in 1993 at the age of sixteen and spent two years as a kitchen assistant at a tennis club. Then, after training and a test, she got a job as a town-service minibus driver in Bath. Two years later she trained for double-decker buses and drove those for two years before being accepted, three years ago, on the coach and tour roster for Western Coach Travel Ltd.
- **Dress** A uniform of navy skirt, light green blouse, bright green sweater, navy tie and navy shoes.
- **Salary** £15,000 a year plus meal allowance of £7,75 per day, ticket commission and occasional tips
- **Monthly spending** partner pays the mortgage; £100 bills; £100 clothes; £50 tennis and trampolining; £30 cinema; £30 home and holidays

Now ask your partner for information about Barbara Barsa Jamison.

- **Name** Barbara Barsa Jamison
- **Age**
- **Occupation**
- **Route to the job**

?
- When did she leave university?
- What was her first job?
- How long did she stay in this job?
- What did she do next?
- How long has she had her present job?
- How many different jobs has she had since she left university?
- How much does she earn?
- How much does she spend on clothes a month?

File Section • (Unit 1)

9c Family relationships
(page 14, Group B)

Look at the list of names in the Grant Family and prepare questions to ask Group A. Find out their family relationships and try to put their family tree together. There are three married couples in this family.

You can only ask "yes/no" questions like:

> Are you …?
> Is … your …?
> Are … your …?

Peter
Anna
Brian
Mary
Steven
Liz
Scott
Amy
Paul

File Section • (Unit 6)

4 An optimist or a pessimist?
(page 57, Partner B)

Ask your partner the following questions:

- Do you like skiing?
- Do you think that we'll still go skiing in 2050?
- Do you think we'll have only battery cars in 2050?
- Do you think we'll have problems with our waste in 2050?

File Section • (Unit 12)

4 Making a booking
(page 114, Student B)

You work at the Citizens' Theatre Box Office.

Some of the information required by the caller is given here; any missing information you will have to make up by yourself.

When you have completed the role play once, switch roles.

**119 Gorbals Street
Glasgow G5 9DS**

Booking
Tickets can be booked at the Citizens' Theatre Box Office, Monday to Saturday from 10am to 9pm, or 10am to 6pm when there is no evening performance. From 22 May to 14 July the Box Office is open Monday to Friday, 10am to 5pm only.

Telephone bookings can be made on:
0141-429 0022

Access and *Visa* accepted.

Ticket prices
£12 Full Price
£ 5 Unemployed, Senior citizens, Registered disabled, Students, School children

Performances
Tuesday – Saturdays: 7.30pm
Free matinees: 2.30pm

Buses to Citizens Theatre
Strathclyde Buses: 5, 5a, 12, 12a, 31, 66, 66a, 66b, 74, M14
Kelvin Central: 67

Underground
Bridge Street

Car parking
There is a free car park next to the theatre. Please do not leave valuable items in cars. We can store them for you during the performance.

Grammar Reference Section

(Unit 1)
1 The Simple Present (1) — 130
2 "have" and "have got" — 130
3 Positive and Negative Statements — 132
4 Questions — 132
   a Yes/No Questions — 132
   b Questions with Question-words — 133
5 The –'s Form — 133
6 "There is" and "There are" — 133

(Unit 2)
1 The Simple Present (2) — 134
2 The Present Progressive — 134
3 Some and Any — 136
4 How much and How many? — 137

(Unit 3)
1 Adverbs of Frequency — 137

(Unit 3+4)
2 The Simple Past — 138
   a Positive and Negative Short Answers — 138
   b Yes/No Questions — 138
   c Questions with Question Words — 139
3 Simple Past of "to have" — 139
4 Simple Past of "to be" — 140
5 Other Irregular Verbs — 140
6 The Past Progressive — 141

(Unit 4)
1 Question tags — 142
   a To check information — 142
   b To sound interested or to show sympathy — 142

(Unit 5)
1 The Present Perfect Simple (1) — 143
2 The Present Perfect or the Simple Past? — 143
3 Pronouns and Adjectives — 144

(Unit 6)
1 The Future in English — 144
   a "will"-Future — 144
   b "Going to"-Future — 145
   c The Present Progressive — 146

(Unit 7)
1 If-sentences — 146
   a If-sentence type 1 — 146
   b If-sentence type 2 for general use — 147
   c If-sentence type 2 for giving advice — 147

(Unit 8)
1 Modal Verbs — 148
   a "Used to" — 148
   b "Must / have to" — 148
   c "Mustn't / not allowed to" — 149
   d "Have to / Don't have to" — 149
   e "may, might, must, can't" — 150

(Unit 9)
1 The Present Perfect Simple (2) — 151
2 The Present Perfect Progressive (or Continuous) — 151
3 For or Since — 152

(Unit 10)
1 Comparative and superlative forms of adjectives — 153
2 Verbal expressions followed by gerunds and/or infinitives — 154
3 The passive — 156

(Unit 11)
1 If-sentences type 3 — 157

(Unit 12)
1 Reported speech — 158
2 Past perfect simple — 159

Prepositions
List of Prepositions — 160

Phrasal Verbs
List of Phrasal Verbs — 161

Irregular Verbs
List of Irregular Verbs — 162

Grammar Reference Section (Unit 1)

1 The Simple Present (1) (ex. 6, page 12)

Positive Form

The verb form is the same for all persons except "he / she / it".
Remember the rhyme you learnt at school: „He/she/it – das S muss mit!"

I / You / We / They	eat	toast every morning.
He / She / It	eats	toast every morning.

Negative Form

Add "do" + "not" to the basic form.

I	don't (do not)		
You	don't (do not)	eat	toast every morning.
We	don't (do not)		
They	don't (do not)		

Add "does" + "not" to the basic form.

He	doesn't (does not)		
She	doesn't (does not)	eat	toast every morning.
It	doesn't (does not)		

"He/she/it – das S muss mit – for the preSent but only once!"

Usage

For a regular habit:
- He eats toast every morning.

To describe something that is always true:
- London stands on the River Thames.
- She speaks German.

2 "have" and "have got" (ex. 1, page 8)

"Have got" sounds strange to German ears, but it is important to learn, as you will hear the question "have you got" a lot in England, but not so much in Scotland and not in America.

Positive Form

I	've (I have) got	a bicycle.
You	've (you have) got	a cold.
He	's (he has) got	a moustache.
She	's (she has) got	two sisters.
It	's (it has) got	a bone.
We	've (we have) got	a lot of time.
They	've (they have) got	a new car.

Negative Form

Add "not". This is usually shortened to "n't" in speech but not in writing.

I	haven't (have not) got	a bicycle.
It	hasn't (has not) got	a bone.
They	haven't (have not) got	a new car.

Question

Invert (change round) the subject (I / you / he / we / they) and the verb (have).

Have	you	got	a new hat?
Have	we	got	a lot of time?

Usage

"have got" describes a state and not an action.

For possession:
- I've got a bicycle. *(Ich habe / ich besitze ein Fahrrad.)*

To talk about relationships:
- She's got two sisters.

To talk about an illness:
- You've got a cold. *(Sie sind erkältet.)*
- I've got a headache. *(Ich habe Kopfschmerzen.)*

In descriptions:
- He's got a moustache.

In common expressions:
- Have you got a light? *(Haben Sie Feuer?)*
- Have you got the time? *(Wie spät ist es?)*
- Have you got a minute? *(Haben Sie Zeit? Ich möchte Sie sprechen.)*
- Have you got change for the phone? *(Haben Sie Kleingeld?)*

The Verb "have"

American speakers use "have" and not "have got":
- I have two sisters.
- She has a new car.

The question form is then as a full verb using "do":
- Do you have a car?

"have" in British English can be used:

In repeated situations:
- I often have headaches.
- We don't usually have beer in the house.

As an action verb, instead of another verb:
- We have breakfast at seven o'clock. *(Wir frühstücken um sieben.)*
- She has a shower every morning. *(Sie duscht jeden Morgen.)*
- He has a shave before he goes to work. *(Er rasiert sich …)*

3 Positive and Negative Statements (ex. 3c, page 9; ex. 5, page 11)

- Mark **likes** maccaroni, but he **doesn't like** red ties.
- I **like** apples, but I **don't like** apricots.
- Helga **is** fond of horse-riding, but she **isn't** fond of English beer.
- I**'m** fond of swimming, but I**'m not** so fond of skiing.

For the complete positive and negative forms of the simple present and the verb "to be" check **1** on **page 130** and **2** on **page 134**.

4 Questions (ex. 4, pages 10–11)

There are two forms of questions which can be used with all the tenses in English:
- Do you play soccer?
- When did you start playing?

a Yes/No Questions

- Do you play soccer?

They are called "yes / no questions" because they expect the answer "yes" or "no". They always begin with an auxiliary verb followed by the subject.

auxiliary verb	subject	rest of question
Do	you	play soccer?
Are	you	called after someone?
Is	that	your proper name?
Can	you	speak Italian?
Have	you	ever been to the US?
Have	you	got the book?
Did	you	learn English at school?
Does	this bus	go into town?

Questions like these are normally answered by "yes" or "no". However, "yes" or "no" on their own don't sound very friendly, and so we usually add two or three words to make our reply sound friendlier.

Do you play soccer?	Yes, I **do**.	No, I **don't**.
Are you called after someone?	Yes, I **am**.	No, I**'m not**.
Is that your proper name?	Yes, it **is**.*	No, it **isn't**.*
Can you speak Italian?	Yes, I **can**.	No, I **can't**.
Have you ever been to the US?	Yes, I **have**.	No, I **haven't**.
Have you got the book?	Yes, I **have**.	No, I **haven't**.
Did you learn English at school?	Yes, I **did**.	No, I **didn't**.
Does this bus go into town?	Yes, it **does**.	No, it **doesn't**.

* Note the change from "that" to "it"!

b Questions with Question-words

- When did you start playing?

These questions always begin with one or more question-words followed by the pattern in **4a**.

question-word(s)	auxiliary verb	subject	rest of question
When	did	you	start playing?
Where	do	you	live?
How	do	you	get here?
How much	was		the book?
Where	does	Werner	work?

Questions like these expect more information than just the answer "yes" or "no".

When did you start playing?	When I was a kid.
Where do you live?	On the other side of town.
How do you get here?	By bus, and then I walk the rest.
How much was the book?	Sorry, I don't know. My wife bought it for me.
Where does Werner work?	In Dresden, I think.

Note: In spoken English we don't always use full sentences when replying to questions.

5 The –'s Form

This form can have three different meanings.
1. John**'s** back.
2. John**'s** back is sore.
3. John**'s** had a sore back for over a week now.

You can see the difference clearly in the following sentences.
1. John **is** back.
2. John's back (**His** back) is sore.
3. John **has** had a sore back for over a week now.

In sentences 1. and 3. the –'s form is a short verb form of **is** (in 1.) and **has** (in 3.).
In sentence 2. it is the possessive form of the noun which it is added to.

The possessive (or genitive) –'s form always comes after the full form of the noun it goes with:
John's back; the **child**'s ball; the **children**'s books; Mr **Smith**'s car; the **boy**'s bike

Note: If the noun already ends in an –'s, you don't add another one: the **boys**' bikes; Mr **Jones**' car.

6 "There is" and "There are" (ex. 6c, page 12)

- There is a cinema in the town.
- There are two pubs in the village.

This is used in English to express the German „*es gibt*".

Note: You cannot say "There are a ..." and so in a long list you use "There is".
- There's a pub, a post office and a bank in the town.

But:
- There **are two** pubs, a post office and a bank in the town.

Grammar Reference Section

Grammar Reference Section (Unit 2)

1 The Simple Present (2)

We looked at the form of the simple present in **Unit 1** and talked about how it is used for a regular habit, a routine.

You also hear the simple present in commentaries because the speaker thinks of the events as a link in a chain of events (ex. 3, page 22).
- He kicks the ball and scores a goal!

"What does he do?" – This question has a special meaning (ex. 4, page 22).

What does he do?	What's his job?	–	He's a doctor.
What does she do?	What's her job?	–	She's a doctor too.
What do you do?	What's your job?	–	I'm a footballer.
What do they do?	What are their jobs?	–	They're actors.

Note: It's more usual to ask the question "What does he do?" than "What's his job?"

Be careful: Notice that you answer these questions with the verb "to be" + a/an + profession.
- I'm **a** footballer.
- She's **a** nurse.

This is different from German.

2 The Present Progressive (ex. 4, page 22 and ex. 5, page 23)

Positive Form

The verb "to be" + -*ing*-form of the verb.

I	'm (am)	
You	're (are)	
He	's (is)	
She	's (is)	enjoying the holiday.
We	're (are)	
They	're (are)	

Negative Form

The verb "to be" + not + -*ing*-form of the verb.

I	'm not (am not)	
You	're not (are not)	
He	's not (is not)	
She	's not (is not)	enjoying the holiday.
We	're not (are not)	
They	're not (are not)	

Usage

We use the present progressive:

to talk about what's happening at the time of speaking. In the picture on page 22 you can see what's happening now.
- Gerard Depardieu is smoking a cigarette.

to talk about an action that's temporary but is not happening at the moment of speaking.
- She's having driving lessons.

Note: Remember the name of this form of the present: the PROGRESSive.
This means we use it when an action is in PROGRESS now or for a limited period of time.

Question Form

Invert the subject and the verb "to be" + *-ing*-form.

Am	I	driving too fast?
Are	you we they	enjoying the holiday?
Is	he she it	

Positive and Negative Short Answers

We use short answers because repeating the information in the question when we answer a "yes / no question" sounds angry or irritated:
- "Is he playing football?" – "Yes, he is playing football!" (What a silly question, I told you five minutes ago!)

Positive Form

Yes,	I am. you are. he is. she is. they are. we are.

Be careful: You can't use short forms in positive short answers!

Negative Form

No,	I'm not you aren't he isn't she isn't we aren't

Be careful: For negative short answers the full form sounds angry:
- "Is he bathing the baby?" – "No, he is not. He's watching football on TV." (So I'm bathing the baby again!)

3 Some and Any (ex. 2, page 21)

Some nouns in English are uncountable and some are countable.

Countable: glass, ski
Uncountable: money, water

You can say "one glass, two glasses", "one ski, two skis" – these nouns are countable.
So you can ask: "I'd like a glass of wine, please."

But "money" and "water" are uncountable nouns. Add "some" in front of uncountable nouns when you ask: "I'd like **some** money, please."

Some – Usage

"Some" is used with plural countable nouns and uncountable nouns in positive sentences:
- I need some eggs.
- I need some water.

"Some" is used with plural countable nouns and uncountable nouns when you are offering something and you expect the answer to be "yes":
- Would you like some tea?
- Would you like some biscuits?
- Would you like to have some fun?

Any – Usage

"Any" is used with plural countable nouns and uncountable nouns in negative statements and questions:
- I'm sorry I haven't got any sausages.
- Have you got any onions?
- We don't need any more white wine.
- Do we need any beer?

"Any" is used when it means "it's not important which":
- Come and see us any time.

The most common compounds of "some" and "any" are:

someone	anyone
something	anything
somewhere	anywhere

Be careful: Some nouns are countable in German but not in English, e.g. advice, information, furniture, news.
- I'd like **some information** about …
- He gave his colleague **a piece of bad news**.

4 How much and How many? (ex. 6 and 7, pages 25–26)

How many – Usage

In questions with countable nouns:
- How many slices of toast do you eat for breakfast?

"Not many" means "not a lot" *(nicht viele)*:
- My children don't eat many sweets. (They only eat them at the weekend).

How much – Usage

In questions with uncountable nouns:
- How much beer do you drink a week?

"Not much" means "not a lot" *(nicht viel)*.

You can use a "a lot of" with countable and uncountable nouns.
- She drinks a lot of whisky. *(viel)*
- She's got a lot of problems. *(viele)*

Grammar Reference Section (Unit 3)

1 Adverbs of Frequency (ex. 3, page 31)

These are little words that answer the question: How often?

always
usually
often
sometimes
seldom
never

Position

These words come before a full verb and after an auxiliary verb.

She seldom buys ice-cream.
It's usually easy to park before 8.

Grammar Reference Section (Unit 3+4)

2 The Simple Past (unit 3, exs. 5 and 6, page 34–35)

Usage

We use the simple past to talk about finished actions or states in the past, often together with time words: "last week", "yesterday", "last Saturday", "in 1999", "two days ago", "three months ago".

Positive Form / Regular Verbs

For all persons add "-d" or "-ed" to the infinitive.

Negative Form / Regular Verbs

Add "did not" (short form "didn't") to the infinitive.

I You	lived didn't live	in Rostock in 1999.
He She We They	cleaned didn't clean	the car yesterday.

Be careful: The regular form always ends in "-ed" but the pronunciation is not always the same.
- elect – elected [ɪd]
- ask – asked [t]
- clean – cleaned [d]
- start – started [ɪd]
- polish – polished [t]
- change – changed [d]

a Positive and Negative Short Answers

Form

| Yes, | I
you
he
she
it
we
they | did. | No, | I
you
he
she
it
we
they | didn't (did not). |

Be careful: The full form of the negative can sound angry:
- "No, I did not leave the door open." – "You did!"

b Yes/No Questions

Form

"Did" + person + infinitive.

| Did | you
she
they | live in Rostock in 1999? |

Note: Remember how you answer "yes / no questions":
- "Did he work for BMW?" – "Yes, he did."

c Questions with Question Words (unit 4, ex. 1, page 42)

Form

Question word + "did" + person + infinitive.

When		you start your job in Bielefeld?
Where	did	he live as a student?
Why		they arrive so early?

3 Simple Past of "to have"

Usage

The past form of "to have" is the same for both "have" and "have got".

It is used to talk about a description in the past:
- He had dark hair.

It is used to talk about a state or an action in the past:
- I had a dog when I was a child. (I possessed a dog.)
- They had breakfast late yesterday. (They ate breakfast late yesterday.)

Positive and Negative Form

The forms are always the same for all persons.

I		
You		
He	had	breakfast late yesterday.
She	didn't have	a dog in 1995.
We		a wonderful holiday.
They		

Question Form

Formed with "did" + person + infinitive. It is the same for all persons.

	I	
	you	
	he	have a moustache?
Did	she	have a dog in 1995?
	we	have breakfast late yesterday?
	they	

Grammar Reference Section **139**

4 Simple Past of "to be"

Usage

To talk about a situation that is finished.
To give a description in the past.

Positive and Negative Form

I		
He	wasn't (was not)	
She	was	
It		about 25.
		drunk yesterday.
You	were	
We	were not (weren't)	
They		

Question Form

Invert the order of the subject and the verb.

	I	
	he	
Was	she	
	it	about 25?
		drunk yesterday?
	you	
Were	we	
	they	

Note: This question form is very irregular as it doesn't form the past tense questions and negatives with "did". This should be easy for you: it's more like the German question form! ("Were you drunk yesterday?" – „Warst du gestern betrunken?")

5 Other Irregular Verbs (Unit 4, exs. 2–4, pages 43–44)

Positive Form

You have to learn the positive form of irregular verbs.
Look at the list on pages 162–163.

Negative and Question Forms and Short Answers

These are all formed in the same way, with "did" as for regular verbs.

They didn't fly Lufthansa.
Did they fly to Singapore?   No, they didn't.
Did they fly to Kuala Lumpur?   Yes, they did.

6 The Past Progressive

Positive and Negative Form

The past of the verb "to be" + (not) + -ing-form.

I	was	
He	was	wearing jeans.
She	was	
It	wasn't (was not)	snowing.
You	were	
We	were	having breakfast.
They	weren't (were not)	

Question Form

Invert the subject and verb + -ing-form.

Were	you	
Was	he	wearing jeans?
Was	it	snowing?

Usage

To give descriptions in the past.

To describe the background action of a story.
- The sun was shining and the birds were singing.

To talk about an action that was in progress at one point of time in the past.
- He was having breakfast at seven o'clock yesterday.

The simple past and the past progressive can be used together (unit 4, ex. 5, page 45)

We use the past progressive to express a longer action that was in progress when a second action began.
- She was driving to the airport when the taxi collided with a bus.

State and action verbs

The verbs "to be" and "have got" describe a state and not an action. We don't usually use them in the progressive form.

Grammar Reference Section

Grammar Reference Section (Unit 4)

1 Question tags (ex. 3, page 44)

We can use question tags in different ways:
- to check information
- to sound interested or to show sympathy

a To check information

If there's a positive statement there's a negative tag and if there's a negative statement there's a positive tag.

Form
Full verbs in the present: the present of the auxiliary "do" + person. • You play football at the weekend, don't you? • You don't watch soap operas on TV, do you?
Full verbs in the past: the past of the auxiliary "do" + person. • You didn't go to Canada last year, did you? • You went to Majorca for your holidays, didn't you?
Auxiliaries in the past and present (including "be" and "have"): repeat the auxiliary or the correct form of "be" and "have" + person. • You're single, aren't you? • You aren't married, are you? • You can speak Spanish, can't you? • You haven't got a brother, have you? • He hasn't got a dog, has he? • You weren't here last week, were you?

b To sound interested or to show sympathy

If there's a positive statement there's a positive tag.
If there's a negative statement there's a negative tag.

Form
Full verbs in the present: the present of the auxiliary "do" + person. • I love English pub food. Do you? • He likes chocolate. Does he?
Full verbs in the past: the past of the auxiliary "do" + person. • I met Claudia Schiffer last year. Did you? • I didn't go away on holiday last year. Didn't you?
Auxiliaries in the past and present (including "be" and "have"): repeat the auxiliary or the correct form of "be" or "have" + person. • He can't swim. Can't he? • We haven't got any children. Haven't you? • He's divorced. Is he? • I'm divorced. Are you? • I was late for work yesterday. Were you?

Grammar Reference Section (Unit 5)

1 The Present Perfect Simple (1) (ex. 1, page 48 and ex. 5, page 51)

Positive and Negative Form

The verb "to have" + (not) + past participle.

To form the past participle of regular verbs add "-d" or "-ed" to the infinitive and for irregular verbs the past participle has to be learnt: see list of irregular verbs on pages 162–163.

I You We They	've (have) haven't (have not)	installed the new alarm system.
He She	has hasn't (has not)	had a car accident.

Question Form

Invert the subject and verb "have" + past participle.

Have	I you we they	installed the new alarm system?
Has	she he	ever had a car accident?

Usage

The present perfect simple is used to talk about an indefinite time that includes the present, as part of your experience. It is used with time words such as "ever, never, three times" etc:
- Have you ever had a car accident?
- I've had two accidents.
- I've never had a car accident.

Or to talk about a recently finished action that has results in the present:
- The factory manager has installed a new alarm system. (It's in the factory now.)
- I've broken my leg. (It's in plaster now.)

Note: The name of this verb form may help you remember how to use it.
It's called the PRESENT perfect and it connects the past and the PRESENT.

2 The Present Perfect or the Simple Past? (ex. 3a, page 49)

If there's no connection with the present then we use the simple past:

If results of past action are no longer visible:
- He broke his leg last year. (But his leg's OK now.)

Definite past:
- Firemen arrived at the scene at six this morning. (Definite time: we know when.)

3 Pronouns and Adjectives (ex. 8, page 53)

	Personal pronouns	Possessive adjectives	Possessive pronouns
I	me	my	mine
You	you	your	yours
He	him	his	his
She	her	her	hers
It	it	its	its
We	us	our	ours
They	them	their	theirs

Usage

We use pronouns **instead of** a noun.
- **The robber** punched the **policeman**. – **He** punched **him**.
- **The blue umbrella** is my **umbrella**. – It's **mine**.

We use adjectives **with** a noun.
- The robber stole the **red** car. – The robber stole **my** car.

Be careful: If you say "It's mine" you can't add anything except a full stop after the possessive pronoun.

Grammar Reference Section (Unit 6)

1 The Future in English

There's no one "future tense" in English but there are ways of talking about the future.

a "will"-Future (ex. 3–4, page 57)

"will"-future is used to talk about:
- the neutral future. Something that you can't change.
- predictions
- a future intention decided at the time of speaking
  (a spontaneous decision / offer / promise)

Be careful: In German you use the present tense to express future intentions decided at the time of speaking. (*Ich rufe dich heute abend an.*)

Positive and Negative Form

"will" + (not) + infinitive.

This is the same for all persons. In speech "will" is usually shortened to "'ll" and "will" not is shortened to "won't" – even in short answers.

I You He She It We They	'll (will) will not (won't)	be 40 in August. rain tomorrow. phone you on Saturday.

Be careful: The full form is used in short answers and in business letters:
- "Will the manager be in the office tomorrow?" – "Yes, he will."
- The manager will be happy to see you for an interview on Tuesday.

In speech the full form of the negative expresses annoyance:
- "Will you be 40 in August?" – "No, I will not. I'll be 35!"

Question Form

Invert the subject and the auxiliary "will".

Will	it you she	rain tomorrow? be 40 in August? phone on Saturday?

"Shall" is seldom used as a future form in speaking.
"Shall I open the window?" is an offer and not the description of a future action.

b "Going to"-Future (ex. 2, page 57)

Usage

"Going to"-Future is used to talk about:

a future plan or intention thought about before the moment of speaking.

a future event for which there's some evidence now:
- Look at that idiot on a motorbike. He's going to have an accident.

Positive and Negative Form

The verb "to be" + (not) + going to + infinitive

I	'm (am) 'm not (am not)		
You We They	're (are) aren't (are not)	going to	recycle rubbish.
He She It	's (is) isn't (is not)		

Question Form			
Invert the subject and the verb "to be".			
Is	she		
Are	you	going to	cycle to the container?
Are	we		

c The Present Progressive (ex. 5, pages 58–59)

Check the form of the present progressive on page 134.

Usage

To talk about definite plans and arrangements.
- We're flying to Alice Springs on 12th.
- I'm going to the dentist's on Wednesday afternoon.

Note: In German you use the present tense for this sort of future too!
(*Wir fliegen am 12. nach Alice Springs.*)

Grammar Reference Section (Unit 7)

1 If-sentences

a If-sentence type 1 (ex. 4, page 70)

- If it snows on Christmas Day, some people will be very happy.

Form and Usage

Conditional sentences are always made up of two parts:
the if-clause which contains the condition and the main clause which describes the result.

if-clause	main clause
If you don't hurry up,	you'll miss the bus.
If I miss the bus,	I'll be late for work.

Note: The comma after the if-clause.

We can, of course, reverse the order and put the main clause first.

main clause	if-clause
You'll miss the bus	if you don't hurry up.
I'll be late for work	if I miss the bus.

Note: There's no comma between the two clauses.

These are what we call **real** conditions because they can still happen.
You can see that from the tenses we use.

if-clause	main clause
simple present	"will"-future

b If-sentence type 2 for general use (exs. 5–6, pages 71–72)

- If the Burtons won the National Lottery jackpot, Ted would retire immediately.

Form and Usage

Here, too, the conditional sentence consists of two parts:
the if-clause which contains the condition and the main clause which describes the result.

if-clause	main clause
If I found a spider in my bed,	I'd probably scream my head off.

In this case you imagine what you would do or what would happen in a particular situation. Some of these situations are more likely than others: we're more likely to lose something than to win the lottery jackpot. But even in this case we can still imagine what we would do. And the tenses we use show that we are talking about an **imaginary** situation.

if-clause	main clause
simple past	would-conditional

If I **found** a spider in my bed, I'd scream my head off. (But I haven't, so I won't!)

c If-sentence type 2 for giving advice (ex. 8, page 73)

- If I were you, I wouldn't lie in the sun too long.

We also use an if-sentence type 2 when we want to give someone some advice or when we think we know better.

Note: The form of the verb in the if-clause: "If I **were** you, …".

Grammar Reference Section (Unit 8)

1 Modal Verbs

The form of modal verbs is the same for all persons. In the present tense there's no "-s" at the end of the verbs after "he / she / it". (This rule is not true for "have to" and "to be allowed to".)

All modal verbs are followed by the infinitive. Some also have "to".

Modal verbs are used in many different ways.

a "Used to" (exs. 1 and 2, pages 74–75)

Usage
To talk about a regular habit or routine in the past.

Positive and Negative Form		
Queen Sylvia	used to	live in Heidelberg.
The children		buy sweets every Saturday.
Mum	didn't use to	come to Watford with us.

Note: "Never" is often used instead of the negative:
- Mum never used to come to Watford with us.

Question Form
What **did** the family **use to** do on Saturdays?

b "Must / have to" (exs. 4–5, page 76)

Usage
"must" is used to talk about general rules and regulations that you see on notices.
"have to" is used to talk about how rules and regulations affect us personally

Be careful: If you can't decide if "must" or "have to" is correct, use "have to"! Remember too that "have to" has different forms in the present tense like a "normal" verb.

The question form "must you?" exists but it's much more usual to say "Do you have to?". See the section on "don't have to".

Form			
Present tense		**Past tense**	
You	must have a valid ticket.		
I / You / We / They	have to wear a uniform at school.	I / You / We / They	had to wear a uniform at school.
He / She	has to wear a uniform at school.	He / She	

c "Mustn't / not allowed to" (exs. 4 and 8, pages 76 and 78)

Usage

"mustn't" is used to talk about what's generally forbidden.

"not allowed" to is used to talk about something that is or was forbidden to us personally.

Be careful: In German "mustn't" is „dürfen nicht" and NOT „müssen nicht". Remember too that to "be allowed to" has different forms in the present tense like a "normal" verb.

Form

Present tense

You	mustn't drink and drive.

I	am	
You	are	not allowed to smoke.
We	are	
They	are	
He	is	not allowed to smoke.
She	is	

Past tense

I		
He	wasn't	allowed to smoke.
She		
You		
We	weren't	allowed to smoke.
They		

d "Have to / Don't have to" (exs. 5 and 6, pages 76–77)

Usage

"have to/don't have to" is used to talk about something that is or was not necessary.

Be careful: In German "don't have to" is „müssen nicht".

Form

Statements in the present and the past.

Present tense

I	
You	don't have to wear a uniform at school.
We	
They	
He	doesn't have to wear a uniform at school.
She	

Past tense

I	
You	
We	didn't have to wear a uniform at school.
They	
He	
She	

Question Form

"must" is very seldom used in questions. The usual question form is "have to".

Do	I you we they	have to wear a uniform? have to clock in and out?
Does	he she	have to wear a tie in the office?
Did	he she	have to wear a tie in the office?

e "may, might, must, can't" (ex. 7, pages 77–78)

Usage

"may", "might", "must", "can't" are used to talk about positive and negative deductions.

Form

Possible	**may**	She may be married.
Improbable	**might** **could**	She might be a flight attendant but she's over forty.
Impossible	**can't**	His first name can't be Pamela. That's a girl's name.
Certain	**must**	He's eighty. He must be retired.

Grammar Reference Section (Unit 9)

1 The Present Perfect Simple (2) (ex. 1c, page 83; exs. 2 and 3, pages 83–84)

Look back at the form of the present perfect simple on page 143.

Usage

To talk about a state or an action that started in the past and continues into the present used with the time words "for" and "since".
- She's (has) been divorced since 2002.
- We've (have) had a dog for a year.
- She's (has) worn glasses since she left university.

The question you can use here is "How long ...?"
- How long has she been divorced? – Since 2002.
- How long have they had a dog? – For a year.
- How long has she worn glasses? – Since she left university.

Be careful: You can also ask "How long ...?" in questions with "did" and "was" but then you are asking about something that's finished, something that isn't true now.
- How long was she married? (She isn't married now.)
- How long did they have a dog? (The dog is dead now.)
- How long did she wear glasses? (She doesn't wear glasses now, she wears contact lenses.)

2 The Present Perfect Progressive (or Continuous)

Positive and Negative Form

The verb "to have" + (not) + been + -ing-form

I You We They	've (have) haven't (have not)	been living in Berlin since 2003.
She He	's (has) hasn't (has not)	been living in Berlin since 2003.
It	's (has) / hasn't	been raining since 8 o'clock.

Question Form

Invert the subject and the verb "to have" + been + -ing-form.

Have	you they	been living in Berlin since 2003?
Has	she	been living in Berlin since 2003?
Has	it	been raining since 8 o'clock?

> **Usage**
>
> To talk about an action that started in the past and is still in progress at the time of speaking.
> - He's (has) been working in the garden since two o'clock. (He's still working in the garden.)
> - She's (has) been living in Berlin since the beginning of 2003.
>
> **Be careful:** If the action is still in progress you **must** use the present perfect progressive. You can't say: "He has worked in the garden all afternoon" if he's still working in the garden.
>
> As with **1 Present Perfect Simple** the question you use here is "How long …?"
> - How long has he been working in the garden? – Since two o'clock.
> - How long has she been living in Berlin? – Since the beginning of 2003.

Note: There's not a lot of difference between:
- She's (has) sung in the chorus of the Deutsches Theater since March.
- She's (has) been singing in the chorus of the Deutsches Theater since March.

However, the second sentence emphasises the continuation of the action, she will probably continue to sing in Berlin for a long time. The former is more neutral.

3 For or Since (ex. 2, page 83)

> **Usage**
>
> We use "for" to say "how long" the action has been happening and we use "since" to say "when" it started.
> - She's (has) been singing **for over ten years**.
> - She's (has) been singing **since she left the academy**.

Note: In German you use the simple present to express this idea of an action that's not finished. In English you use the present perfect simple or present perfect progressive/continuous. How can you remember this?

> **Form**
>
> Try thinking of this: The present perfect connects the **present** and the **past** and so it must have **two** parts.
>
> The **present** of the verb "to have" and the **past** participle:

Present perfect simple:
- They **have had** a dog since 1995.

Present perfect progressive/continuous:
- They **have been working** for the same company for ten years.

Grammar Reference Section (Unit 10)

1 Comparative and superlative forms of adjectives
(ex. 2, page 95; exs. 3c-d, page 97; exs. 6-7, page 100)

Form

All adjectives have three forms: **basic**, **comparative** and **superlative**.

1. Adjectives with one syllable add **-er** and **-est** to the basic form.

2. Adjectives with two syllables ending in *-y* change the *-y* to *-i* and add **-er** and **-est** to the basic form.
   The two-syllable adjectives "clever", "narrow", "quiet" and "simple" also add **-er** and **-est**.

3. All other adjectives form the comparative and superlative by putting **more** and **most** in front of the basic form.

4. Some adjectives have special comparative and superlative forms.

	basic	comparative	superlative
1.	fast	faster	fastest
	big	bigger	biggest
2.	easy	easier	easiest
	simple	simpler	simplest
3.	comfortable	more comfortable	most comfortable
	inconvenient	more inconvenient	most inconvenient
4.	good	better	the best
	bad	worse	the worst
	far	further	the furthest
	much/many/a lot	more	the most
	little/not much	less	the least
	little/small	smaller	the smallest

Comparisons

We often use adjectives in all three forms – basic, comparative and superlative – to compare two or more people or things.

- My new boss is **as old as** I am. (basic form)

- Our last flat was **more inconvenient** for taking the underground. (comparative form)

- The **cheapest** and the **most exciting** taxi ride I've ever had was in Hong Kong. (superlative form)

Grammar Reference Section 153

2 Verbal Expressions Followed by Gerunds and/or Infinitives

(ex. 2, pages 95–96; ex. 8, page 101)

- I enjoy cycling on holiday. *(gerund)*
- We hope to visit New Zealand next year. *(infinitive)*
- I hate travelling/to travel in the rush-hour. *(gerund and infinitive)*

Gerunds

These are some of the most common verbal expressions followed by gerunds:

to admit	to be fond of	to look forward to	to suggest
to avoid	to give up	to mind	what/how about
to enjoy	to imagine	to practise	
to finish	to keep(on)	to regret	

- Would you mind **shutting** the window?
- She just kept on **talking** while I was trying to read the paper.
- I can't imagine you **hitchhiking**.

Form

The gerund is formed by adding *-ing* to the infinitive form of the verb:

talk + *-ing*	talking
hitchhike + *-ing*	hitchhiking (no "e"!)
shut + *-ing*	shutting (double "t"!)

Infinitives

These are some of the most common verbal expressions followed by infinitives:

to afford	to manage	to seem
to decide	to offer	to threaten
to hope	to plan	to want
to learn	to promise	

- We can't afford **to buy** a new car this year.
- You promised **to get** home earlier tonight.
- My boss offered **to take** us out for dinner.

Gerund and Infinitives

Verbs of liking and disliking can normally be followed by either a gerund or an infinitive:

- I don't like **taking/to take** the car to work.
- I prefer **taking/to take** the bus.

However, the forms "would / wouldn't like / hate" and "would love / prefer" are **always** followed by the **infinitive**.

- I wouldn't like / would hate **to take** the cross-Channel ferry to England.

- I would love / would prefer **to take** the Shuttle.

These verbs can be followed by the gerund or the infinitive without any change in meaning:

to begin
to continue
to intend
to start

- They began **building/to build** the new harbour bridge last year.
- They'll continue **working/to work** on it for the next two years.
- They intend **charging/to charge** a toll for all private vehicles.
- They've started **making/to make** a survey on the percentage of private and public transport using the old bridge.

These verbs have a different meaning when followed by the gerund or the infinitive:

to remember
to stop
to try

- I remembered **to close** all the windows before I left the house. (I didn't forget to do it.)
- I remember **closing** all the windows before I left the house. (I have a picture of it in my head.)
- I stopped **smoking** last year. (I don't smoke any more.)
- I stopped **to have** a cup of coffee. (I interrupted what I was doing in order to have a cup of coffee.)
- I tried **to answer** all the questions in the exam, but some of them were just too difficult. (I tried very hard, but I couldn't.)
- I tried **cooking** the pudding without sugar, but the kids didn't like it. (It was an experiment which failed.)

Grammar Reference Section

3 The Passive (ex. 5, page 99; ex. 9, page 101)

- Most new cars **are fitted** with airbags.
- The new ferry route to Scotland **was introduced** in 2002.
- A new intranet system **has been installed** at our office.
- The dishwasher you ordered **will be delivered** next Thursday.

Form

The passive form of the verb is made up of two parts: the appropriate form of the verb "to be" (depending on the subject and the tense) and the past participle.
Check the list of irregular verbs on pages 162–163.

"to be"	past participle
are	fitted
was	introduced
has been	installed
will be	delivered

Only transitive verbs (verbs which take an object) have a passive form.
There is a passive form of these verbs for most tenses.

Most new cars **are fitted** with airbags.	*simple present*
A new salary payment system **is being developed** by our company.	*present progressive*
The fire brigade **was called** immediately.	*simple past*
Our road was closed yesterday because the holes **were being filled**.	*past progressive*
All patients' data **have been recorded** on computers since 1995.	*present perfect simple*
His new car **had been stolen** before he even got it home.	*past perfect simple*
The new harbour bridge **will be completed** in two years.	*will -future*
The old army camp **is going to be turned** into a leisure centre.	*going to-future*

Usage

We use the passive form of the verb instead of the active form when we don't know or don't want to say who did something, or when it's not important.
- His new car **had been stolen** before he even got it home. (We don't know who stole it.)
- The fire brigade **was called** immediately. (It's not important to know who called it.)

We also use the passive form to describe what things are made of.
- Most phones **are made of** plastic.
- That's an interesting watch. What's it **made of**?

The passive form places the emphasis on the action and not on the person or thing that carried out the action.
- **The telephone was invented by** Alexander Graham Bell. (emphasis on the invention of the telephone)
- **Alexander Graham Bell invented** the telephone. (emphasis on the inventor)

Grammar Reference Section (Unit 11)

1 If-sentence type 3 (exs. 2b–d, pages 104–105; ex. 5, page 108)

- The fire would not have happened if they had kept the matches away from the children.

As with the conditional sentences described in **Unit 7** there are two parts to the sentence: the if-clause which contains the condition and the main clause which describes the result.

Form and Usage

if-clause	main clause
If they had kept the matches away from the children,	the fire would never have happened.
If you had phoned first,	I would have baked a cake.

We use this form of the conditional to describe what would or would not have happened in other circumstances. The situation we are describing is in the past and cannot be changed, and so we call these **unreal** conditions. This is also clear from the tenses we use.

if-clause	main clause
past perfect	would have-conditional

When we use "would" or "wouldn't have" in an if-sentence type 3, we are absolutely sure. When we are not so sure, we use "might" or "mightn't have".

- If they had kept the matches away from the children, the fire might never have happened.

However, something else might have started the fire, or the children might have found some matches somewhere else.

Grammar Reference Section (Unit 12)

1 Reported Speech (exs. 2b-c, pages 112-113; exs. 8-9, pages 116-117)

- The teacher warned them that they would be sent home for bad behaviour.
- The children said they didn't have enough money.
- Father Kipling's housekeeper asked him how he had enjoyed the film.

Usage

We use reported speech (or indirect speech) to tell others what someone has said. We take that person's direct words and put them into a new framework.
- "You'll be sent home for bad behaviour."
  The teacher warned them that they would be sent home for bad behaviour.
- "We haven't got enough money."
  The children said they didn't have enough money.
- "How did you enjoy the film?"
  Father Kipling's housekeeper asked him how he had enjoyed the film.

To introduce the reported speech we need the person who spoke the direct words:
- the teacher
- the children
- Father Kipling's housekeeper

In some cases we use the word "someone" because we're not sure who said it:
- Someone said the government was going to increase VAT. (It's really not important who said it.)

We also need an introductory verb:
- The teacher **warned** them …
- The children **said** …
- Father Kipling's housekeeper **asked** …

The most common of these verbs are:

to say	to tell	to ask

However, there are also some other, more expressive, introductory verbs which we can use:

to admit	to explain	to warn
to complain	to insist	to wonder
to confess	to promise	
to demand	to remind	

If a personal pronoun is used in direct speech, this often changes in reported speech if the person reporting is different from the original speaker.
- "**You**'ll be sent …"   The teacher warned them that **they** would be …
- "**We** haven't got …"   The children said **they** didn't have …
- "How did **you** enjoy …?"   Father Kipling's housekeeper asked **him** how **he** had enjoyed …

Form

If the introductory verb is in the past, then there is usually a change in the tenses of the verbs taken from the direct speech.

- "You'll be sent ..."   The teacher warned them that they **would be** ...
- "We **haven't got** ..."   The children said they **didn't have** ...
- "How **did** you **enjoy** ...?"   Father Kipling's housekeeper asked him how he **had enjoyed** ...

Direct speech	Reported speech
Simple Present	Simple Past
Present Progressive	Past Progressive
Simple Past	Past Perfect Simple
Past Progressive	Past Perfect Progressive
Present Perfect Simple	Past Perfect Simple
Present Perfect Progressive	Past Perfect Progressive
Past Perfect Simple	Past Perfect Simple
Past Perfect Progressive	Past Perfect Progressive
will, can, may	would, could, might

The following modal verbs **don't** change their form:

would	could	might	must	should
would have	could have	might have	must have	should have

If what we are reporting is something that is still true at the time of reporting, then there is no change in the tenses.
- "I **love** you."   He said he **loves** me.

2 Past Perfect Simple (ex. 6, page 115; ex. 7, page 116)

- Mrs Dukes made a 900-mile dash across the country after her son **had left** on a school-trip without his favourite toy.
- I was surprised when I heard that they **had chosen** an American actress for the leading role.

Form

The past perfect simple is formed with "had" (for all persons) and the past participle. Check the list of irregular verbs on pages 162–163.

The negative form is "hadn't" + past participle.

Question Form

How many different places **had you lived** in before you settled in the Lake District?

Usage

We use the past perfect simple to express the idea that something had or hadn't happened at an earlier time in the past than the one we are talking about.
- When Lesley got to the bus stop, the bus **had** already **left**.
- They **had lived** in different parts of the world before they decided to settle in the Lake District.

In sentences like this we often use words like "after", "before", "already" and "still" as indicators of the different times.

Grammar Reference Section **159**

Grammar Prepositions

Prepositions are used with a great deal of variety in English, and throughout the book, from Units 1 to 12 you'll find lots of examples. It's a good idea to learn the use of prepositions in context in English because very often there will be quite a difference compared with your own language.

about	for	over
after	from	since
at	in	to
before	into	under
between	of	until
by	off	with
during	on	without

Usage

Prepositions are used to show how other words are connected and are usually followed by a noun, a pronoun or a gerund.
- We gave our old car **to** the Transport Museum.
- Has the electrician been here? I spoke **to** him this morning.
- We're really looking forward **to** seeing you next weekend.

They are used to express different kinds of relationships.
The most common are **time** and **place**:
- I'll see you   **about** five o'clock.
  after work.
  at the weekend.
  before class.
  between lectures.
  by March at the latest.
  during the break.
  for five minutes this afternoon.
  from 2 **to** 2.30.
  in the evening.
  on Tuesday.
- I haven't seen him **since** Christmas, and I won't see him again **until** Easter.
- I'll meet you   **at** the pub.
  between the bank and the post office.
  by (near) the car park.
  in the park.
  on the boat.
  under the bridge.

More detailed information about the use of prepositions can be found in any good English-English dictionary. See also the use of prepositions in phrasal verbs on page 161.

Note: The following verbs take direct objects **without** a preposition: to discuss, to enter, to phone
- We'll **discuss the problem** tomorrow.
- The burglar **entered the house** as quietly as possible.
- I think you've got a temperature. I'll **phone the doctor**.

Grammar Phrasal Verbs

Phrasal verbs are very common in English, and as with prepositions (see above) it's a good idea to learn them in context. There are lots of examples throughout the book, and as with the prepositions it's a good idea to learn and use them as you go along.

Form

Phrasal verbs are made up of a verb plus an adverb and/or a preposition.

- I **got up** in a rush this morning. (1)
- I think I'**ve taken on** too much responsibility with this job. (2)
- Don't forget **to put** the milk bottles **out**. (3)

Just like other verbs they can be used transitively (with an object, as in nos. 2 + 3) or intransitively (without an object, as in no. 1).

Intransitive Phrasal Verbs

We don't usually **get up** early at the weekend.
My husband doesn't **get on** too well with his brother. (They don't agree.)
The children **got out** of school early today.
Prices are **going up** all the time.
The thief **made off** with the old lady`s handbag. (He ran away with it.)
First they quarrelled, then they kissed and **made up**.
I **can't put up** with this noise any longer! (I can't stand it.)
The caller **rang off** before I could ask for his number.
The fans **turned out** in great numbers to welcome the Cup winners back home.
Why can't you be more punctual? You **turn up** late for everything.

Transitive Phrasal Verbs

Here you are, Mrs Wilson. I'**ve made up** the cough mixture for your daughter.
I'**ve put on** weight instead of **taking** it **off**.
Would you mind **putting out** that cigarette? This is a no-smoking compartment.
When Mr Harvey retired, he **took up** woodwork as a hobby.
I'm exhausted! I **must have tried** 15 dresses **on** this afternoon.
Have you **tried out** any new recipes lately?
Don't forget to **turn** the lights **off** before you go to bed.
I usually **turn on** the computer as soon as I come home.
Could you **turn** the heating **up** a bit? It's rather cold in here.
Ssh! Don't **wake up** the baby!

Position

There are usually two possible positions for the object with transitive phrasal verbs:
- Don't **wake up** the baby!   or   Don't **wake** the baby **up**!
- I **tried on** 15 dresses.   or   I **tried** 15 dresses **on**.

However, if the object is a **pronoun**, then it must come **between** the verb and the adverb/preposition:
- Don't wake **her/him** up!
- I tried **them** on.

Grammar Irregular Verbs

Here is a list of the most common irregular verbs.
Add verbs to the list if you find more when you are reading.

Infinitive	Simple Past	Past Participle	
be	was/were	been	*sein*
beat	beat	beaten	*schlagen*
become	became	become	*werden*
begin	began	begun	*starten, anfangen, beginnen*
bite	bit	bitten	*beißen, stechen*
bleed	bled	bled	*bluten*
blow	blew	blown	*blasen*
break	broke	broken	*(zer)brechen, kaputtmachen*
bring	brought	brought	*(her)bringen*
build	built	built	*bauen*
burn	burnt*	burnt*	*(ver)brennen*
buy	bought	bought	*kaufen*
catch	caught	caught	*fangen, erreichen (Zug)*
choose	chose	chosen	*(aus)wählen, (aus)suchen*
come	came	come	*kommen*
cost	cost	cost	*kosten*
cut	cut	cut	*schneiden*
deal	dealt	dealt	*handeln, sich beschäftigen mit, geben*
dig	dug	dug	*graben, bohren*
do	did	done	*tun, machen*
draw	drew	drawn	*zeichnen, zuziehen (Vorhang)*
dream	dreamt*	dreamt*	*träumen*
drink	drank	drunk	*trinken*
drive	drove	driven	*fahren*
eat	ate	eaten	*essen*
fall	fell	fallen	*fallen*
feel	felt	felt	*(sich) fühlen*
fight	fought	fought	*(be)kämpfen*
find	found	found	*finden*
fly	flew	flown	*fliegen*
forbid	forbade	forbidden	*verbieten*
forget	forgot	forgotten	*vergessen*
freeze	froze	frozen	*frieren*
get	got	got	*bekommen*
give	gave	given	*geben*
go	went	gone	*gehen, fahren*
grow	grew	grown	*wachsen, anbauen, züchten*
hang	hung*	hung*	*(auf)hängen*
have	had	had	*haben*
hear	heard	heard	*hören*
hide	hid	hidden	*(sich) verstecken*
hit	hit	hit	*schlagen, treffen*
hold	held	held	*halten*
hurt	hurt	hurt	*verletzen, schmerzen*
keep	kept	kept	*behalten*
know	knew	known	*wissen, kennen*
lay	laid	laid	*legen*
lead	led	led	*führen*
learn	learnt*	learnt*	*lernen*
leave	left	left	*verlassen, abfahren*

* means that a regular form exists alongside the irregular form (e.g. burnt or burned)

lend	lent	lent	*leihen*
let	let	let	*lassen, erlauben*
lie	lay	lain	*liegen*
light	lit*	lit*	*(be-, er-)leuchten, entzünden, (an)zünden*
lose	lost	lost	*verlieren*
make	made	made	*machen, tun*
mean	meant	meant	*bedeuten*
meet	met	met	*(sich) treffen, abholen, kennenlernen*
pay	paid	paid	*(be)zahlen*
put	put	put	*legen, stellen*
read	read	read	*lesen*
ride	rode	ridden	*fahren, reiten*
ring	rang	rung	*klingeln*
rise	rose	risen	*steigen, sich erheben*
run	ran	run	*laufen, rennen, verwalten*
say	said	said	*sagen*
see	saw	seen	*sehen*
sell	sold	sold	*verkaufen*
send	sent	sent	*senden, schicken*
shake	shook	shaken	*schütteln, geben (Hand), zittern*
shine	shone	shone	*scheinen, glänzen*
shoot	shot	shot	*schießen*
show	showed	shown*	*zeigen*
shut	shut	shut	*schließen*
sing	sang	sung	*singen*
sink	sank	sunk	*(ver)sinken, untergehen*
sit	sat	sat	*sitzen, sich setzen*
sleep	slept	slept	*schlafen*
slide	slid	slid	*gleiten, rutschen*
smell	smelt*	smelt*	*riechen, duften*
speak	spoke	spoken	*sprechen*
spell	spelt*	spelt*	*buchstabieren*
spend	spent	spent	*verbringen (Zeit), ausgeben (Geld)*
spoil	spoilt	spoilt	*verwöhnen, verderben*
stand	stood	stood	*stehen*
steal	stole	stolen	*stehlen*
stick	stuck	stuck	*steckenbleiben, kleben*
sting	stung	stung	*stechen*
strike	struck	struck	*schlagen, stoßen*
swear	swore	sworn	*schwören*
sweep	swept	swept	*kehren, fegen*
swell	swelled	swollen	*(an)schwellen*
swim	swam	swum	*schwimmen*
swing	swung	swung	*schwingen, schaukeln*
take	took	taken	*nehmen, (hin)bringen, dauern (Zeit)*
teach	taught	taught	*unterrichten*
tear	tore	torn	*(zer)reißen*
tell	told	told	*erzählen, sagen*
think	thought	thought	*denken, glauben*
throw	threw	thrown	*werfen*
understand	understood	understood	*verstehen*
wake	woke	woken	*(auf)wecken, (auf)wachen*
wear	wore	worn	*tragen (Kleidung)*
win	won	won	*gewinnen*
write	wrote	written	*schreiben*

Tapescripts

Unit 1

4a Names aren't everything

- Have you done an English course before?
- Yes, I have.
- When was that?
- Oh, about three years ago.

- Did you have English at school?
- Yes, I did.
- Is this your first English course?
- No, it isn't. I did an intensive course on Malta last year.

- Where did you learn to speak English?
- At the vhs.
- Have you ever been to England?
- No, I haven't, but I've been to Ireland.

- Do you need English at work?
- Not at the moment, but perhaps later.
- Why are you taking this course?
- Well, I'm planning a trip to New Zealand, and I think it would be good for my job prospects.

- Have you got the book?
- Yes, I have.
- Where did you get it?
- At the bookshop next to the railway station.
- How much was it?
- Oh, I can't remember. Let me have a look. Perhaps the price is still on it.

- Do you know the teacher?
- No, I'm afraid I don't. But she looks very nice. I wonder if she's English.
- Can you speak any other foreign languages?
- Not very well. I had French at school, but that's a long time ago now.

- Do you live near here?
- Not really. It takes about 15 minutes to get here.
- How do you get here?
- By car.

6a Commuters

David Carr commutes the sixty miles from his home Finstock in Oxfordshire to London to give his family a better life. He lives with his wife Hilary and their three teenage children and two poodles in a four-bedroomed house worth about £300,000, and they have a large garden that he works in at the weekend. "It helps me to relax", he says. He gets up early, at 6 o'clock, and leaves the house at 6.25 and drives into Oxford. There isn't a bus at that time in the morning. His first class train ticket costs him £431.20 a month, just over £5,000 a year. The time he spends on train journeys adds up to 39 days a year!

6c The commuter's wife

Finstock's a very friendly village. There's always something going on here. There's the local history society, the Finstock singers and an active church community. We have all the facilities we need, too. There are two pubs and there's a small shop and post office though I have to admit that I do most of my shopping in Witney. There's a small primary school in the village itself and there are good comprehensive schools in Witney and Chipping Norton. There's some beautiful countryside all around Finstock where we can take the dogs for walks and, of course, we're not far from Woodstock and Blenheim Palace as well as Oxford, all great attractions with any visitors.

8 A phone call

J = Jane / S = Sheila

J Hello, Sheila, it's Jane. How are you? How's your back? Any better?
S Not much, no, not really. I think I'll have to go back to the doctor's this week.
J Oh dear, sorry to hear that. How's Mum? Is she helping you with the children?
S Oh, yes, she's been a great help. She takes Roddy to school every morning and gives Emily her bath at night. I'll be sorry to see her go.
J When is Bill coming home?
S He should be back on Friday if there are no problems.
J Oh good. Can I speak to Mum, please, Sheila?
S Sorry, Jane, but she's just taken Emily to the park. Can I give her a message?
J Yes, please. Will you tell her that I'll collect her at the railway station on Saturday? David has got a seminar this weekend.
S That's no problem, Jane. I'll tell her as soon as she comes back. In fact, she can give you a ring to check times and so on.
J Thanks, Sheila, I'll be in all day. Take care. I hope your back will be better soon. And love to the children.
S I will, Jane, and thanks for phoning. Love to David. Bye.
J Bye.

15c Word stress

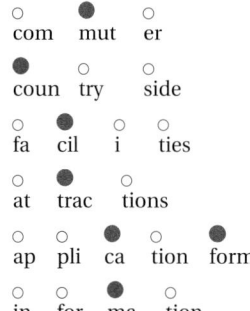

Unit 2

3 The commentary

1.
Oh, surely that ball was on the line. Mills goes over to the umpire, but John Talbot is shaking his head. Mills throws his racket to the ground and breaks it, and, yes, the umpire gives him a warning. Let's hope he doesn't lose his concentration now. He's not serving as fast as he normally does, but he's volleying well, and he's winning a lot of points with his forehand. He returns to his end of the court and thunders a service of 160 kilometres an hour over the net, but Andersson is prepared and takes the ball early for a clear winner down the line. Thirty fifteen.

2.
And she comes round the corner. She's travelling about 75 kilometres an hour and taking a very good line. And now the jump. She takes that well, and her time at the half-way point is just two tenths of a second slower than her nearest rival, the Austrian. Can she make up the time on the bottom half of the course that's a bit icy? She tucks into the egg position again letting the skis run. She's looking good, and, yes, she takes the lead in a time of 2 minutes 4.6 seconds.

3.
A good match, both teams are playing well, but there is still no score with less than two minutes to go. Rangers on the attack again. Gascoine is now on the right wing and goes outside his man. A high cross, but it's too long. Goal kick for United. The keeper takes the kick. A short one to Richards, but he loses it. What a disaster! Now Barnes is running down the left wing, but Evans brings him down. Oh, what a foul. Yes, it's a free kick just outside the box. Gascoine takes it, a good one, and Roberts is there and heads the ball into the back of the net. The crowd go wild as the referee blows the final whistle. The UEFA cup final is over, and Rangers are the champions.

5a Four phone calls

Call 1

A 67887
B Mrs Dickson?
A Yes.
B This is Andrew. Is Angela there please?
A I'm sorry, Andrew, she's playing tennis with her friends at the moment.
B Oh, of course, I forgot, she plays every Friday. Never mind. I'll phone back later.

164

Call 2

A Airton 478.
B Gill?
A Yes.
B Hi, this is Ian.
A Hi, Ian, how are you?
B Fine. Can I speak to John, please.
A Hold on. He's washing the car. I'll just get him.
B Thanks.

Call 3

A Cheltenham 61334
B Mr McIntosh?
A Yes.
B Hello, this is Helen. Can I speak to Melanie, please?
A I'm afraid she's not in. She's having a piano lesson.
B Oh, of course, she has a lesson every Wednesday, doesn't she?
A Yes. Do you want her to phone you back?
B Oh, er, yes, please.
A Fine. I'll tell her, Helen.

Call 4

A 634859. Hello.
B Is that Trish?
A Yes.
B Oh, hello, Trish. This is Pam. Is Alan there?
A Well, he's watching the football on TV. Hold on, and I'll get him.
B Oh, don't bother. It's not urgent, and I know he doesn't often watch it. I'll phone back in an hour.
A OK. Bye.

9 Shopping

Dialogue 1

A I'd like something for a headache, please.
B Ask at the pharmacy counter over there. We only sell shampoo, soap and toothpaste here.
A Oh – er, thank you. Have you got anything for a headache, please?
C Yes. We've got aspirin or paracetomol.
A Paracetomol, please.
C It's 42p for a packet of 16 capsules.
A Fine.
C Anything else?
A No, that's all thanks.

Dialogue 2

A Five cards is it mate. That'll be £1.25.
B Can I buy stamps here, too?
A No, sorry, but there's a post office just round the corner.
B Thanks.

B How much is it for a postcard to Germany?
C 37 pence.
B And a letter?
C The same if it's not more than 20 grams.
B Ten 37p stamps then, please.
C Anything else?
B No, that's all, thanks.

Dialogue 3

A A street map of London, please.
B Right you are. This A to Z is very good.
A Fine. And have you got a map of the tube?
B There's one on the back of the A to Z, love.
A Oh, good.
B Anything else?
A A copy of 'Hello' magazine, please.
B Coming up.
A And do you sell German newspapers?
B Well, I do but I've only got one from yesterday at the moment. Today's will be in at about 10 o'clock.
A OK, I'll leave it then.
B Sorry.
A Never mind.
B So, £1.65 for 'Hello' magazine and £5.75 for the A to Z. That'll be £7.40 altogether, please.

Unit 3

4b I'm in love with a big blue frog

I'm in love with a big blue frog
A big blue frog loves me.
It's not as bad as it appears
He wears glasses and he's six foot three.

I'm not worried about our kids
I know they'll turn out neat.
They'll be great lookers cos they'll have my face
Great swimmers cos they'll have his feet.

I'm in love with a big blue frog
A big blue frog loves me.
He's not as bad as he appears
He's got rhythm and a PhD.

Well I know we can make things work
He's got good family since
His mother was a frog from Philadelphia
His daddy an enchanted prince.

The neighbours are against it
And it's clear to me.
And it's probably clear to you
They think value on their property will go right down
If the family next door is blue.

Well I'm in love with a big blue frog
A big blue frog loves me.
I've got it tattooed on my chest
It says P-h-r-o-g Phrog and me,
P-h-r-o-g.

9 Listening

Dialogue 1

A Where were you on 29th June 1995?
B I've no idea.

Dialogue 2

A Where were you at ten o'clock yesterday?
B In the morning or in the evening, officer?
A In the evening.
B I was at the pub.
A Were you alone?
B No, my mates were with me. We were playing darts.

Dialogue 3

A Where were you between six o'clock and midnight on Saturday evening?
B At a disco.
A What, the whole time?
B Yeah, that's right.
A What were you doing there?
B Playing the drums.

10 Dialogues

Dialogue 1

A Yes, madam.
B Half of cider, please.
A Sweet or dry?
B Dry, please.

Dialogue 2

A Excuse me, is there a chemist's near here?
B I'm sorry, I'm a stranger here, too.

Dialogue 3

A Can I change a traveller's cheque here?
B Over there, madam, at the foreign counter.

Dialogue 4

A Excuse me, is there a garage near here?
B Yes. First left and then second right.
A Thanks.

Dialogue 5

A Yes, sir.
B A pint of lager, please.
A Bottled or draft?
B Draft, please.

Dialogue 6

A Can I change a traveller's cheque here?
B Yes, certainly. Can you countersign it, please?
A What's the rate of exchange at the moment?
B 1 Euro is $1.10.

Tapescripts

Revision Unit 1

6 Pronunciation

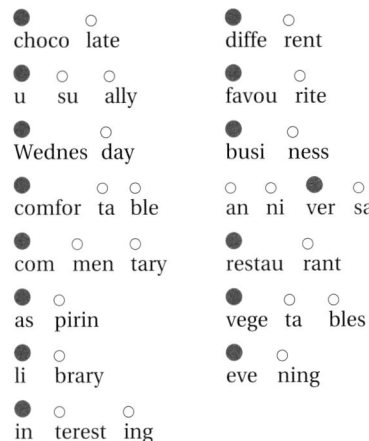

7 Matching and listening

I = interviewer / T = Tommy

(fade in ... to lead such an interesting double life)

I: Now, our next news story comes from the race-course in Virginia City where the international camel races are now into their second day. Yep, that's right, folks, camel races; no horses, no cars. OK, here we go with a quick interview with one of the participants, Tommy Dupont.
Hi there, Tommy, what are you doing right now?
T: I'm training for the next race.
I: So, how many races do you take part in each year?
T: About 10–12.
I: And how old were you when you rode your first race?
T: 18.
I: 18, not bad. Tommy, where was your last race?
T: Alice Springs, at the US-Australia Cup. It's a great event.
I: So, Tommy, tell us. What do you do?
T: Well, I'm a camel jockey, I guess.
I: But that's not all, is it? What else do you do?
T: Some of the time I also train camels for Safari treks.
I: And which do you prefer?
T: What do you think? The races, of course.
I: Yes, I can believe that. OK, Tommy, just one last question. Who do you work for?
T: For myself. I have my own company.
I: Well, that just shows that camel-racing is a profitable business. Thank you, Tommy, for answering my questions and good luck for the rest of the tournament.

Unit 4

3a Sound interested

1. I always fly Lufthansa.
   Do you? What's the service like?
2. I flew to Dubai last weekend.
   Did you? Did you stay in the world's only 7-star hotel?
3. I went to Edinburgh on business last year.
   Did you? Did you have good weather?
4. I love English beer.
   Do you? Most people prefer their beer cold.
5. I had an awful journey.
   Oh dear. Did you? What was the problem?

4 Something different

Last year it was Mr and Mrs Lang's 10th wedding anniversary, and they went on a wonderful holiday to Kenya. They flew Malaysian Airlines from London Heathrow to Kuala Lumpur. They flew first class. When they arrived, they spent four nights in the Majestic Hotel in Kuala Lumpur and then took a bus to the new luxury resort on Pangkor Island. Their bedroom looked out over the sea, and, of course, it was air-conditioned. Temperatures in Malaysia rose to 26 degrees during the day, and even in the evening it was 20 degrees. Every morning after a breakfast of fresh mangoes, rolls and butter and tea they relaxed on the verandah of their room or by the pool and drank their cold drinks and wrote letters to their friends in Germany. In the evening they went snorkelling and saw wonderfully coloured fish and twice they had a demonstration of how to fly a Malaysian kite. In the evenings they usually listened to Malaysian music, but once they watched a Chinese puppet play. They only stayed for three weeks, and the holiday passed very quickly.

5 The flight attendant

A What do you do?
B Well, I'm a nurse now, but I was a flight attendant for five years.
A Why did you change your job?
B Well, it's a hard job, especially on long flights, and you never stay in exotic countries very long. Well, er, I was getting tired of my job, and then one day I delivered a baby in the airplane.
A A baby?!
B Yes, a baby! I was working for Singapore Airlines, and we were flying between Abu Dhabi and Singapore, when suddenly a passenger complained of labour pains.
A What did you do?
B Well, there were no doctors on board, so the senior stewardess and I cleared a space in the back of the business class area that was near the kitchen, so we could get lots of boiling water. No-one in the economy cabin knew there was a problem. They were watching the film. I think it was an old western, you know the sort of thing, the Indians were attacking the fort and the soldiers were shooting the Indians when suddenly the passengers heard the cry of a new-born baby.
A Did you panic?
B No, I didn't. We didn't have time!
A But I thought airlines didn't accept very pregnant passengers.
B No, that's right. We don't carry people after they are thirty-four weeks pregnant, not on long flights, anyway. This lady was thirty-two weeks gone, but she was travelling to the airport when her taxi collided with a bus. She was OK, but the shock brought on the labour apparently.
A So this experience persuaded you to become a nurse.
B I suppose it did, yes.

10 Be an interested listener

1. I met Claudia Schiffer last year.
   Did you? What was she wearing?
2. We always go wind-surfing when we go on holiday.
   Do you? Where do you go?
3. We spent Christmas in Florida last year.
   Did you? What was the weather like?
4. We went to Berlin for the millennium celebrations.
   Did you? Did you take any photographs?
5. I lost my passport when I was on holiday in Spain last year.
   Did you? Did you go the police station?
6. I had a car accident last week.
   Oh dear. Did you? Not serious, I hope.
7. Our daughter got a divorce last year.
   Oh, did she. I'm sorry. Has she got any children?

Unit 5

3 On a Sunday!

A Have you ever mowed the lawn on a Sunday?
B Yes, I have.
A When was that?
B Last year. We came back after three weeks' holiday and the lawn was very long, so we mowed it.
A And did anything happen?
B Yes. One of our neighbours, we don't know which, called the police.

6 The news

Fires have destroyed large areas of a national park in Southern Spain. Strong winds have made the firemen's jobs very difficult, and the fires are not yet under control. Many families in the danger area have left their homes. Police think that picnickers dropped some matches and that they set fire to the very dry grass. They have issued new guidelines for visitors to the park and have threatened to fine people who don't follow them.

Art thieves have stolen two Lowry paintings from the Manchester City Art Gallery. There is a large exhibition of Lowry's paintings in the Manchester gallery to mark the twentieth anniversary of his death. Police have talked to customs officers at Manchester airport, and the Art Gallery has offered a reward for the safe return of the paintings.

The police have seized 10 kilos of heroin hidden in a lorry carrying tulips from Holland. Sniffer dogs found the heroin during a routine search of the lorry at Dover. Local drug officers have taken the driver to the police station for questioning.

And now for tomorrow's weather …

7 Wednesday Morning 3 am

I can hear the soft breathing of the girl that I love
As she lies here beside me asleep with the night
And her hair in a fine mist floats on my pillow
Reflecting the glow of the winter moonlight.

She is soft, she is warm, but my heart remains heavy
And I watch as her breasts gently rise gently fall
For I know at the first light of dawn I'll be leaving
And tonight will be all I have left to recall.

Oh, what have I done? Why have I done it?
I've committed a crime. I've broken the law.
For twenty five dollars and pieces of silver
I held up and robbed a hard liquor store.

My life seems unreal, my crime an illusion
A scene badly written in which I must play.
Yet I know as I gaze at my young love beside me
The morning is just a few hours away.

8a The lost property office

Dialogue 1

A Good morning madam – can I help you?
B Yes, I've lost an umbrella, a blue, erm, a blue umbrella.
A Blue. Mmm. Where exactly do you think you lost it?
B I think I left it on a number 7 bus yesterday afternoon.
A Well, there's nothing about a blue umbrella in the book, but I'll have a look. Well, this is the only blue umbrella we have at the moment. Is this yours?
B No, that's not mine. Mine's dark blue.
A Well, let me take the details, someone might hand it in.

Dialogue 2

A 'ello lads. What can I do for you?
B We've, er, lost our school bags.
A What sort of bags?
B Well, his is a black bag with Benetton colours on it, and mine's the same but, er, dark blue.
A Black, dark blue, Benetton colours. Right, and where did you lose 'em?
B Well, er, we were playing football at the bus stop this mornin', and when the bus came we, er, forgot all about 'em.
A A bit silly, eh.
B Yeah well …
A Let's see what's in the book. You're lucky, lads. An old lady handed two bags in an hour ago. Do these look like yours?
B Yeah. Brill!
A 'old on a minute. I just 'ave to check. What was in your bags?
B Well, there were some school books in mine, er, a walkman, two cassettes, no, three cassettes, oh, and two pens.
C There was a lot of dirty washing in mine, a pair of football boots, a pair of shorts, a T-shirt, some dirty football socks and, erm, a comic.
A OK. 'ere you are. Play football on a field in future, eh?

12 Short forms

A Where's Phillip?
B He's gone to the police station.
A Why? What's happened? Is he OK?
B Don't panic, he's fine, but he's lost his driving licence. He thinks he dropped it in the post office yesterday because he used it then as a form of identification.
A Has he asked there?
B Yes, he has, but no luck.
A I've never lost mine, touch wood. I hope he's lucky, and someone's handed it in.
B Yeah. Let's hope so.

Unit 6

2a Green Olympics?

Interviewer: I think many Australians and indeed sports enthusiasts from all over the world will remember the Sydney Olympics as the good will games, the games during which there was a spirit of reconciliation. It was important that Cathy Freeman, the aboriginal 400 metre runner carried the Olympic flame as a symbol of this spirit. In the planning phase, however, the organising committee thought of them as the green Olympics. How did that come about?

Roberts: The 'green games' is something that came out of the architectural competition that was held to design the Olympic village. One of the winners was the official entry from Greenpeace. So we worked with Greenpeace on the design of the village. The IOC had asked the bid cities to try to respond to the environment in their planning and it was something that the media just loved. So we took it further. We were surprised that there was so much interest in it. Every second developer in the world was contacting us and wanted to see the amazing village that had been designed. There was nothing new about solar energy or water recycling in individual houses, but to do it on a scale like that of 2,500 units, a whole new suburb within the context of the Olympics set a great example to the world. We issued environmental guidelines to all sites that weren't virgin sites and tried to use industrial land to build our sites and any trees that came down had to be moved or replaced. There were also a number of wetland species that had to be protected. It was a very challenging planning project.

Interviewer: And a very successful one indeed.

Roberts: We certainly think it was.

7 A good holiday?

I = interviewer / G = Alistair Grant

I I have in our studios today Mr Alistair Grant who works for the Great Barrier Reef Marine Park Authority based in Townsville, Queensland. So welcome, Mr Grant.
G Hi, it's good to be here.
I Mr Grant, can you tell us something about the work of the authority?
G Well, it was founded in 1975. Er, interest in the great barrier reef and the possibilities it offered for snorkelling and scuba diving began in the fifties and sixties and has grown a lot since then. We wanted to welcome tourists, but we also wanted to protect this area of great natural beauty.
I And how can you do both?
G Well, we divided the area of the reef, all 344,000 square kilometres of it, into zones. Certain ones are for scientific research only and others are open to the public. You can visit Marine National Park Zone B, for example, but as it is a "look but don't touch zone", fishing and shell collecting are forbidden. Then there are what are known as the recreational areas where there are the big new resorts and sports facilities of all kinds. Of course, no commercial spearfishing is allowed in any of these areas.
I And has the damage to the reef decreased since the park was founded?
G Well, yes and no. The number of visitors is rising every year, and so, of course, there will be damage to the reef, but we think that it's under control.
I What causes the damage exactly?

Tapescripts

G Erm, I suppose one of the main causes of problems to the reef itself is reef walking. However careful you are if you walk on it, you'll kill certain parts of it, and kids often pick up shells and take them home.

I But that's OK, isn't it? I mean, you can buy shells in the shops.

G Oh, yes I know, and I can understand that it's wonderful to take a souvenir home with you, but I think shells are best left in the sea. You can buy great T-shirts of the islands, and they make good souvenirs. You can show your friends when you wear them that you've visited the reef.

I Is that the only problem?

G Well, most people are very careful when they come camping here, they know that the reef is very special, but there are always some people who leave litter and don't use a stove at the camp-sites, but light fires anywhere. Also on Lady Elliott and Heron Islands lights left on in the resort at night can disorient turtles that come there to lay their eggs.

I You make the tourists sound the bad man of all this.

G Well, it isn't just the tourists, commercial fishing boats from Asia often try to collect giant clams from the reef. Most of our tourists, as I said, come to enjoy the wonders of the reef and know that if they destroy it, it won't be there for their grandchildren to see, I think that in Australia we have at last understood this.

I Thank you.

G Thank you.

11 Running together of sounds

1. Carolyn and her boyfriend are travelling round Australia for eight weeks. They've been to Sydney and Melbourne, and they're taking the bus to Alice Springs next.
2. Walter and his family want some sun this year. So they're going to Turkey. They went to Istanbul in 1995, so this year they've booked a flight to Antalya.
3. Mike's going on a business trip to Ottawa next month.
4. David Quarrie's visiting Europe for the first time this summer, and his first visit will be to Rome.
5. Gill's going on holiday for two weeks to Edinburgh.
6. Sheila's having a winter holiday. She's going skiing with friends. Not to Garmisch this year but to Aspen, Colorado.
7. Charles and his wife Barbara are going to Turkey, to Istanbul.
8. Bruce Foster's visiting Greece for the first time in July. He's flying to Athens and then hopes to go on a cruise round the Greek islands.
9. Mrs Hatton's flying to Garmisch on Friday because her daughter's in hospital there. She broke her leg, no, not skiing but when she was getting off a bus!
10. Helen's flying from Alice to Melbourne next Friday.

Unit 7

2 Weather forecasts

And here is tomorrow's weather forecast. It will be hot and sunny. England and Wales will start fine with a little mist in places. This will clear quickly before it becomes another hot day. Some isolated thunderstorms will develop, especially in the southwest.

Scotland and Ireland will start fine and dry. Northern Ireland will remain dry with sunny intervals, but isolated thunderstorms are expected in the south later in the day. Central and southern Scotland will enjoy the best of the Scottish weather tomorrow.

Temperatures will be high, reaching 30 degrees in places. Winds will be light to moderate.

We'll be back with the weather update after the ten o'clock news. Until then we hope you'll enjoy a pleasant evening's viewing with …

5b Money isn't everything!

R = Interviewer / T = Ted / I = Irene /
A = Andrew / L = Alison / S = Sally

R Good evening, ladies and gentlemen. This evening we're visiting the Burton family from Skegness who have played the National Lottery every week since it started. That's quite a record. So far they've not been lucky, but, as Ted Burton says, it's the luck of the draw, and they're not giving up. Now, Ted, I understand you've formed a family syndicate. Is that right?

T Yes, it is. There's my wife, Irene, and myself, of course. Then there's our daughter, Alison, she's 19, and our son, Andrew, who's 17. And not to forget the wife's mother, Sally, but I won't tell you how old she is!

R Right then, Ted. Now tell me, how would you divide up the money if you ever won?

T Oh, fair and square. There are five of us, and we'd divide the money into five equal shares.

R Well, that sounds fair enough to me. Does that mean that you all pay the same amount every week?

T Yes, that's right, a pound each for all five of us, which means each person fills in one board with six different numbers.

R I see. Well, what our listeners would also like to hear is what you would do with the money if you were finally successful. Irene, what about you? Any ideas?

I Oh, yes. If we won the jackpot, Ted would retire immediately. We'd buy a big house in the country with a huge garden, and we'd breed horses. I've always wanted to do that.

T Maybe you have, but I haven't. Yes, I'd retire straight away, but we wouldn't move to the country. We'd buy ourselves a nice little castle in France, where we'd grow wine. That's what I've always wanted to do.

R Well, let's hope you have time to come to an agreement before you make the big money. Now then, the youngest member of the Burton family. Andrew, what would you do?

A I'd buy myself a BMW 500cc motorbike and all the leather gear, and the rest of the money I'd put in the bank till I was 30.

R Very wise, too, if I may say so. And what about you, Alison? Would you put your share in the bank, too?

L No, I wouldn't. I'd go on a world tour. I'd stay at all the best hotels and buy all the latest designer model clothes.

R Hm, I don't think your money would last very long if you spent it like that.

L I wouldn't care. I just want to enjoy life while I'm young.

R OK, Alison. Thank you. And now the person we've all been waiting to hear from, Sally, our lottery grandmother of the country! Sally, what would you do with your share if you won the jackpot?

S Well, I'd leave enough money in the bank so that I could play bingo every day for the rest of my life, and with the rest I'd go to California to see my brothers and sisters that I haven't seen for over forty years. I'd give a huge party for them and my nephews and nieces and their wives and husbands and their children. And I wouldn't come back until I had spent every penny.

R Sounds wonderful! Let's hope you mark the six right numbers this week. Good luck to you all, and thank you for taking part.

Unit 8

2a Saturdays

I used to really like Saturdays. Why? Well, er, … I don't really know exactly. They were very boring, in fact, because we always did the same thing. We used to go to Watford with Dad. Everyone knows Watford now because it's off the M25 motorway, the ring road round London, and there are lots of signs to Watford that you can read if you are in a traffic jam. Of course, there was no M25 when I was young, in fact there wasn't even the M1, so we used to drive along little country lanes. Well, we, that is my Dad, my sister and I, used to go to Watford. Mum? Oh, she used to stay at home and do the cleaning while we were out of the way. First we used to change our library books. I liked historical novels when I was young, but I'm not so keen on them now. I don't remember exactly what sort of books my sister liked, but I do know that she used to read very, very quickly, so we had to choose very thick books for her so that they would last her until the next Saturday. Dad chose non-fiction books for himself, and then he used to choose novels for Mum to read. She never complained about his choices, believe it or not. What I really remember was that we used to buy sweets every Saturday from a little shop near the library. It's closed down now, a lot of little shops have closed in that area because big new superstores are opening outside the town centre. It seems a pity. The old man from Pakistan who ran the shop in those days was so friendly. My favourite sweets were jelly babies, and my sister used to like smarties. We only used to have sweets on a Saturday, so if we ate them all on the way home in the car then that was that for another week. We used to get home about one o'clock, and lunch was always the same. We used to have a thick oxtail soup with lots of vegetables in it that we called Saturday stew. I always re- member Saturday stew. There was some- thing very comforting about it and oxtail soup still reminds me of my childhood.

Unit 9

1b A journalist and then an opera singer

Isabel was born in Berlin, but, when she was five, her parents moved to Britain, and she went to school and university there. She got a degree in journalism in 1988 and worked as a reporter for the Bradford Echo for a year. She hated the work and decided to go back to college and try to make a career out of a hobby. She was very lucky to get a place to study voice at the Royal Academy of Music in London. Isabel was an excellent pupil, and, after she left the Academy in 1992, she sang in the chorus of the theatre in Leeds for three years. Then in the 1996/97 winter season she went on tour with the Welsh National Opera Company. On this tour she met an American tenor who was taking a year off and travelling round Europe. He came to every performance the company gave. When the tour finished, he asked Isabel to marry him. She said no at first as her career was very important to her, but in August 1998 she agreed, and the couple moved to New York where he sang in the chorus of the Metropolitan Opera House. She didn't like their ground floor flat in East River Drive, but she loved life in New York and the big American cars. She used to drive a Lincoln Continental. It was, however, very difficult for Isabel to get a job as a singer in America and she became very unhappy. At the end of 2002 the couple got divorced. They didn't have any children, so at the beginning of 2003 Isabel said good-bye to her ex-husband and her cat called Marmalade and moved to Berlin, where in March 2003 she joined the chorus of the Deutsche Oper. She likes being back in Berlin, although she thinks her Golf is a very small car and she's sad that she's not allowed to have a cat in her flat in Grazer Straße. Speaking German again was difficult at first, as she last spoke this language regularly with her parents when she was a child.

9 Word stress

personnel
questionnaire
lemonade
cigarette

invitation
sentimental
conversation
presentation

personal
optimist
programmer
heroin
tolerant

organizer
advertising
interviewer
journalism
ceremony

photographer
impossible
competitive
emergency

promotion
committee
develop
election

Revision 3

1 The weather

1. What beautiful weather we're having!
2. It's rather cold for the time of year.
3. It rained all day yesterday. Wasn't it awful?!
4. I hope there won't be any fog tomorrow. I have to drive up north.
5. Oh no, that sounds like thunder. I'm afraid of thunderstorms.
6. What a storm there was last night. I couldn't get to sleep all night.
7. We got stuck in a snowdrift coming back from our skiing trip.
8. It's so hot today! If only there were a nice breeze.

Unit 10

1d

1. Hi, my name's Ronnie, and I live and work in London. My partner and I share a flat in W1, which is very central, really great for eating out or going to a show, things like that. We don't have a car, well, for one thing, where would we park it? And then with this new congestion tax they've introduced in central London, that just makes it more expensive, doesn't it? Anyhow, I work in Canary Wharf, so I take the Tube, sorry, the underground. Everyone in London calls it the Tube. I have to change trains once, but that's OK. The service is pretty good, and it's much faster than crawling through London by car.
2. Hello there, I'm Sharon, and I live in Sydney. I use my car to go shopping and when we go on trips, but not to get to work. You see, I work on the other side of the bay, and the easiest way to get to work is to take a ferry. It's a very popular method of travel with Sydneysiders because it's cheap and efficient and much more relaxing than getting stuck in a traffic jam every day. I just love watching the skyline of the city from the bay.
3. My name's Michael, but most people call me Mickey. I have to drive through the centre of Belfast every day to get to the office. That's a real pain with the amount of traffic on the road these days. So, you're probably wondering why I do it every day, Monday to Friday? Well, the main reason is that I hate public transport. It's uncomfortable and takes just as long. At least in my own car I can listen to the radio or some of my favourite music, and I don't have to listen in to other people's telephone calls. Yeah, altogether I'd say it's more convenient and worth the money.
4. Hi there, my name's Christine. I'm an English teacher at a secondary school in Hong Kong. I would love to have a car, but I can't really afford it, and, anyway, the public transport system here is excellent, and pretty cheap, too. I use the MTR to get to school. MTR? Well, that stands for Mass Transit Railway, and I suppose it's a combination of underground and railway. Of course, the trains are often busy, but they have air-conditioning, and they're very fast.
5. Hi. I'm Sally, and I live in Rolling Hills, Los Angeles with my husband and our three children. We have two cars, and I use mine to get to work, take the kids to school, and collect them, of course, do the shopping, go to the fitness centre, visit my Mom in downtown LA, take the kids to training and the weekly ball games. I just couldn't live without my car. The local transport system is so

Tapescripts **169**

Tapescripts

inconvenient, and I need to get to so many different places every day. It just makes life so much easier.

4b Hi-tech home defences

S = Sales Accountant / H = Houseowner

S Good afternoon, sir. Can I help you?
H Yes, I'm looking for some kind of home protection system. A friend of mine told me to come to you.
S Well, you've come to the right place if I may say so. Now then, sir, is it for a flat or a detached property?
H A semi-detached house with a back and front garden and a driveway leading to an attached garage.
S Is there a door from the garage to the house?
H No, there isn't. The main entrance is through the front door, but there are also patio doors leading from the dining room to the back garden.
S And what's behind the back garden, sir?
H The back gardens of the houses behind us.
S I see. Well, in that case, sir, what about a conventional burglar alarm fitted above the front door with a second one above the patio doors?
H No, thank you. We've already got something like that, and it doesn't work. It keeps going off for no reason. The neighbours hate it, and the police ignore it! Our house has just been broken into for the third time. Everyone thought it was a false alarm again. No, this time I want something better, something which is really burglar-proof.
S Right, sir. I think I've got just what you're looking for. Our latest alarm system goes a step further. It doesn't just make a noise, it booms out a repeated warning message. Let me play it for you: "Police have been called! Police have been called!" *(very loud!)*
H No, I don't think that's what I'm looking for. The neighbours would love us even more for that!
S What about our smoke alarm system? As soon as a burglar enters your home, the room is filled with high-density smoke.
H And how does the system know the difference between a burglar and my wife? No, thank you. Haven't you got anything a bit more hi-tech?
S Well, we have, but it's not too popular with the police. It's an electric wire system which is hidden behind the walls of your house. When the system is set, any intruders who touch the wall are shocked or burnt.
H I can see why the police don't like it. I wouldn't like it either! Well, thank you very much, but I don't think you've got what I'm looking for. My wife was right after all. We'll just have to get a couple of geese!

Unit 11

3c "Green or Greenish?"

I = Interviewer / S = Sue / M = Martin

I Good evening, ladies and gentlemen, and welcome to our weekly challenge programme "Green or Greenish?", in which we are once again trying to find our Green couple of the week. Tonight's first contestants are Sue and Martin Bingley from Huntingdon in Cambridgeshire. *(Applause)* Sue is 28 and works for the Inland Revenue. Martin is 31 and a self-employed accountant.

In the meantime our other two couples are sitting in their soundproof cubicles waiting for their turn. At the end of the programme the couple with the highest score will be our Green couple of the week and the winners of this week's surprise Green prize! *(Applause)*

Right then, Sue and Martin, you know the rules of the game. There are ten questions which either of you can answer. For each answer you give the members of our studio audience will press one of two buttons – "Green" or "Greenish". Remember you need a 60% vote to win the "Green" point.
So here we go. Question No.1.
Where do you buy your fruit and veg?

S From our local greengrocer because it's always fresh and unpacked.
I OK, no.2. Martin, do you use an electric shaver?
M Well, as you can see, I've got a full-face beard, which Sue trims for me with a pair of scissors. So the answer's no.
I Right. Now for no.3, a bit personal this one. Do you share the bath? *(Laughter)*
M That's a tricky one. I don't really like baths. I prefer to take a shower. Sue sometimes has a bath after a hard day at the office, but generally speaking she uses the shower. And, em, no, we've never shared the shower. *(Laughter)*
I Well, that was a pretty honest answer. OK, next question. Do you use cotton hankies?
S Well, Martin does, and he washes them by himself, too. I don't really use hankies, although I do keep a packet of tissues in my handbag just in case.
I Right. Here we go with question no.5. Has your flat got double glazing?
M Unfortunately not. It's quite an old flat, and our landlord has so far refused to have double glazing put in. He says it's too expensive, but then he doesn't have to pay the heating bills.
I And that brings me to the next question. How many rooms do you heat at a time?
S Only the room we live in, and the bathroom, of course. There are no heaters in the kitchen or bedroom, and the one in the hallway just doesn't work.
I OK; question no. 7. Which washing cycles do you use?
M Well, it's usually me who does the washing since Sue's out all day. I tend to use only one washing cycle, the warm wash on 40°, for practically everything. It's easier that way.
S Yes, that's a point we don't really agree on. I've had to ask him not to wash my wooly jumpers in the machine. I do them by hand in the wash-hand basin.
I I see. Well, let's move on to the next question. Do you buy drinks in non-returnable bottles?
S We try not to, but there are some drinks which you just can't buy in returnable bottles in this country. Not like Denmark. We went there on holiday last year and were very impressed. All their drinks are in returnable bottles.
I Right. A tip for the Minister of the Environment there. OK, two more questions to go. Have you got a car?
M Yes, we have, but we hardly ever use it. I have a bike which I use to get around Huntingdon, and Sue takes the train to Peterborough. There's a good commuter service. I suppose we use the car about two or three times a month, mainly for longer journeys, – oh yes, and for going to the bottle bank.
I And now for the final question in tonight's first round to find our Green couple of the week. How do you squeeze your toothpaste tube? *(Laughter)*
S I'm afraid that's another point we don't quite see eye to eye on. I'm very careful about squeezing the tube from the bottom and rolling it up as I use it. That's the way I was taught to do it as a child. However, Martin just squeezes it right from the top, and, if I'm not careful, he throws the tube out when it's really still half-full. He doesn't seem to have the same patience as I do.
I Well, I don't suppose you are the only couple who has fought over the toothpaste tube *(Laughter)*. Sue and Martin, thank you for being so honest with your answers. You deserve a big round of applause. *(Applause)* Now, if you would just take a seat over here while I introduce our next contestants …

Unit 12

3b What's it about?

1. 'Well, of course, I am a Hugh Grant fan, and I think this is one of his best. I remember when I saw it for the first

time, I kept wondering who was going to get him in the end. I think I would have been quite disappointed if he had married 'Duck-face'.'
2. 'I don't know how many times I've watched this film. I've got it on video and on DVD, but I think I must have seen it at least three or four times on TV and, of course, at the cinema when it first came out back in the Sixties. I like the music, too.'
3. 'This is the film where you suddenly see a field full of warriors with their faces painted blue and white, and Mel Gibson as William Wallace is right at the head of them. I wonder if the Scots really did paint their faces before they went into battle?'
4. 'I read the book first, and I thought I might be disappointed when I saw the film. You know how that happens sometimes. But I wasn't. The special effects were fantastic, and they are important in this kind of film. But the scenery was great, too. They did the filming in New Zealand.
5. 'Hugh Grant again, but this time he plays the 'baddie', well, not the nice Englishman type that he plays in some of his other films. I was surprised when I heard that they had chosen an American actress for the leading role, but there wasn't a trace of an American accent to be heard.'

5b

'Carol Dukes, a 41-year-old mother-of-two from Berkshire, has told reporters how she made a 900-mile dash across the country after her son had left on a school trip without his trusty Gameboy. She spent £150 on planes and taxis in pursuit of Charlie, aged eleven, who was headed for Iona, off the west coast of Scotland. According to his mother, Charlie couldn't have lasted a whole week without the game.

Charlie and 39 classmates were bound for Iona to learn about life without modern amenities. When his mother managed to overtake the train carrying the school party and eventually delivered the toy at the station in Dumbarton, Charlie was understandably embarrassed. Mrs Dukes said she wasn't an over-indulgent mum but had felt guilty after re-packing Charlie's bag and forgetting to replace the game. "I wanted him to have a good time, and the only option I had was to get the Gameboy to him in person," she said.

Key

Unit 1

4a

1. **Have you** done an English course before?
2. **When** was that?
3. **Did you** have English at school?
4. **Is this** your first English course?
5. **Where/When did you** learn to speak English?
6. **Have you** ever been to England?
7. **Do you** need English at work?
8. **Why are you** taking this course?
9. **Have you** got the book?
10. **Where did you** get it?
11. **How much** was it?
12. **Do you** know the teacher?
13. **Can you** speak any other foreign languages?
14. **Do you** live near here?
15. **How do you** get here?

4c

1. Where do you live?
   Where do you work?
   Where were you born?
   Where do you come from?
   Where did you go to school?
2. When do you get up?
   When do you start work?
   When do you finish work?
   When do you get home?
   When did you finish work today?
3. What's your sister-in-law's name?
   What's your wife's name?
   What's your daughter's name?
   Who was your best friend at school?
   Who did you sit next to at school?

4f

Where does Werner live?
Where does he work?
Where does he go to school?
Where does Werner come from?

5

Partner A

- How old is Betsy?
- Who does she work for?
- Is she married?
- What's her husband's name?
- Has she got any children?
- Where does she live?
- What sort of house does she live in?
- How much does she pay for the house?
- What sort of car does Betsy drive?
- How does she get to work?
- How far is her house from the factory?
- How many shifts are there at the factory?
- How long does each shift last?
- How many hours a week does Betsy work?
- How many days' holiday does Betsy have?
- How much does Betsy earn?

Partner B

- How old is Oscar?
- Who does he work for?
- Is he married?
- What's his wife's name?
- Has he got any children?
- Where does he live?
- What sort of house does he live in?
- How much does he pay for the house?
- What sort of car does Oscar drive?
- How does he get to work?
- How far is his house from the factory?
- How many shifts are there at the factory?
- How long does each shift last?
- How many hours a week does Oscar work?
- How many days' holiday does Oscar have?
- How much does Oscar earn?

6a

commutes, lives, works, helps, gets, leaves, drives, costs, spends, adds.

6c

Atmosphere:	friendly
Activities:	History society, Finstock singers, church
Facilities:	2 pubs, small shop and post office
Schools:	primary school in the village and comprehensive schools in the nearby towns
Area:	Beautiful countryside
Tourist attractions:	Woodstock and Blenheim Palace and Oxford

8

1. False
2. False
3. Possible
4. False
5. True
6. False
7. Possible
8. False
9. Possible
10. Possible

9a

Tom is Isobel's husband.

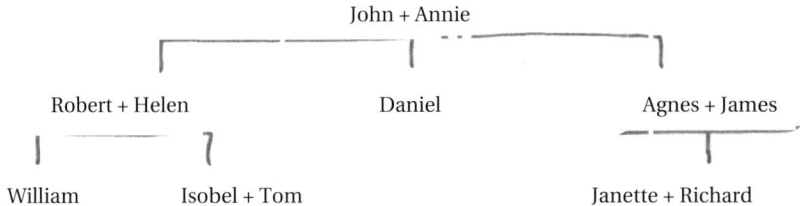

9b

male	female
grandfather	grandmother
father	mother
son	daughter
brother	sister
uncle	aunt
nephew	niece
cousin	cousin
grandson	granddaughter
husband	wife
father-in-law	mother-in-law
son-in-law	daughter-in-law
brother-in-law	sister-in-law
step-father	step-mother

12

1. Where **do** you live?
2. The express bus **doesn't** stop here.
3. **Have** you **got** a spare pen?
4. **What does** "spare" mean?
5. **Is there** a phone in this building?
6. Sorry, I **don't** know your name.
7. **What's** your address?
8. I just **don't/can't** understand this exercise!

13a

- The house costs £185,000.
- No, she works as a vet.
- He just has a cup of coffee.
- No, he only has breakfast with the children at the weekend.

1. successful
2. four-bedroomed semi-detached
3. locally
4. second class season
5. snatched
6. sparkling
7. only

15d

- gel, gin, glen
- he, hen, hinge, his
- in, is, isle
- leg, lie, line
- nil, Nile
- she, shin, shine, shingle, sign, sin, singe

Unit 2

2b

- Some jockeys, in Australia, catch, break in and train wild camels for racing ...
- Anyone over the age of 18 ...
- ... but you don't have any turning or braking equipment, ...
- If a camel stops suddenly, there isn't really anything a jockey can do.
- Sure you take some risks ...
- ... and if there aren't any risks there isn't any fun.
- Would you like to have some fun, kids?
- ... a camel doesn't have any water in its hump ...
- ... at the camel ball that raises some money ...

Statement 1, 3: true
Statement 2: false

3

1. tennis
2. downhill skiing
3. football

4a

Gerard Depardieu is an actor.
He's smoking a cigarette.

5a

	Phone call? person calling? number?		person in? What's she/ he doing?
1	Andrew	67887	no playing tennis
2	Ian	Airton 478	yes washing the car
3	Helen	Cheltenham 61334	no having a piano lesson
4	Pam	634859	yes watching football on TV

The grid

Answer the phone
3559. (Hello.)
Speaking. *or:* No, this is ...
I'm sorry she's not in.
Can I take a message?
Hold on. I'll just get her/ him.
(I'll tell her /him you called). Bye.

Make a phone call
Hello. This is X.
(Is that) Barbara?
Could I speak to ... please?
Can I leave a message?
Thanks.
Thanks (for your help). Bye.

6a

- What's your first name / surname?
- How old are you?
- What do you do?
- Are you married?
- Have you got any children?
- How much (money) have you got in your purse / wallet?
- What do you spend a lot of money on?
- What don't you spend much money on?

7a

countable:
bars of chocolate, eggs, bottles, glasses, cups, slices of toast, tomatoes, biscuits, chops

uncountable:
water, beer, lemonade, orange juice, coffee, wine, tea, sugar, butter, salad, meat

7b

much / many / much / many / much / many / much / much / many / many / much / many

8

a bar of:	soap, chocolate
a bottle of:	beer, lemonade, wine, orange juice
a box of:	chocolates, washing powder, eggs, matches
a can of:	beer, coke
a carton of:	orange juice, milk
a crate of:	beer, lemonade
a glass of:	wine, orange juice, lemonade, beer
a jar of:	honey, jam
a litre of:	wine, orange juice, lemonade, mineral water
a packet of:	cigarettes, sweets, crisps, soup, tea, rice, washing powder, biscuits
a slice of:	ham, bread, bacon, pineapple, toast
a tin of:	soup, peas, pineapple, tomatoes
a tube of:	tomato puree, toothpaste

9a

Kiosk/Post office: 5 postcards, 10 stamps
Pharmacy counter: a packet of paracetamol
Newsagent: street map of London, 'Hello' magazine

9b

1. Possible
2. True
3. True
4. True
5. True
6. False

10

many, some, much, any, some, some, any, some, much, many, many, some, much, any

11

1. is studying / works / enjoys / meets
2. teaches / teaches / isn't teaching / is teaching / enjoys / plays / spends / is having
3. works / is working / spends / enjoys / isn't drinking

Unit 3

2

1 C, 2 H, 3 A, 4 G, 5 E, 6 D,
7 M, 8 F, 9 K, 10 L, 11 O, 12 B,
13 J, 14 N, 15 I

3a

always, always, never, always, sometimes

4b

Fill in the gaps in the song:
loves, glasses, kids, face, feet, mother, daddy, down, family, chest

5c

regular verbs:
walked, liked, helped, loved, attended, travelled, talked, died, accepted, studied, moved, hoped, waited, washed, worked, qualified, re-trained, finished, explained, started

irregular verbs:
was/were, had, got, gave, became

8

eyes, tongue, smell, ears, taste, hear, walk, head, work, think, eat, thirsty, sleep, eat, drink

10

1. at the pub   4. in the street
2. in the street   5. at the pub
3. in the bank   6. in the bank

Revision Unit 1

1

1b; 2a; 3a; 4c; 5d; 6c; 7c; 8d; 9a; 10d

Key

3a

1. expensive
2. supporter
3. married
4. vet
5. semi-detached
6. pub
7. hairdresser
8. sweet
9. teenager
10. commuter

3b

(suggestions)

1. is not married
2. helps you find your way when you're driving
3. who rides camels in races
4. which you do in your free time
5. which doesn't cost much money
6. who works in a bank
7. which contains bottles of mineral water or beer
8. you can buy aspirins, shampoo and toothpaste
9. you can get money
10. you don't know

4

Here are some suggested dialogues:

Carolyn: But he doesn't drink alcohol.
Friend: Yes, but he watches football and holiday programmes on TV.
Carolyn: Yes, but he's allergic to cats, and I've got two cats. And he likes fish. I'm allergic to fish. He likes mountain-biking and I hate it and he doesn't like holidays by the sea.
Friend: Yes, but he speaks English and Italian.
Carolyn: Yes, but I don't speak German.

Robert: Well, she's 25 and that's a good age but she doesn't like mountain-biking or fish.
Friend: Yes, but she likes reading and she watches football and holiday programmes on TV.
Robert: Yes, but she's got two cats, and you know I'm allergic to cats. She drinks wine and I don't drink any alcohol and she doesn't like holidays in the mountains.
Friend: Yes, but she speaks Italian and English.
Robert: Yes, but she doesn't speak German.

5

1E; 2A; 3G; 4C (any, any); 5D (anything); 6F (some); 7H (some); 8I; 9B

7

1e; 2g; 3b; 4c; 5a; 6h; 7d; 8f

Unit 4

1a

Here are some suggested questions that can be formed from the prompts given:

- What does your boss / your partner wear at work?
- What does your boss / your partner have for supper?
- What does your boss / your partner cook for supper?
- When does your boss / your partner have lunch?
- When does your boss / your partner cook lunch?
- Where does your boss / your partner have lunch?
- When does your boss / your partner start / finish work?
- How does your boss / your partner get / travel to work?
- Where does your boss / your partner spend her/his holidays?

2b

Questions for partner B:
- Where did they go to?
- Where did they fly to in Malaysia?
- How did they get to (the luxury resort on) Pangkor island?
- What did they eat for breakfast?
- Where did they relax?
- What did they write to their friends?
- What did they see (when they went snorkelling)?
- What did they watch on their last evening?

Questions for partner A:
- How did they fly?
- How many nights did they spend in the Federal Hotel (in Kuala Lumpur)?
- How high did temperatures rise?
- What did they drink for breakfast?
- What did they drink by the pool?
- What did they do in the afternoon?
- What did they usually watch in the evening?
- How long did they stay?

5a

Sentences you hear on the CD:
- I was getting tired of my job.
- I delivered a baby.
- I was working for Singapore Airlines.
- We were flying between Abu Dhabi and Singapore.
- The passengers were watching a film.
- The Indians were attacking the fort.
- The soldiers were shooting the Indians.
- They heard the cry of a new-born baby.
- She was travelling to the airport.
- Her taxi collided with a bus.

6

began, saw, took, sat, ate, lost, shot, brought, caught, spent, heard, flew, forgot, knew, found, slept, cut, gave, shut

8

1. didn't lie
2. didn't go
3. didn't buy
4. didn't hire
5. didn't take
6. didn't enjoy

10

1. Did you?
2. Do you?
3. Did you?
4. Did you?
5. Did you?
6. Did you?
7. Did she?

Unit 5

2a

Possible questions:

Have you ever …
- driven more than 60 km/h in a town?
- travelled on the underground without a ticket?
- parked illegally?
- taken home stationery from the office?
- taken part in a protest march?
- mowed the lawn on a Sunday?
- washed your car in the street in front of your house?
- played loud music after 12 o'clock at night?
- found something valuable in the street and taken it to the police?
- had a car accident?

4b

1c.; 2a.; 3d.; 4f.; 5g.; 6b.; 7e.

6a

- The police have seized 10 kilos of heroin.
- The police have taken the lorry driver to the police station.
- Art thieves have stolen two paintings.
- Fires have destroyed large areas of a national park.
- Strong winds have made the firemen's jobs very difficult.
- The art gallery has offered a reward.
- Many families have left their homes.

8

item • description • where/when

an umbrella • dark blue • on a number 7 bus / yesterday afternoon

2 school bags • Benetton colours / black, blue • at the bus stop / this morning

9

1. has broken, broke, hit
2. have lost, dropped, had, did you talk, did, has handed it in
3. has fallen
4. has stolen, did you park, did you lock, did

10

Heard at …
1. the football stadium
2. the airport
3. the station
4. the lost property office
5. the hotel
6. the hospital
7. the police station
8. the bank
9. the garage
10. home

11a

What is it?
1. a car
2. a dog

11b

1. your
2. his
3. mine
4. mine / ours
5. your; my

Unit 6

5a

You could:
go on a cruise, go birdwatching, visit the flying doctor service, climb Ayers Rock, visit a vineyard in the Barossa valley, buy an opal.

There are:
lots of Aboriginal sites in the national parks, some good vineyards in the Barossa valley.

There's:
the Barrier Reef, a hotel shaped like a crocodile in Kakadu, the Sydney opera House.

5b

The diary
27 April   flight to Cairns
28-4   cruise round the Barrier Reef
5–11 May   Kakadu National Park Jabiru
12 May   flight to Alice Springs
17–23 May   Adelaide Hughes family
24 May   flight to Sydney
24–1   stay with family in Sydney

7a

1. The park was founded in 1975 to welcome tourists but also to protect the reef.
2. Zones for scientific research, zones where you can visit (and can't touch anything) and recreational zones.
3. Tourists: walk on the reef and pick up shells; light fires anywhere and leave litter.
4. No. Fishing boats from Asia collect clams.

8

Dialogue 1

■ Hemel Hempstead 58023 (**A**)
● Is that Brian? (**D**)
■ Yes. (**E**)
● Hi, this is Peter (**G**)
■ Oh, hello Peter. How are you? (**H**)
● Fine. Look Brian, Kate, Jean and I are going to a pop concert near Avesbury next week. Would you like to come? (**I**)
■ Yes, I'd love to. How are you getting there? Are you driving down? (**K**)
● Yes, we're leaving at about 4 on Friday. (**M**)
■ Fine. (**N**)
● I'll pick you up just before 4 then, OK? (**O**)
■ Great. See you then. Bye. (**P**)
● Bye. (**Q**)

Dialogue 2

■ 0171 242 1437 (**T**)
● Jane? (**B**)
■ No, this is Alice. (**C**)
● Oh, Alice I didn't recognize your voice. This is Roy. Is Jane there, please? (**L**)
■ No, she's not, I'm afraid. She's gone to the cinema with Pam. (**J**)
● Any idea when she'll be back? (**U**)
■ Well, the film finishes at 8.30, I think, so she should be back at about 9. (**F**)
● OK. Can you tell her I phoned, and I'll phone again about 9.15. (**V**)
■ Yes, I'll tell her. Bye. (**R**)
● Thanks. Bye. (**S**)

9

1. Congratulations.
2. Good luck.
3. Nothing serious, I hope.
4. The lucky man!
5. Have a good journey.
6. What a shame!
7. No, I didn't get a ticket, unfortunately.
8. OK, have a good holiday.
9. Oh, that's a nuisance.
10. We'd love to.

10

- There'll be a strike of air-traffic controllers. They always go on strike in the summer.
- You'll frighten the fish.
- You won't like the food.
- You'll never get to the top at your age!
- There won't be enough wind at this time of year.

11

Gill / Edinburgh
Charles / Istanbul
Mike / Ottawa
Mrs Hatton / Garmisch
Sheila / Aspen
Walter / Antalya
Carolyn / Alice Springs
David Quarrie / Rome
Bruce Foster / Athens
Helen / Melbourne

Revision Unit 2

1

go	went	gone
lose	lost	lost
eat	ate	eaten
write	wrote	written
hear	heard	heard
sing	sang	sung
think	thought	thought
steal	stole	stolen
pay	paid	paid

Five have three different forms and four have only two.

2a

a broken / hurt
b eaten / cooked / tasted
c driven
d met / shaken hands with
e drunk
f climbed
g had / witnessed
h watched / taken part in

2b

1. got (f)
2. had (a)
3. grew up (c)
4. shook (d)
5. celebrated (e)

Key **175**

Key

6. (b)
7. drove (g)
8. came, marched (h)

3

Possible sentences:

- She / he was driving to work when she / he ran out of petrol / had an accident.
- She / he was flying to Florida when she / he met his wife. (She met her lover's wife!)
- He was travelling abroad when a mugger stole his passport / when he met his wife / when his lover had an accident! / when his lover met his wife!
- She / he was reading a newspaper when the postman brought a parcel.
- She / he was having a bath when the postman brought a parcel.

4

- I'm seeing my dentist …
- I'm meeting a friend for lunch …
- She'll probably be late. / We're going to have lunch …
- It'll be nice to see her. / I'm taking the children swimming …
- She'll be seven in two weeks. / We're having a birthday party … / She hasn't decided how many people she's going to invite. / I'll be exhausted.

5a

1. Angela and Alan: Radfords Country Hotel
2. Rod and his family: The Fox Inn, Dorset
3. George and Sandra: Coastal Cottages
4. Jim and Mieke: Master Builder's Hotel
5. Sarah, Andrew, David and Ruth: Acorn holidays or Anglican Activity Breaks
6. Marjorie and Robert Stevens and Vanessa and Brian Thomas: Old Manor Estate

5b

Dear Sir or Madam,
I saw your advertisement in The Sunday Times of February 12. Could you please send me a colour brochure. I would also like a price list and details of accommodation available in July for a family of 2 adults and a young daughter. Thank you for your help.
Yours sincerely

Unit 7

2a

Weather chart on the right-hand side (on **page 68**).

2c

And here is tomorrow's weather forecast. It will be overcast in most places. Wales and the south of England will be mostly cloudy. Later in the day a few bright intervals may develop, especially in the west. The rest of England will remain overcast with some rain in places.

Scotland will be overcast with rain in central and northern parts of the country. During the afternoon some bright intervals may develop in the south-west.

Ireland will be mainly dry with sunny intervals in the south. Temperatures will be lower than today, from 14 degrees in the north to 20 in the south-west. Winds will be mainly moderate.

3b

1. A cold snap is a sudden period of very cold weather.
2. Bookmakers take bets.
3. A punter is someone who places a bet.

3c

1. True
2. True
3. False
4. False
5. Possible
6. True
7. True
8. Possible

4b

1. I'll call you tomorrow if I can't come.
2. We'll take the train if the weather is bad.
3. You'll get sunburnt if you stay in the sun too long.
4. I'll be late for work if I miss the bus.
5. The hole in the ozone layer will get bigger if we don't stop using CFC's.
6. They'll go on a world trip if they win the lottery.
7. She'll do well in the exam if she studies hard.
8. The milk will go sour if you don't put it in the fridge.

5a

1. £5.00
2. £1.00
3. 9 August 2003
4. Estimated Jackpot £8m

7a

cloudy, showers, bright, sunny, misty, rain, drizzle, dry, thunderstorms, windy

7b

England and Wales **will be** mostly cloudy. Scotland and Northern Ireland **will be** misty. It **will be** less windy than today.

will-future
"may" plus the full verb: This tells us that it is not certain, but possible.

8

Possible advice:

If I were you, …
- I wouldn't lie in the sun at this time of the day.
- I'd leave that until the drought was over.
- I'd take the blue one.
- I'd check the petrol.
- I'd throw it out.
- I wouldn't take so much cash with me the next time.
- I wouldn't do that.
- I'd join an English course.

9

1. If the weather **stays** like this, we**'ll have** a barbecue at the weekend.
2. She**'ll come** back home if she **finds** a job. (The chances are good.)
   She **would come** back home if she **found** a job. (The chances are not so good.)
3. There **would be** fewer road accidents if everyone **drove** more carefully.
4. If you **follow** the signs, you **won't lose** your way. (Giving directions)
   If you **followed** the signs, you **wouldn't lose** your way. (The 'you'-person loses her/his way quite a lot because she/he doesn't follow the signs.)
5. We**'ll buy** a new car if the prices **fall** by the end of the year.
6. The Prime Minister **will resign** if he **doesn't get** a clear majority in the next election. (The PM has said so.)
   The Prime Minister **would resign** if he **didn't get** a clear majority in the next election. (Someone else's opinion.)
7. I**'d die** if I **got stuck** in a lift.
8. If you **give** me your number, Ms Henderson **will call** you back as soon as possible.
9. The milk **will boil** over if you **don't turn down** the gas!
10. I **would write** more often if only I **had** more time.

Unit 8

1
Sting used to be an English teacher.
Sabine Christiansen used to be a flight assistant.
Sean Connery used to be a dock worker.
J.K. Rowling used to be unemployed.
Reinhold Messner used to be a Maths teacher.
Queen Sylvia used to be a hostess.

2a
She used to:
read historical novels, eat jelly babies, buy sweets once a week

Her sister used to:
read thick books, eat smarties, buy sweets once a week

Her father used to:
drive to Watford along country lanes, choose books for her Mum

Her mother used to:
stay at home, do the cleaning, prepare the same Saturday lunch every week

4a
- You mustn't smoke.
- You mustn't touch the exhibits.
- You mustn't park your car in front of the entrance.
- You must be careful because of pick-pockets.
- You mustn't enter this room.
- You must buy a ticket.
- You mustn't play music in the station.

6
Do you have to …?
Yes, I have to…/No, I don't have to …
Sabine has to …/Sabine doesn't have to …

Are you allowed to …?
Yes, I'm allowed to …/No, I'm not allowed to …
Olaf is allowed to …/Olaf isn't allowed to …

7
Ms J. Allmark
- She might be married: Why doesn't she call herself Mrs?
- She may be divorced: We don't know if she is married, single or divorced.
- She might be a flight attendant, but she's not wearing a flight attendant's uniform.
- She might be a bus driver, but why is she wearing such smart clothes?
- She may be the manageress of a supermarket: This is possible.

Miss P. Sutton
- She may be called Pamela. This is a woman's name.
- She can't be called Paul. This is a man's name.
- She might be a good swimmer. But she doesn't look very strong.
- She can't be still at school. She's not wearing a uniform.
- She can't be a policewoman. She's too short.
- She may be a dentist. She's wearing a white coat.

11a
In the supermarket:
Express checkout 5 items or less.
No credit cards at this checkout.
Please pay here.
Cash only at this checkout.

In the park:
Dogs must be kept on a lead
No ball games
Do not drop litter – Penalty £25.
Do not feed the ducks

On the bus / at the bus stop:
Queue here
Please give up this seat if an elderly person needs it
Do not talk to the driver
Please tender exact fare

11b
1. true
2. true
3. true
4. false
5. true
6. true

12
1. mustn't
2. mustn't
3. had to
4. must
5. had to
6. don't have to
7. wasn't allowed to
8. has to
9. had to
10. had to, don't have to
11. don't have to
12. have to

Unit 9

1b
- She used to be a journalist and now she is an opera singer.
- She used to be married and now she is divorced.
- She used to live in New York and now she lives in Berlin.
- She used to drive a Lincoln Continental and now she drives a Golf.
- She used to sing at the theatre in Leeds and now she sings at the Deutsche Oper in Berlin.
- She used to speak English all day and now she speaks German.

1c
For one year.
Since she left the Royal Academy in 1992.
For over 4 years.
Since 2003.
For four years.
Since 2003.

2a
- How long was she a journalist / did she work as a journalist? – For a year.
- How long has she been an opera singer? – Since she left the Royal Academy in 1992.
- How long was she married? – For over four years.
- How long has she been divorced? – Since the end of 2002.
- How long did she live on East River Drive? – For over four years.
- How long has she been living in Grazer Straße? – Since 2003.
- How long did she drive a Lincoln Continental? – For over four years.
- How long has she been driving a Golf? – Since 2003./Since she moved to Berlin.
- How long did she sing at the theatre in Leeds? – For three years.
- How long has she been singing at the Deutsche Oper? – Since March 2003.
- How long did she speak English? – For a long time./For many years.
- How long has she been speaking German? – Since she went back to Germany./Since she got a job at the Deutsche Oper.

3
Jenny Dickson
- How old is she? She's 26.
- When did Jenny Dickson leave school? In 1993 at the age of 16
- What does she do? (It is not usual in English to ask: What is her occupation?) She's a coach driver.
- What was her first job? A kitchen assistant at a tennis club.
- How long did she stay in her first job? 2 years
- What did she do next? She was a town-service mini-bus driver.

Key

- How long has she had her present job? Three years.
- How many different jobs has she had since she left school? Four.
- How much does she earn? £ 15,000 a year
- How much does she spend on clothes a month? £100

Barbara Barsa Jamison
- Age: She's 38.
- Occupation: She's the Vice President of Membership Rewards for American Express.
- 1989
- Assistant Product Manager
- 3 years
- She was Product Manager of seven dog-food lines.
- Since 2002
- Seven
- £85,000 a year
- £250

4

to do shift work
to work at the weekend
to wear a uniform
to earn a competitive salary
to travel to foreign countries
to need good communication skills
to send e-mails
to have a degree
to sit at a desk
to be creative
to have a lot of responsibility
to solve problems
to understand technology
to be computer literate

6a

since the spring election of 2003
since she left school
since the beginning of the winter term
since they won a million Euro
for over three years
since the cat ran away
for two weeks
for an hour

6b

1. ... since they won a million Euro.
2. ... since she left school.
3. ... for an hour.
4. ... for two weeks.
5. ... since the spring election of 2003.
6. ... since the cat ran away.
7. ... since the beginning of the winter term.
8. ... for over three years.

7a

1b.; 2k.; 3c.; 4e.; 5i.; 6d.; 7a.; 8g.; 9f.; 10h.; 11j.

9

○ ○ ●
personnel
lemonade
questionnaire
cigarette

○ ● ○ ○
photographer
impossible
competitive
emergency

● ○ ○ ○
organizer
advertising
interviewer
journalism
ceremony

● ○ ○
personal
optimist
programmer
heroin
tolerant

○ ○ ● ○
invitation
sentimental
conversation
presentation

○ ● ○
promotion
committee
develop
election

Revision Unit 3

1

1. beautiful weather
2. rather cold
3. rained; awful
4. fog
5. thunder; thunderstorms
6. storm
7. snowdrift
8. hot; breeze

2

1. If you took your medicine, you'd feel much better.
2. The room would look more inviting if you put the armchair over there.
3. I'll give you a call if I can't make it in time.
4. You'll miss the bus if you don't hurry!
5. If you don't turn down the music; I'll (have to) call the police.
6. If I were you, I'd find out a bit more about their bonus scheme.

3

1. He has had a house in Erfurt since 1994. He has been living in Erfurt since 1994.
2. He has had a Mercedes for three years. He has been driving a Mercedes for three years.
3. She has been the Personnel Manager for two years.
4. He has been married since 1986.
5. He has had a CD ROM drive for a year.
6. He has been playing tennis for five years. / He has been a member of the village tennis club for five years.
7. She has been working / she has worked as an editor for a local newspaper since January 1993.
8. They have been fishing for three hours.
9. She has been wearing glasses / she has worn glasses since she was at university.
10. She has been studying engineering since October 2000.
11. They have been divorced for six months.
12. He has been digging the garden since three o'clock.

4a

1. You mustn't smoke here.
2. You mustn't cross the road now.
3. You don't have to pay to go in.
4. You mustn't take photos here.
5. You don't have to be a resident of the hotel.

4b

1. Company employees mustn't smoke at the workplace.
2. Company employees mustn't park at the front of the building.
3. Company employees don't have to wear a shirt and tie.
4. Company employees have to hand in a timesheet each week.
5. Company employees mustn't use recycled paper in the photocopier.
6. Company employees have to take 2 weeks' holiday at Christmas.
7. Company employees don't have to pay for the wine at the Christmas party.

5a

Harald:	Multimedia
John:	Hippers
Alex:	For Women – but has she had enough experience?
Barbara:	For Women
Jane, Angela, Mike:	Kingston Smith
Joanna:	Hippers, but has she got enough experience and the right interpersonal skills?
Frank:	Hippers, but what about all the travelling to London?
Pat:	Hippers because she can work on Saturdays.
Peter:	Multimedia, if he's got experience in Macintosh programming or CD-i.

5c

1. True
2. False
3. False
4. Love from; Best wishes; Yours

178

Unit 10

1d

1. Ronnie: London; the underground; service is good and it is faster than going by car
2. Sharon: Sydney; the ferry; it is cheap and efficient and much more relaxing
3. Michael: Belfast; the car; public transport is uncomfortable; car is more convenient
4. Christine: Hong Kong; MTR (underground and train); public transport is excellent, it is pretty cheap and very efficient
5. Sally: Los Angeles; the car; local transport is so inconvenient; car makes life so much easier

2a

1. True
2. False
3. True
4. True
5. False

2d

1. I enjoy going by …
2. Do you prefer travelling / to travel …
3. Would you like to fly …
4. I don't mind walking …
5. Some people like driving / to drive …
6. My neighbour hates travelling / to travel …

3a

1a.; 2c.; 3d.; 4 a.; 5b.; 6c.; 7b.; 8d.; 9a.; 10d.; 11b.; 12a.; 13d.; 14c.; 15b.

3c

basic	comparative	superlative
long	longer	the longest
short	shorter	the shortest
expensive	more expensive	the most expensive
cheap	cheaper	the cheapest
exciting	more exciting	the most exciting

4b

1. False; 2. True; 3. True; 4. False; 5. False; 6. True; 7. True; 8. False; 9. False; 10. False

5a

1. have been called
2. is filled
3. is hidden
4. is set / are shocked, burnt

5b

1. is fitted
2. was told / had been given
3. was broken into
4. are written
5. has been made
6. will be delivered
7. are used
8. has been cancelled

6

Matthew is (14 minutes) older than Mark.
Matthew is (2 cm) shorter than Mark.
Matthew is (1.5 kg) heavier than Mark.
Matthew has less money in the bank than Mark.
Matthew's school grades are not so good as Mark's.
Mark is (14 minutes) younger than Matthew.
Mark is (2 cm) taller than Matthew.
Mark is (1.5 kg) lighter than Matthew.
Mark has more savings than Matthew.
Mark is better at school than Mark.

7

Possible sentences:

1. most wonderful
2. most thrilling
3. richest
4. saddest
5. youngest
6. heaviest
7. most important
8. most brilliant

8a

gerund	infinitive	gerund or infinitive
enjoy	hope	like
don't mind	would like	begin
look forward to	promise	prefer
give up	want	hate

8b

1. seeing
2. closing/opening/shutting
3. to do
4. cycling/driving/flying/smoking
5. going dancing
6. to call/to phone
7. chasing/frightening
8. to move

9

1. The fire brigade was called as soon as the fire broke out.
2. My car has been stolen.
3. The painting was given to me when I retired.
4. The dishwasher will be delivered on Wednesday.
5. The exam results are sent straight to the candidates.
6. A man has been arrested in connection with the Baker Street bank robbery.
7. In hospital you are always wakened so early.
8. This is the worst meal I have ever been served.

Unit 11

1c

Possible sentences:

It might be a good idea if you …
- got more sleep.
- ate more fresh fruit and vegetables every day.
- got some regular exercise.
- gave up smoking.
- had regular medical check-ups.
- went to the dentist's at least once a year.
- didn't work such long hours.
- took more time to relax with your family and friends.
- didn't drink more than two cups of coffee a day.
- didn't worry so much.

2c

Possible sentences:

The accident / explosion / fire wouldn't have happened if they …
- had stayed by the pan when frying the chips.
- had had their chimney swept at least once a year.
- had had enough electrical sockets.
- had known how to wire a plug correctly.
- had kept the entranceway well lit.
- had replaced the worn carpet.
- had kept the pills in a lockable cabinet.

4

Possible sentences:

1. Neither do I.
2. So do I.
3. Neither will I.
4. So have I.
5. So did I.
6. Neither would I.
7. So could I.
8. So am I.

Key

7

Possible sentences:

Do's
- Turn the hi-fi level down after 11pm.
- Think about your neighbours when you are doing something noisy.
- Leave a key with someone who can be called to deal with false operation of alarms.

Don'ts
- Don't use domestic appliances late at night.
- Don't have frequent late parties in the same house or flat.
- Don't leave a dog alone for long periods.
- Don't sound car horns, rev engines and slam doors late at night.
- Don't carry out noisy DIY after 9pm on any day and before 10.30 am on weekends.

Unit 12

2a

- things had come to a pretty bad pass
- to indulge in
- indignant
- to scrutinize
- grimy
- shrivelled
- bewildered
- guardian
- an urchin
- disgust

2c

1. She/He said the car wouldn't start because there was no petrol in the tank.
2. She/He asked me if I had seen the latest Kevin Costner film.
3. She/He suggested I should have a rest.
4. She/He told me she/he was going into hospital the following week.
5. She/He promised she/he would call me as soon as she/he got there.
6. She/He wanted to know what the problem was.
7. She/He said I could borrow her/his car if I wanted to.
8. They said they were sorry they couldn't come. They were having visitors on Saturday.

3b

1. Four Weddings and a Funeral
2. Goldfinger
3. Braveheart
4. The Lord of the Rings
5. Bridget Jones's Diary

5c

1. False; 2. True; 3. False; 4. Possible; 5. False; 6. False

6

made / was surprised – past simple; had left / had chosen – past perfect

7

1. had just got; rang
2. arrived, had given
3. was not; had sown/had sowed
4. had they unpacked; came on
5. had always wanted; ruined
6. had had; went
7. opened; had taken
8. had lived; decided
9. knew; had dialled; heard
10. woke up; had had

8

1. He asked her where she came from.
2. He admitted that the investment fund was two million in the red.
3. She wondered where the strange smell was coming from.
4. The teacher warned them that they would be sent home for bad behaviour.
5. The children said that they didn't need any money.
6. I told him that it was too early to tell.
7. John reminded me that there were still some charts to complete.
8. We complained that the heating had been turned off.

9

1. Where do you come from?
2. The investment fund is two million in the red.
3. Where is the smell coming from?
4. You will be sent home for bad behaviour.
5. We don't need any money.
6. It is too early to tell.
7. There are still some charts to complete.
8. The heating has been turned off.

Revision Unit 4

1a

2, 4, 5, 3, 1

1b

1. False. He had driven hundreds of times before.
2. True. She didn't have to pay; she was asked to make a voluntary donation.
3. Possible. The collection box was bolted securely to the floor.
4. False. Sarah was only joking.
5. Possible. She compares him to Dean Martin when he was a very successful and popular film star.
6. False. He also drives the taxi on his day off.
7. False. He describes them as 'endless'.
8. Possible. We're not told.

1c

1. to clamber
2. donation
3. to gesture
4. bolted
5. to hail
6. heyday
7. to angle
8. parishioner
9. diocesan
10. schtick

1d

(suggestions)
charming, humorous, honest, pleasant, realistic

2

1. hope
2. look forward to (more formal); are looking forward to (more informal)
3. likes; loves; enjoys
4. would ... like
5. do ... like; prefer; enjoy
6. start; stop; give up
7. doesn't mind
8. hate
9. offered
10. want

Vocabulary Unit by unit

Phonetic alphabet

These phonetic symbols mean that:
[ː] the previous sound is long.
['] the primary stress is on the following syllable.
[ˌ] the secondary stress is on the following syllable.
[‿] the two sounds are linked together.

[ʌ] bus [bʌs], run [rʌn]
[ɑː] last [lɑːst], park [pɑːk]
[aɪ] my [maɪ], nice [naɪs]
[aʊ] out [aʊt], how [haʊ]
[æ] back [bæk], stand [stænd]
[e] egg [eg], best [best]
[eɪ] late [leɪt], name [neɪm], safe [seɪf], pay [peɪ]
[eə] air [eə], where [weə]
[ə] about [ə'baʊt], member ['membə]
[əʊ] own [əʊn], so [səʊ]
[ɜː] firm [fɜːm], word [wɜːd]
[ɪ] it [ɪt], film [fɪlm]
[ɪə] near [nɪə], here [hɪə]
[iː] please [pliːz], see [siː]

[ɒ] not [nɒt], long [lɒŋ]
[ɔɪ] boy [bɔɪ], noise [nɔɪz]
[ɔː] all [ɔːl], north [nɔːθ]
[ʊ] book [bʊk], good [gʊd]
[ʊə] sure [ʃʊə], tour [tʊə]
[uː] who [huː], school [skuːl]
[ŋ] young [jʌŋ], thing [θɪŋ]
[r] right [raɪt], friend [frend]
[s] sir [sɜː], Miss [mɪs]
[z] busy ['bɪzɪ], please [pliːz]
[θ] thing [θɪŋ], both [bəʊθ], nothing [nʌθɪŋ]
[ð] that [ðæt], with [wɪð], another [ə'nʌðə]
[ʃ] shop [ʃɒp], fresh [freʃ]
[ʒ] television ['telɪvɪʒn]
[v] visit ['vɪzɪt], love [lʌv]
[w] well [wel], what [wɒt], always ['ɔːlweɪz], quiet [kwaɪt]
[tʃ] church [tʃɜːtʃ]
[dʒ] Germany ['dʒɜːmənɪ]

Within the units the words appear in alphabetical order.

Unit 1

activity [æk'tɪvɪtɪ]		Aktivität, Übung
add (up to) [æd]		zusammenzählen, ergeben
additives ['ædɪtɪvz]	Some people are allergic to all kinds of ~ in food and drink.	Zusätze
admit [əd'mɪt]	I ~ my mistake.	zugeben
afford [ə'fɔːd]	I can't ~ a BMW. It's too expensive.	sich leisten
allergic to [ə'lɜːdʒɪk]		allergisch sein, allergisch reagieren auf
application form [ˌæplɪ'keɪʃən 'fɔːm]	Fill in this application form for a language school.	Bewerbungsformular
application [ˌæplɪ'keɪʃən]		Bewerbung
area ['eərɪə]		Gegend
around [ə'raʊnd]	There are ~ 750,000 words in the English language.	ungefähr
average (an ... of) ['ævrɪdʒ]	He works an ~ of 35 hours a week. The ~ car worker in England doesn't live in a flat.	durchschnittlich, (im) Durchschnitt
back [bæk]	I was working in the garden all day yesterday, and now I've got a sore ~.	Rücken
	John's going on a business trip tomorrow, but he'll be ~ on Friday.	zurück
	At the ~ of the book.	hinten
be afraid [ə'freɪd]	Do you know where room 42 is? – No, I'm ~ I don't.	leider; es tut mir Leid
be fond of [fɒnd]	I'm not very ~ of cats. What about you?	gern mögen, gern haben
be married ['mærɪd]		verheiratet sein
be on a business trip ['bɪznɪs trɪp]	Are you here on holiday? – No, I'm on a ~.	auf einer Geschäftsreise sein
be worth [wɜːθ]	The house is worth £300,000. It's worth it for those extra fifteen minutes in bed!	wert sein; sich lohnen (es lohnt sich)
be wrong [rɒŋ]	1+2+3+4+5+6+7+8+9=44. – No, that's ~; it's 45.	nicht stimmen, Unrecht haben
behind [bɪ'haɪnd]	Where's Maren? – She's standing ~ you.	hinter
carefully ['keəfəlɪ]	Drive ~! The roads are very icy.	vorsichtig
case (in any ...) [keɪs]		in jedem Fall
century ['sentʃərɪ]	We're now at the end of the 20th ~.	Jahrhundert
check [tʃek]	Did you ~ that the door was locked?	kontrollieren
choose [tʃuːz]	Choose a colour: red, blue, green or yellow?	wählen
clue [kluː]	What's got no legs, but always runs? – I don't know. Can you give me another ~?	Hinweis, Anhaltspunkt
collect [kə'lekt]	I'll ~ her at the railway station on Saturday./Can you ~ me after work? She ~s post cards.	abholen; sammeln
community [kə'mjuːnətɪ]		Gemeinde
commuter [kə'mjuːtə]	The five o'clock train is always packed with ~.	Pendler

Vocabulary Unit by unit

compare [kəm'peə]	~ your answers with the key on page 99.	vergleichen
comprehensive school [ˌkɒmprɪ'hensɪv]		etwa: Gesamtschule
count (off) [kaʊnt]	The sports teacher counted off pairs of children for the ski lift.	(ab)zählen
countryside ['kʌntrɪsaɪd]	There's some beautiful ~ round Finstock.	Landschaft
dictionary ['dɪkʃən,rɪ]	Can you find this word in the ~ ?	Wörterbuch
dishwasher ['dɪʃwɒʃə]		Spülmaschine
divorced [dɪ'vɔːst]	Anna and Dave got married in 1985, but they've been ~ for six years now.	geschieden
during ['djʊərɪŋ]	How are you going to learn vocabulary ~ your course?	während
earn [ɜːn]		verdienen
enclose [ɪn'kləʊz]		(mit) einschließen
equipment [ɪ'kwɪpmənt]	They tested all their ~ before they left for the Himalayas.	Ausrüstung, Ausstattung, Geräte
exchange [ɪks'tʃeɪndʒ]	I'd like to ~ this jumper for a different colour. Exchange your information.	(aus-, um-)tauschen
facilities [fə'sɪlətɪz]		Einrichtungen, Gelegenheiten, Möglichkeiten
father-in-law ['fɑːðər_ɪn lɔː]		Schwiegervater
favourite ['feɪvrɪt]		Lieblings-; beliebt; am liebsten
female ['fiːmeɪl]	The ~ form of waiter is waitress.	weiblich
fit [fɪt]	Can I bring the jumper back if it doesn't ~?	passen
flat [flæt]		Wohnung
foursome ['fɔːsəm]	My three friends and I often go out in a ~ on Saturday evening.	Vierergruppe, zu Viert
get (here) [get]	How do you ~ to work? – By bus. How do you ~ to your English class?	(hierher)kommen kommen
get up [get 'ʌp]	We usually ~ up between eight and nine at the weekend.	aufstehen
however [haʊ'evə]	I can't come to the class next week. ~, I'll phone someone to get the homework.	jedoch, aber
husband ['hʌzbənd]	My ~ and I have been married for ten years now.	(Ehe)mann
imagine [ɪ'mædʒɪn]		(sich) vorstellen, sich denken, annehmen
improve [ɪm'pruːv]		verbessern
in fact [ɪn 'fækt]	I don't really like cats; ~, I hate them!	eigentlich
introduce [ɪntrə'djuːs]	Come with me, and I'll ~ you to the others. Introduce your partner to the group.	(sich/jmd.) vorstellen; einführen
journey ['dʒɜːnɪ]		Fahrt; Anreise; Bus-, Zugfahrt
jumper ['dʒʌmpə]	This ~ is made of pure cashmere.	Pullover
lazy ['leɪzɪ]	Sunday is a ~ day with us: we do as little as possible.	faul
lease [liːs]	You can buy a car or you can ~ one.	hier: ein Auto leasen
locally ['ləʊkəlɪ]	His wife works ~.	am, vor Ort
look (to have a ... at) [lʊk]	Doctor, would you have a ~ at my right leg. It's very sore.	sich etwas anschauen
look forward to [lʊk 'fɔːwəd]		sich freuen auf
ludo ['luːdəʊ]	The first person to get all four men home at ~ is the winner.	Mensch-ärgere-dich-nicht(Spiel)
maintenance ['meɪntɪˌnəns]	The ~ department works with machines.	Instandhaltung
member ['membə]		Mitglied, Angehörige(r)
message (to give s.o. a ...) ['mesɪdʒ]	Sorry, Frank isn't in right now. Can I give him a ~?	jmd. etwas ausrichten
missing ['mɪsɪŋ]	In this exercise you have to find the ~ verbs.	fehlend
mortgage ['mɔːgɪdʒ]	He pays £5,000 for the ~.	Hypothek
necessary ['nesəsrɪ]	Do you really think it's ~ to have a route finder in your car?	notwendig
nephew ['nefjuː]		Neffe
niece [niːs]		Nichte
occupation [ˌɒkjʊ'peɪʃn]	And your ~, sir? – Teacher.	Beruf, Tätigkeit
over there [ˌəʊvə 'ðeə]	Excuse me, where's the English course? – In the room ~.	dort drüben
overtime ['əʊvəˌtaɪm]	She works one hour ~ every week.	Überstunden
pavement ['peɪvmənt]		Gehweg, Bürgersteig, Bodenbelag
percentage [pə'sentɪdʒ]	A relatively high ~ of Germans speak English.	Prozentsatz
perhaps [pə'hæps]	Are you coming to the party on Saturday? – I don't know, ~.	vielleicht
pork [pɔːk]		Schweinefleisch
present ['preznt]	No, that's my old address. My ~ address is 6 Ashton Lane, Bradford.	jetzig, aktuell, gegenwärtig
primary school ['praɪmərɪ]		Grundschule
probably ['prɒbəblɪ]	United are playing well. They'll ~ win.	wahrscheinlich
proper ['prɒpə]		eigentlich, richtig, anständig
railway station ['reɪlweɪ ˌsteɪʃn]	Waterloo is one of the biggest railway stations in London.	Bahnhof
rather ['rɑːðə]		ziemlich
recent ['riːsnt]	I enclose a ~ photo of myself.	jüngste(-r, -s)
regret [rɪ'gret]		Bedauern
relationship [rɪ'leɪʃnʃɪp]	Tom's ~ to his father-in-law is not very good.	Verhältnis, Beziehung; Verwandtschaft

remember [rɪˈmembə]	Sorry, I can't ~ your name.	sich erinnern an
rent [rent]	He pays £590 a month ~.	Miete
score [skɔː]	How many points did you ~ ?	erzielen, punkten, bekommen, schießen
season ticket [ˈsiːzn ˌtɪkɪt]		Fahrschein für eine bestimmte Zeit
semi-detached house [ˌsemɪdɪˈtætʃt]		Doppelhaushälfte
shift [ʃɪft]		(Arbeits-) Schicht
signature [ˈsɪgnətʃə]	Could I just check your ~ on your bank card, please?	Unterschrift
similar [ˈsɪmɪlə]		ähnlich
sister-in-law [ˈsɪstər ɪn lɔː]		Schwägerin
snore [snɔː]		schnarchen
sore (a ... leg) [sɔː]	I've had a ~ leg since playing squash last week.	weh tun; schlimm
spare [speə]	Our new house has got a ~ bedroom for when we have visitors.	übrig, frei, Ersatz-
spare time [speə ˈtaɪm]		Freizeit
stockbroker [ˈstɒkbrəʊkə]		Börsenmakler
successful [səkˈsesfl]	To be a ~ tennis player you have to train for hours every day.	erfolgreich
suitable [ˈsuːtəbl]		passend
take care [teɪk ˈkeə]	Take ~ when you cross the road!	aufpassen
	Bye. Take care.	Pass auf dich auf!
tax [tæks]	Everybody has to pay lots of ~es these days.	Steuern
thatched roof [θætʃt ruːf]	The ~ is made of straw.	Strohdach, Reetdach
tie [taɪ]	In Britain you normally have to wear a ~ with your school uniform.	Krawatte
useful [ˈjuːsfl]	The word "nice" is one of the most ~ words in the English language. You can use it in so many different situations.	nützlich
vegetable [ˈvedʒtəbl]		Gemüse
vet [vet]		Tierarzt
village [ˈvɪlɪdʒ]		Dorf
wife [waɪf]		Ehefrau
wonder [ˈwʌndə]	I ~ if it'll rain tomorrow.	sich fragen, gespannt sein
worry [ˈwʌri]	I can't find my keys. – Don't ~. They're probably in your bag.	sich Sorgen machen

Unit 2

accelerator [əkˈseləreɪtə]	You press the ~ and the car goes faster.	Gaspedal
actor [ˈæktə]	Gerard Depardieu is an ~.	Schauspieler
adult [ˈædʌlt]	You are not a child, you are an ~.	Erwachsener
advertising executive [ˈædvətaɪzɪŋ ɪgˌzekjʊtɪv]		leitender Angestellter, der bei einer Werbeagentur arbeitet
attack [əˈtæk]	Players who are in a position of trying to score in a game. The players are on ~ again.	angreifen
bacon [ˈbeɪkən]		Schinkenspeck
bank clerk [ˈbæŋk ˌklɑːk]	A person employed in a bank to keep records, accounts etc.	Bankangestellte(r)
bar [ˌbɑːr əv ˈsəʊp]	A ~ of soap.	Stück (Seife)
be fit [fɪt]		fit sein, in Form sein, gesund
bother [ˈbɒðə]	Don't ~! It's not urgent.	Nicht nötig! / sich (nicht) die Mühe machen
box of chocolates [bɒks]		Schachtel Pralinen
braking equipment [ˈbreɪkɪŋ ɪˌkwɪpmənt]	If you want to stop a machine, you use the ~.	Bremse(n)
branch [brɑːntʃ]	There's a ~ of Lloyds bank in every town.	Filiale
busy [ˈbɪzi]	We've been terribly ~ at work recently.	viel beschäftigt
can of coke [kæn]		Dose Cola
car park [ˈkɑː pɑːk]		Parkgarage, Parkplatz
carton of orange juice [ˈkɑːtn əv ˈɒrɪndʒ dʒuːs]		Karton Orangensaft
central heating [ˌsentrəl ˈhiːtɪŋ]		Zentralheizung
charity organisation [ˈtʃærɪti ˌɔːgənaɪˈseɪʃən]	Misereor is a ~.	Wohltätigkeitsorganisation
commentary [ˈkɒməntri]	Our reporters will give us a ~ of the results of the last matches.	aktueller Bericht vom (Sport-)reporter
confirm [kənˈfɜːm]	When asked, Helen ~ed that she was on the phone.	bestätigen
copy [ˈkɒpi]	Have you got a ~ of Hello magazine?	Exemplar
corner [ˈkɔːnə]	The skier comes round the ~.	Ecke, Kurve, (Fußball: Eckball)
crate [kreɪt]	A ~ is a large (wooden) container for transporting goods or for storing bottles.	Kiste
crisps [krɪsps]		Kartoffelchips
Cup Final [ˈkʌp faɪnl]		Pokalendspiel
current [ˈkʌrənt]	Have you got a ~ copy of the newspaper?	aktuelle

Vocabulary Unit by unit

decide [dɪ'saɪd]	It's difficult to ~ between the two.	entscheiden, sich entschließen
excitement [ɪk'saɪtmənt]	The film isn't boring, there is a lot of ~.	Aufregung, Spannung
extravagance [ɪk'strævəgəns]		Luxus, Verschwendungssucht
faint-hearted [feɪnt 'hɑ:təd]	If you are ~, you would never play rugby.	zaghaft
false [fɔ:ls]	This statement is ~.	falsch
forehand ['fɔ:hænd]	She hit the ball to my ~.	Vorhand
forget [fə'get]		vergessen
free [fri:]	He doesn't pay for the whiskey. It's ~.	kostenlos
grid [grɪd]	A ~ is a network of lines crossing each other to form a series of squares.	Tabelle, Raster
guideline ['gaɪdlaɪn]	Use the following ~s to help you.	Angabe(n), Richtlinie(n), Hilfslinie(n)
ham [hæm]		Schinken
have sth. left over [left 'əʊvə]		etwas übrig haben
headache ['hedeɪk]		Kopfschmerzen
Hold on! ['həʊld 'ɒn]	(on the telephone:) ~! I'll get him in a minute.	Bleiben Sie dran./Warten Sie.
honey ['hʌnɪ]		Honig
hump [hʌmp]	A camel has two ~s.	Höcker
inside [ɪn'saɪd]		drinnen
investment adviser [ɪn'vestmənt ˌædvaɪzə]	An expert giving her/his opinion about what sb. else should do with their money.	Anlageberater
jar [dʒɑ:]	a jar of honey	Glas
jump [dʒʌmp]		springen
kick [kɪk]		mit dem Fuß stoßen, kicken, treten
lead [li:d]	The German skier is in the ~.	(in) Führung (sein)
map [mæp]	You need a ~ if you want to find your way around in a city you don't know.	(Straßen-)Karte
mean ['mi:n]	Pat Smith is too ~ to go the hairdresser's more often.	geizig
meanness ['mi:nɪs]	She is not willing to give or share things, e.g. money.	Geiz
member ['membə]	He's a ~ of the tennis club.	Mitglied
net [net]		Netz
Never mind!		Macht nichts, ist doch egal. / Schon gut, ist ja auch egal.
out of order ['ɔ:də]	Don't use the hair dryer, it's ~.	kaputt; außer Betrieb
outside [aʊt'saɪd]		draußen
packet ['pækɪt]		Päckchen, Tüte
phone card ['fəʊn ˌkɑ:d]	Phone cards are handy because you don't need small change to make a call.	Telefonkarte
pineapple ['paɪnæpl]		Ananas
popular ['pɒpjʊlə]	Skiing isn't a very ~ sport in Britain.	beliebt
pottery ['pɒtərɪ]		Töpfern, Töpferei, getöpfert(-e,-es)
prefer [prɪ'fɜ:]	I like wine. I ~ red to white.	vorziehen
questionnaire [ˌkwestʃə'neə]	A ~ is a written list of questions to be answered – normally by a number of people.	Fragebogen
racing ['reɪsɪŋ]	Hockenheim is famous for motor~.	hier: Autorennen
racket (tennis ...) ['rækɪt]		(Tennis-) Schläger
referee [ˌrefə'ri:]	The ~ of a football match controls it.	Schiedsrichter
ride [raɪd]	Can you ~ a horse?	reiten
rules [ru:lz]	I don't understand the ~ of football.	Regeln
salad ['sæləd]		gemischter Salat
score (no ...) [skɔ:]		ohne Treffer; 0 zu 0-Spielstand
security guard [sɪ'kjʊərətɪ ˌgɑ:d]		Sicherheitsbeauftragte(-r), Wächter
slice [slaɪs]	A ~ of bread.	Scheibe
soap [səʊp]		Seife
solicitor [sə'lɪsɪtə]	A lawyer who advises clients on legal matters and prepares legal documents, e.g. for the sale of land or buildings.	Rechtsanwalt (-anwältin)
spend [spend]	to spend money on	Geld für etwas ausgeben
teach [ti:tʃ]		unterrichten
thirsty ['θɜ:stɪ]		durstig sein, Durst haben
throw [θrəʊ]		werfen
tin [tɪn]		Dose
true [tru:]		wahr
tube [tju:b]		Tube
unit ['ju:nɪt]	Phone calls cost 20p per ~. / This book has got 12 ~s.	Einheit
unusual [ʌn'ju:ʒʊəl]	Camel racing is an ~ sport.	ungewöhnlich
urgent ['ɜ:dʒənt]	It is most ~ that I see you today.	dringend
use [ju:z]		brauchen, gebrauchen
volunteer [ˌvɒlʌn'tɪə]	He's a ~ fireman in his free time.	Freiwilliger
wallet ['wɒlɪt]	You use a ~ for your paper money and credit cards.	Portemonnaie, Brieftasche
warning ['wɔ:nɪŋ]	The player receives a ~.	Warnung

what about ...-ing [ˌwɒt_əˈbaʊt]	What about going to the cinema?	wie wär's mit?
whistle [ˈwɪsl]	The referee blew his ~.	Pfeife

Unit 3

accept [əkˈsept]	to accept a cheque	annehmen
ago [əˈgəʊ]	Twelve years ~.	vor
appear [əˈpɪə]	He ~s tired.	scheinen
attend [əˈtend]	He ~ed Eton school.	besuchen, teilnehmen an
bark [bɑːk]		bellen
be lucky [ˈlʌkɪ]	You were lucky to escape injury.	Glück haben
be responsible for [rɪˈspɒnsəbl]		verantwortlich sein für
behaviour [bɪˈheɪvjə]	The way you behave towards other people. Your ~ is socially acceptable and polite.	Benehmen, Verhalten
blank [blæŋk]	Fill in the ~s in this sentence.	Lücke
born-again Christian [bɔːn əgeɪn krɪstɪən]		Evangelikal-Christen, (wörtlich: Wiedergeborene Christen)
change [tʃeɪndʒ]	Some ~s in society are difficult to understand.	(Ver-)Änderung
cheerful [ˈtʃɪəfəl]	He's never sad, he's always ~.	munter, fröhlich
chest [tʃest]		Brust
choice [tʃɔɪs]	The prize is a holiday of your own ~.	Wahl
cider [ˈsaɪdə]		Apfelwein
citizen [ˈsɪtɪzən]		(Staats-)Bürger
column [ˈkɒləm]		Spalte; Säule
countersign [ˈkaʊntəsaɪn]	You have to ~ the cheque, please.	gegenzeichnen
crowd [kraʊd]		Menschenmenge
currently [ˈkʌrəntlɪ]	at the moment	zur Zeit
describe [dɪˈskraɪb]	Can you ~ the man who stole your purse?	beschreiben
description [dɪˈskrɪpʃn]		Beschreibung
draft beer [ˌdrɑːft ˈbɪə]		gezapftes Bier, Bier vom Fass
draughtsman [ˈdrɑːftsmən]		(Technischer) Zeichner
drums [drʌmz]	My son plays the ~ in a jazz band.	Trommel
election [ɪˈlekʃn]	In 1996 there was an ~ for president in the USA.	Wahl
employ [ɪmˈplɔɪ]	She ~s a gardener.	beschäftigen, einstellen
enchanted [ɪnˈtʃɑːntɪd]	You don't meet ~ princes in real-life situations.	bezaubernd
except [ɪkˈsept]	The restaurant is open every day ~ Monday.	außer
foreign language [fɒrɪn ˈlæŋgwɪdʒ]	She's French, so, for her, German is a ~.	Fremdsprache
foreigner [ˈfɒrənə]	A person from a country other than your own./ A person who is regarded as not belonging to a particular community.	Ausländer, Fremder
freezer centre [ˈfriːzə ˌsentə]		Fachgeschäft für Gefriergeräte
fridge [frɪdʒ]	Do your keep your eggs in the ~?	Kühlschrank
go down [ˌgəʊ ˈdaʊn]	The value of their house went down because of the new motorway near it.	fallen, runtergehen, sinken
groceries [ˈgrəʊsərɪz]	Mrs Hatton buys the ~ at the supermarket in town.	Lebensmittel
guess [ges]	You don't know. You're just ~ing.	raten
hate [heɪt]		hassen
heaven [ˈhevn]	~ is a place believed to be the home of God and good people after death.	Himmel
jacket [ˈdʒækɪt]		Jacke
job applicants [dʒɒb ˈæplɪkənts]	We interviewed 100 ~ for this job.	Bewerber
kids [kɪdz]	children	Kinder
library [ˈlaɪbrərɪ]		Bibliothek
liver [ˈlɪvə]	Too much alcohol isn't good for your ~.	Leber
look up [lʊk ˈʌp]	Look up the words in the word list.	nachschlagen, nachschauen
loud [laʊd]		laut
no idea (I've ...) [aɪˈdɪə]		(Ich habe -) Keine Ahnung.
obvious [ˈɒbvɪəs]	Something that is easily seen and understood; that is clear.	offensichtlich, klar
officer [ˈɒfɪsə]	When you talk to a policeman you call him ~.	hier: Herr Wachtmeister
official residence [əˈfɪʃl ˈrezɪdəns]	Buckingham Palace is the Queen's ~ in London.	Hauptresidenz
open s.o.'s eyes to sth. [ˈəʊpən ... aɪz]		jmd. die Augen öffnen (für etwas)
operate [ˈɒpəreɪt]	She ~d the cash machine.	bedienen, handhaben
opponent [əˈpəʊnənt]		Gegenspieler, Gegner
order [ˈɔːdə]	In the correct ~.	in der richtigen Reihenfolge
peace [piːs]		Frieden

Vocabulary Unit by unit

performance [pə'fɔ:məns]	They saw a ~ of Hamlet.	Vorstellung
PhD [,pi: eɪtʃ 'di:]	He's got a ~.	Er hat seinen Doktor gemacht./Er hat einen Doktortitel.
pick up [pɪk ʌp]	The thief picked up Mrs Hatton's purse.	aufheben
pierced [,pɪəsd]	She's got ~ ears.	durchgestochen(e)
poverty ['pɒvətɪ]		Armut
pray [preɪ]		beten
property ['prɒpətɪ]	~ in the London area is more expensive than in the north of England.	(Wohn-)eigentum, Grundeigentum, Besitz, Immobilien
rate [reɪt_əv ɪks'tʃeɪndʒ]	What's the ~ (of exchange) for the euro?	Wechselkurs
real [rɪəl]	They call him Bill but his ~ name's William.	eigentlich(-e, -er)
realise ['rɪəlaɪz]	He didn't ~ his mistake.	sich bewußt werden, bemerken, begreifen
really ['rɪəlɪ]	What do you need? Nothing ~.	Was brauchst du? Eigentlich nichts.
run off with [,rʌn_'ɒf wɪð]		sich mit etwas davon machen
scholarship ['skɒləʃɪp]	He got a ~ to study at the university.	Stipendium
seldom ['seldəm]	not often; rarely	selten
smell [smel]		riechen
smile [smaɪl]		lächeln
stranger ['streɪndʒə]	A person you do not know.	Fremde(r)
surprised [sə'praɪzd]		überrascht
sweet [swi:t]		Bonbon
taste [teɪst]		schmecken
three times [θri: taɪmz]		dreimal
unless [ən'les]	if ... not; on the condition that	es sei denn; wenn ... nicht
value ['vælju:]	The worth of s.th. in terms of money. / Moral standards of behaviour: cultural, family, social etc.	Wert(e)
vary ['veərɪ]	It varies.	unterschiedlich sein, abweichen von
violence ['vaɪələns]		Gewalt
welcome ['welkəm]	She's ~ to stay here whenever she likes. / We've been made most ~ in the village.	willkommen heißen
whole time [həʊl taɪm]		die ganze Zeit

Revision 1

ability [ə'bɪlɪtɪ]		Fähigkeit
archery ['ɑ:tʃərɪ]	Are you interested in ~?	Bogenschießen
be of assistance [bi: əv ə'sɪstəns]	Please call if we can ~.	behilflich sein
continue [kən'tɪnju:]	Now ~ the conversation.	fortsetzen
current affairs ['kʌrənt ə'feəz]	Are you interested in ~?	Aktuelles
foaming ['fəʊmɪŋ]		schäumend
hestitate ['hezɪteɪt]	Don't ~ to ask for help.	zögern
housekeeper ['haʊski:pə]	I'll ask the ~ to bring you another towel.	Haushälterin
immediately [ɪ'mi:dɪətlɪ]	I'll ask the housekeeper to bring you another towel ~.	sofort
introductory [ɪntrə'dʌktərɪ]		Einführungs-
outing ['aʊtɪŋ]	It's our office ~ tomorrow.	Ausflug
pet [pet]	Did you have a ~ as a child?	Haustier
range [reɪndʒ]	There's a wide ~ of activities at the leisure club.	Auswahl, Angebot
rapids ['ræpɪdz]		Stromschnellen
reception [rɪ'sepʃən]	Ring ~ if there's a problem with your room.	Empfang
ring [rɪŋ]	Don't hesitate to ~ again.	anrufen
swirling [swɜ:lɪŋ]		herumwirbelnd
towel [taʊəl]	Could I have another ~, please?	Handtuch
What's the trouble? [wɒts ðə 'trʌbl]	What's the problem?	Was ist das Problem?
whether [weðə]	There are activities for everyone, ~ old or young.	ob

Unit 4

air-conditioned ['eə kən,dɪʃnd]		klimatisiert
airline ['eəlaɪn]		Fluggesellschaft
art gallery ['ɑ:t gælərɪ]		Kunstgalerie
available [ə'veɪləbl]	What accommodation is ~ in July?	frei, verfügbar
beach [bi:tʃ]		Strand
budget ['bʌdʒɪt]	Accommodation to suit all ~s.	Etat, Haushaltsplan, Geldbeutel (es passt für jeden Geldbeutel)
building ['bɪldɪŋ]		Gebäude
cabin staff ['kæbɪn stɑ:f]		Kabinenbesatzung

celebrate ['selɪbreɪt]	It's my birthday – let's ~.	feiern
celebration [selɪ'breɪʃən]	When they won there was a big ~.	Feier
clear [klɪə]	to clear a space	Platz schaffen
collide with [kə'laɪd]	The car ~d with a bus.	zusammenstoßen mit
complain [kəm'pleɪn]	to complain of pains	über etwas klagen
cottage ['kɒtɪdʒ]		Häuschen, Hütte
cover ['kʌvə]	Christo ~ed the parliament building in Berlin.	(ab-, zu-, ver-)decken
currency ['kʌrənsɪ]	The euro is the ~ in most of Europe.	Währung
degree [dɪ'gri:]	The average temperature in London in the summer is 19 ~s.	Grad
deliver [dɪ'lɪvə]	The flight attendant ~ed a baby.	hier: entbinden, zur Welt bringen
demonstration [ˌdemən'streɪʃn]	They saw a ~ of how to fly a kite.	Vorführung, Demonstration
details ['di:teɪlz]		Einzelheiten
die [daɪ]		sterben
different ['dɪfrənt]		anders
enjoyable [ɪn'dʒɔɪəbl]	The holiday was very ~.	angenehm, unterhaltsam
especially [ɪ'speʃəlɪ]		besonders
flight attendant [flaɪt_ə'tendənt]		Stewardess
get tired of [get 'taɪəd]	They got tired of discussing the same problem over and over again.	einer Sache müde oder überdrüssig werden
host [həʊst]	Munich ~ed the Olympics in 1972.	Gastgeber sein (bei)
hurt [hɜ:t]		weh tun, sich weh tun
interested ['ɪntrestɪd]	I'm not ~ in politics.	interessiert sein an
intonation [ˌɪntəneɪʃən]	The ~ of "good morning" is important if you want to sound friendly.	Betonung
invent [ɪn'vent]	Not all the characters in the book are ~ed.	erfinden
kite [kaɪt]	Children play with ~s when it's windy.	Drachen
link [lɪŋk]	The hotel has a ~ with British history.	Verbindung
notice ['nəʊtɪs]		bemerken
nurse [nɜ:s]		Krankenschwester
pain [peɪn]		Schmerz
particularly [pə'tɪkjʊləlɪ]	They are ~ interested in history.	besonders
pass [pɑ:s]	The holiday ~ed very quickly.	vergehen
peaceful ['pi:sfəl]		ruhig
pickpocket ['pɪk pɒkɪt]		Taschendieb
please yourself [pli:z]		tun was einem gefällt
proud [praʊd]	Anthea's parents were very ~ of her when she got a place at Oxford University.	stolz (auf)
puppet play ['pʌpɪt pleɪ]		Marionettenspiel
recently ['ri:səntlɪ]	Not long ago. She has ~ been made director.	neulich
rent [rent]	They ~ a cottage for their summer holiday.	mieten
resort [rɪ'zɔ:t]	A place where a lot of people go on holiday. Brighton is a popular coastal ~.	Urlaubsort
reunification [ˌri:ju:nɪfɪ'keɪʃn]		Wiedervereinigung
rise [raɪz]	Temperatures rose to 35° during the day.	steigen
sensible ['sensɪbl]	making sense	sinnvoll; vernünftig
serious ['sɪərɪəs]	She looked very ~ when she heard the news. / Please be serious for a minute, this is important.	ernst, ernsthaft
shoot [ʃu:t]		schießen
shout [ʃaʊt]		schreien
snorkelling ['snɔ:klɪŋ]		schnorcheln
sound [saʊnd]	Does this sentence ~ right?	klingen
space [speɪs]	to clear a space	Platz
spicy ['spaɪsɪ]	Do you like ~ food?	scharf, würzig
spoil yourself [spɔɪl]	Have another chocolate – go on, ~.	sich verwöhnen
stressful ['stresfəl]		stressig
suit [su:t]	A holiday to ~ all budgets.	geeignet sein für
supper (for ...) ['sʌpə]	The last meal of the day. What's for supper?	zum Abendessen
sympathetic [sɪmpə'θetɪk]	He was enourmously ~ when my grandfather died.	mitfühlend, teilnahmsvoll
treat yourself to sth. [tri:t]		sich etwas leisten, gönnen
unspoilt [ʌn'spɔɪlt]		unverdorben
unusual [ʌn'ju:ʒʊəl]	Different from what is usual or normal.	außergewöhnlich, ungewöhnlich
veal [vi:l]		Kalbfleisch
wear [weə]	A policeman ~s a uniform.	tragen (von Kleidung)
wedding anniversary ['wedɪŋ æniˌvɜ:sərɪ]	They're celebrating their (golden) ~.	Wiederkehr des Hochzeitstages, Jahrestag

Vocabulary Unit by unit

Unit 5

ambulance ['æmbjʊləns]	I'll go and call an ~.	Krankenwagen
arrest [ə'rest]	The police ~ed the thief outside the shop.	verhaften
asleep [ə'sli:p]	Don't wake her up – she's fast ~.	schlafen(d)
be sure [ʃɔ:]		sicher sein
break in [breɪk]		einbrechen
breathe [bri:ð]	It's good to ~ in fresh country air.	atmen
breathing ['bri:ðɪŋ]		Atemzüge
charge [tʃɑ:dʒ]	To charge someone with murder.	gegen jmd. Anklage erheben
commit [kə'mɪt]	He ~ed a crime.	begehen
connection [kə'nekʃən]	How long will the ~ on my new phone take? / What is the ~ between the two ideas? / The flight was late, so I missed my ~.	Verbindung
cordless ['kɔ:dləs]	A ~ phone.	schnurlos
couple ['kʌpl]	A couple of days.	ein paar, einige
crime [kraɪm]	The police play an important role in detecting ~.	Straftat
dawn [dɔ:n]		Morgendämmerung
delivery [dɪ'lɪvrɪ]	Your order is ready for ~. / We have two postal deliveries a day.	Lieferung
destroy [dɪ'strɔɪ]		zerstören
driving licence ['draɪvɪŋ ˌlaɪsəns]		Führerschein
eavesdropper ['i:vzˌdrɒpə]	Someone who listens to a private conversation is an ~.	Lauscher
emergency [ɪ'mɜ:dʒənsɪ]		Notfall
escape [ɪ'skeɪp]		entkommen
exactly [ɪg'zæktlɪ]	Please tell me ~ where you are.	ganz genau
excitement [ɪk'saɪtmənt]	His eyes were wide with ~.	Aufregung
fine [faɪn]	A sum of money you have to pay as a punishment.	Geldstrafe
fireman ['faɪəmən]		Feuerwehrmann
float [fləʊt]	Her hair ~s on the pillow.	schweben, (auch: schwimmen, treiben)
four-wheel drive [ˌfɔ: wi:l 'draɪv]		Allradantrieb
gaze [geɪz]		(verliebt) anstarren
give a statement ['steɪtmənt]		eine Aussage machen
glow [gləʊ]		glühen
goal [gəʊl]	He scored a ~ in the football match.	Tor
hand something in [hænd]		etwas abgeben
hold up [həʊld]	He held up the liquor store.	überfallen
horrified ['hɒrɪfaɪd]	To shock sb. greatly. We were ~ by what we saw.	entsetzt
hug [hʌg]		umarmen
identification [aɪˌdentɪfɪ'keɪʃn]		Dokumente, um sich ausweisen zu können
illegally [ɪ'li:gəlɪ]		illegal
increase [ɪn'kri:s]	An ~ of 50% on last year. / Some ~ in working hours may be necessary.	vermehren, zunehmen; Zunahme, Steigerung
install [ɪn'stɔ:l]		installieren
insurance [ɪn'ʃʊərəns]		Versicherung
introduce [ɪntrə'dju:s]	The company has introduced robots in the factory.	einführen
investigate [ɪn'vestɪgeɪt]		untersuchen
issue ['ɪʃu:]	to issue guidelines	ergehen lassen, erteilen
join [dʒɔɪn]	Her daughter ~ed her.	sich jmd. anschließen
kiss [kɪs]		küssen
last [lɑ:st]	How long does the film ~?	dauern
last [lɑ:st]	When did you ~ go to the cinema?	zum letzten Mal
law and order [lɔ: ənd ɔ:də]		Gesetz und Recht
lawn [lɔ:n]		Rasen
liquor store [lɪkə stɔ:]	You buy wine and whisky at a ~.	Spirituosengeschäft
lock [lɒk]	Did you ~ the car?	(ab-, zu-)schließen, zusperren
lost property office [ˌlɒst 'prɒpətɪ ɒfɪs]		Fundbüro
miss [mɪs]	To ~ a train. The flight was late, so I ~ed the connection.	verpassen
mist [mɪst]		Nebel
mistake (by ...) [mɪs'teɪk]	I took your bag instead of mine ~.	aus Versehen
moonlight ['mu:nlaɪt]		Mondschein, Mondlicht
mow [məʊ]		mähen
murderer ['mɜ:dərə]	If a person shoots someone dead, this person is a ~.	Mörder
painting ['peɪntɪŋ]		Gemälde
persuade [pə'sweɪd]	She ~d her to see a doctor when she was ill.	überreden
pick up [pɪk 'ʌp]	The scanner can ~ conversations.	hier: empfangen
pillow ['pɪləʊ]		Kopfkissen
prevent [prɪ'vent]	Your prompt action ~ed a serious accident.	verhindern
prevention [prɪ'venʃn]		Verhinderung

prison ['prɪzn]		Gefängnis
profit ['prɒfɪt]		Gewinn
public (the ...) ['pʌblɪk]	Should the ~ help prevent crime?	die Öffentlichkeit
punch [pʌntʃ]	To hit sb. or sth. hard with the fist.	schlagen
punishment ['pʌnɪʃmənt]	The ~ should fit the crime.	Strafe
recognize ['rekəgnaɪz]	She has a new hairstyle. I didn't ~ her.	(wieder) erkennen
reflect [rɪ'flekt]	See how beautifully the river ~s the trees. / Certain laws need changing to ~ the changing of attitudes in society.	widerspiegeln
remain [rɪ'meɪn]	to stay	bleiben
return (the ...) [rɪ'tɜ:n]	The art gallery has offered a reward for the safe ~ of the painting.	(sichere) Rückgabe
reward [rɪ'wɔ:d]	A £10,000 ~ has been offered for the return of the painting.	Belohnung
robbery ['rɒbərɪ]		Diebstahl
save [seɪv]	He jumped into the water and ~d the child.	retten
seize [si:z]	The police have seized the heroin.	beschlagnahmen
set [set]	to set a date for the crime	festlegen, festsetzen
sheriffs office ['ʃerɪfs ˌɒfɪs]		Polizeiwache (in USA)
soft [sɒft]		sanft
stationery ['steɪʃənrɪ]	Materials for writing, e.g. paper, pens and envelopes.	Bürobedarf
sun roof ['sʌn ru:f]		Schiebedach
suspect [səs'pekt]	The police ~ one of the men who lost his job.	verdächtigen
take part in [teɪk 'pɑ:t]		teilnehmen an
thief [θi:f]		Dieb
threaten ['θretn]	The attacker ~ed her with a gun. / The employee was ~ed with dismissal.	drohen, bedrohen
trouble (in ...) ['trʌbl]		in Schwierigkeiten sein
umbrella [ʌm'brelə]	When it rains you need an ~.	Regenschirm
unemployed [ˌʌnem'plɔɪd]	He hasn't got a job. He is ~.	arbeitslos
unreal [ʌn'rɪəl]		unwirklich
valuable ['væljʊəbl]	We're wasting ~ time.	wertvoll
voice [vɔɪs]	I can hear ~s through the wall. / "There you are", said a ~ behind me.	Stimme
witness something ['wɪtnəs]	They were witnessing an accident. / Europe witnessed massive political change in the 1980s.	Zeuge von etwas sein, etwas bezeugen
word stress [wɜ:d stres]		Wortbetonung

Unit 6

amazing [ə'meɪzɪŋ]	I find it ~ that you can speak five languages.	erstaunlich
anymore (not ...) [ˌnɒt ... enɪ'mɔ:]	It isn't called Ayers Rock anymore.	nicht mehr
air traffic controller [ˌeə træfɪk kən'trəʊlə]		Fluglotse
anyway ['enɪweɪ]	I don't know exactly what sort of ticket it is. ~, it's cheap.	auf jeden Fall; wie dem auch sei
architectural [ˌɑ:kɪ'tektʃərəl]		in Bezug auf die Architektur
authorities [ɔ:'θɒrətɪz]	The ~ are investigating the matter.	Behörde(n)
be under someone's feet [fi:t]		jmd. im Wege sein
beginning [bɪ'gɪnɪŋ]	At the ~ of October.	Anfang
bid [bɪd]	Berlin made a ~ for the summer Olympics.	Angebot
biodegradable [ˌbaɪəʊdɪ'greɪdəbl]	Nowadays you can buy ~ cleaning products.	biologisch abbaubar
break down [breɪk 'daʊn]	My washing machine's broken down.	versagen, kaputt gehen, Panne haben
can't wait (I ...) [weɪt]	I can't wait to see you.	auf etwas gespannt sein
catch [kætʃ]	to catch a train	erreichen
cause [kɔ:z]	What ~ed the explosion?	verursachen
certain ['sɜ:tən]	~ beautiful birds live in the area.	gewisse
champion ['tʃæmpjən]		Sieger
chief [tʃi:f]	the chief organizer	Haupt-; Leiter
chop down [tʃɒp 'daʊn]	to chop down trees	fällen
clam [klæm]		Venusmuschel
climb [klaɪm]	Dad's going to ~ Ayers Rock.	besteigen
cold [kəʊld]	She's got a ~.	Erkältung, erkältet sein
competition [ˌkɒmpə'tɪʃn]		Wettbewerb
copy ['kɒpɪ]	Many developers are going to ~ the idea of the Olympic village.	nachahmen, nachmachen
cruise [kru:z]		Kreuzfahrt
damage ['dæmɪdʒ]	This could cause serious ~ to the country's economy.	beschädigen
decrease [dɪ'kri:s]	The damage to the reef has decreased.	zurückgehen
design [dɪ'zaɪn]		Entwurf, Konstruktion
developer (property ...) [dɪ'veləpə]		Entwickler; Grundstücksmakler

Vocabulary Unit by unit

diary ['daɪərɪ]		Terminkalender
disagree [ˌdɪsə'griː]	To have a different opinion. Even friends sometimes ~. / I ~ with spending so much money on the project.	anderer Meinung sein; nicht zustimmen
disappointed [ˌdɪsə'pɔɪntɪd]	Sad or not pleased. He was ~ to hear they were not coming.	enttäuscht
divide [dɪ'vaɪd]		teilen
diving (scuba ...) ['skuːbə ˌdaɪvɪŋ]		Tauchen
environment [ɪn'vaɪrənmənt]	We can all do something to protect the ~.	Umwelt
found [faʊnd]	The city was ~ed in 1378.	gründen
frighten ['fraɪtən]	Sorry, I didn't mean to ~ you.	erschrecken
fun [fʌn]	It's not much ~ going to the cinema alone.	Spaß machen
get married ['mærɪd]		sich vermählen, heiraten
habitat ['hæbɪtæt]		Lebensraum
harmful ['hɑːmfəl]	You can read about the ~ effects of smoking in the latest publication.	schädlich
have a go at something		Versuch machen, etwas versuchen
headquarters [ˌhed'kwɔːtəz]		Hauptsitz
hole in the ozone layer [həʊl ɪn ðiː 'əʊzəʊn ˌleɪə]		Ozonloch
invitation [ˌɪnvɪ'teɪʃn]		Einladung
invite [ɪn'vaɪt]	She ~d her for a meal.	einladen
launderette [ˌlɔːndə'ret]		Waschautomat
lay [leɪ]	The turtles ~ their eggs on the beach.	legen
life (bird ...) [laɪf]	In Australia there is wonderful bird life.	Vogelwelt
make arrangements [ə'reɪndʒmənts]	She made arrangements to meet her friend for lunch.	sich verabreden
mean [miːn]	Do you understand what I ~?	etwas sagen wollen
media ['miːdɪə]	The main means of communication, e.g. TV, radio and newspapers.	Medien
meet [miːt]	Can you ~ us from the airport?	abholen
mention ['menʃən]	Did she ~ it?	erwähnen
mixed up [mɪkst 'ʌp]		durcheinander
national lottery [ˌnæʃnəl 'lɒtərɪ]		Lotto
nuisance ['njuːsəns]	What a nuisance!	Wie ärgerlich!
pick up [pɪk 'ʌp]	Can you pick us up from the airport?	abholen
please [pliːz]	You can't please everyone all the time.	zufriedenstellen
polite [pə'laɪt]	It is ~ to say please and thank you.	höflich
predict [prɪ'dɪkt]	It's too early to ~ who will win.	voraussagen
protect [prə'tekt]	Make sure the young plants are ~ed from frost.	schützen
puncture ['pʌŋktʃə]	A small hole in a tyre. The car had a ~.	Reifenpanne (kaputter Reifen)
recognize ['rekəgnaɪz]	I ~d her by her red hair. / They failed to ~ the problem.	erkennen
reef [riːf]		Riff
research [rɪ'sɜːtʃ]	Careful study or investigation. In industry a lot of money is spent on ~.	Forschung
returnable [rɪ'tɜːnəbl]	Take the empty ~ bottles back to the shop, please.	Pfandflaschen
rubbish ['rʌbɪʃ]	Do you sort your ~?	Müll
save [seɪv]	We must try to ~ our planet.	retten
shaped like [ʃeɪpt]		in Form von
share [ʃeə]	~ your ideas with the group.	erzählen, teilen
site [saɪt]	a building site	(Bau)stelle
stop-over ['stɒpəʊvə]		Zwischenstation machen
take place [teɪk 'pleɪs]		stattfinden
turtle ['tɜːtl]		Schildkröte
until [ən'tɪl]	We are going to stay with our friends ~ 24th.	bis
usual (as ...) [əz 'juːʒl]		wie normal, wie gewöhnlich
visitor ['vɪzɪtə]	~s can see the patients every afternoon.	Besucher
waste [weɪst]	The goods should be handled carefully to avoid ~. / Why ~ money on clothes you don't need?	Abfall; verschwenden
water ['wɔːtə]		gießen
What a shame! [wɒt_ə'ʃeɪm]		Schade!

Revision 2

abroad [ə'brɔːd]	Have you ever worked ~?	im Ausland
accommodation [əˌkɒmə'deɪʃn]	What kind of hotel ~ would you like?	Unterkunft
appointment [ə'pɔɪntmənt]	I have an ~ at the bank at 10am.	Termin

beauty treatment ['bju:tɪ ˌtri:tmənt]		Behandlung bei einer Kosmetikerin
celebrate ['selɪbreɪt]	Let's ~ now that the exams are finished.	feiern
cottage ['kɒtɪdʒ]	We like to spend our summer holidays in a ~ by the sea.	Häuschen
famous ['feɪməs]	Have you ever met a ~ person?	berühmt
free-house [fri: haʊs]		Gasthaus, das nicht an eine bestimmte Brauerei gebunden ist.
grow up [grəʊ ʌp]	My husband grew up in Australia.	aufwachsen
in advance [ɪn əd'va:ns]	Do you normally book your holiday ~?	im voraus
make yourself at home ['meɪk jəˌself ət 'həʊm]	Come in and ~!	es sich bequem machen, sich wie zu Hause fühlen
octopus ['ɒktəpəs]		Tintenfisch
run out of [rʌn aʊt əv]	Oh no! I've run out of petrol.	ausgehen
seafood ['si:fu:d]	I'm allergic to ~.	Meeresfrüchte
shake hands with [ʃeɪk hændz wɪð]	Do you ~ your friends every time you see them?	jmd. die Hand geben
slide [slaɪd]		Rutsche
unfortunately [ʌn'fɔ:tʃənətlɪ]	Do you often go to the theatre? - ~ not.	leider

Unit 7

abroad [ə'brɔ:d]	We usually spend our holidays ~, but this summer we stayed in Britain.	im Ausland, ins Ausland
according to [ə'kɔ:dɪŋ]	~ a weather expert summers will get hotter.	zufolge, laut
advice [əd'vaɪs]	Take my ~ and stay out of the sun.	Rat, Ratschlag
afford [ə'fɔ:d]	More people can now ~ a holiday abroad.	sich leisten
amount [ə'maʊnt]	The Burton family pay the same ~ for their lottery ticket each week.	Betrag; Menge
autumn ['ɔ:təm]	~ is a windy time of the year.	Herbst
ban [bæn]	In hot, dry summers there is often a ~ on water sprinklers.	Verbot
barbecue (to have a ...) ['ba:bɪkju:]	Our neighbours have ~ in their garden every evening in summer.	grillen
be entitled [ɪn'taɪtl]		den Titel haben; berechtigt sein
beat [bi:t]	You can't ~ British tea!	hier: Es geht nichts über britischen Tee!
bet [bet]	I ~ you 10 euro it snows tomorrow.	wetten
biting ['baɪtɪŋ]	~ winds can make temperatures seem even colder.	eiskalt
boil [bɔɪl]	Wait till the water boils before you make the tea.	aufkochen; überkochen
bookmaker ['bʊkmeɪkə]	~s usually make a lot of money from bets.	Buchmacher in Wettbüros
breed [bri:d]	You need a lot of money to ~ horses.	züchten
bright [braɪt]	It's nice and ~ today. Let's go for a walk.	heiter; hell
care [keə]	I don't ~ if it rains.	(nichts) ausmachen
CFC [ˌsi: ef 'si:]	chlorofluorocarbon	FCKW
chart [tʃɑ:t]	The weather ~ shows tomorrow's temperatures.	Karte
clear [klɪə]	The early morning mist will ~ by noon.	sich legen, sich auflösen
cloud [klaʊd]	There's not a ~ in the sky today.	Wolke
college ['kɒlɪdʒ]	Our son is going to technical ~ after school.	Hochschule
continue [kən'tɪnju:]	Some people ~ to water their garden even when it rains.	etwas weiter tun
demand (for) [dɪ'mɑ:nd]	In summer there is a greater ~ for ice-cream than in winter.	Nachfrage
develop [dɪ'veləp]	Heavy rain will ~ later in the day.	aufziehen; (sich) entwickeln
disappointed [dɪsə'pɔɪntɪd]	I'll be ~ if I lose my bet.	enttäuscht
dress [dres]	That's a nice ~ you're wearing.	Kleid
drizzle ['drɪzl]	a light rain	Nieselregen
drought [draʊt]	a long, dry period without enough water	Dürre
during ['djʊərɪŋ]	We had no rain for ten weeks ~ the summer.	während
equal ['i:kwəl]	Cut the cake in four ~ parts.	gleich
expect [ɪks'pekt]	Have you heard? Liz Jones is expecting a baby.	erwarten
extend [ɪks'tend]	They've decided to ~ shop opening hours in Germany.	verlängern
face [feɪs]		mit etwas rechnen müssen
fair and square [ˌfeər ən 'skweə]	equally	gleichmäßig
fairly ['feəlɪ]	It will be ~ cool tomorrow.	ziemlich, recht
forecast ['fɔ:kɑ:st]	What's the weather ~ for the weekend?	Vorhersage
freezing-point ['fri:zɪŋ pɔɪnt]	Temperatures were at ~ yesterday.	Gefrierpunkt
gear [gɪə]	I can't find my football ~.	Sachen, Zeug
get rid of [get 'rɪd əv]	Have you any idea how I can ~ my cold?	los werden
get stuck [stʌk]	I got stuck in a lift once for six hours and have never used one since then.	stecken bleiben
give up [gɪv ʌp]	When are you going to ~ smoking?	aufgeben
government ['gʌvnmənt]	The last Labour ~ was in 1980.	Regierung

Vocabulary – Unit by Unit **191**

Vocabulary Unit by unit

headline ['hedlaɪn]	Have you seen the ~ on the front page of today's paper?	Schlagzeile
healthy ['helθɪ]	I swim and walk a lot. It keeps me ~.	gesund
highlight ['haɪlaɪt]	~ the new words in the text with a marker.	markieren
hosepipe ['həʊzpaɪp]	Some people wash their car with a ~.	Wasserschlauch
huge [hju:dʒ]	very big	riesig; gewaltig
immediately [ɪ'mi:dɪətlɪ]	Don't wait till later. Do it ~!	sofort
jail [dʒeɪl]	The bank robber was sent to ~ for five years.	Gefängnis
lack (a ... of) [læk]	A millionaire has no ~ of money – or friends!	Mangel
lift [lɪft]	I never take the ~; I always use the stairs.	Aufzug
like [laɪk]	What was your holiday ~? – Very good!	Wie (war) …?
likely ['laɪklɪ]	can be expected	wahrscheinlich
luck [lʌk]	Winning the lottery is a question of ~.	Glückssache
magazine [,mægə'zi:n]	There are a number of interesting articles in this month's motoring ~.	Zeitschrift
majority [mə'dʒɒrətɪ]	The ~ of lottery winners play again.	Mehrheit
met office ['met ɒfɪs]		Wetterdienst
miss [mɪs]	I don't want to ~ the next episode of "Phsycho".	verpassen
mist [mɪst]	There was some ~ on the hills this morning again.	Nebel
motorway ['məʊtəweɪ]	Take the M1 ~ when you leave London.	Autobahn
move [mu:v]	My grandparents have never moved house.	umziehen
occasional [ə'keɪʒənl]	Will it rain all day tomorrow? – No, the forecast says only ~ rain showers.	gelegentlich
offer ['ɒfə]	The firm has offered my husband a job in Mexico.	anbieten
only child ['əʊnlɪ]	I'm an ~. I've no brothers or sisters.	Einzelkind
outskirts ['aʊtskɜ:ts]	We live on the ~ of Bristol.	Stadtrand
place a bet [pleɪs ə bet]	Have you ever placed a bet on a football or tennis match?	auf etwas wetten
pleasant ['plezənt]	What's your new colleague like? – Very ~.	nett, angenehm
practically ['præktɪklɪ]	nearly, almost	fast, so gut wie
prediction [prɪ'dɪkʃən]	The general ~ is for hotter summers.	Vorhersage
prefer [prɪ'fɜ:]	I ~ autumn to winter.	vorziehen, lieber mögen
punter [pʌntə]	A ~ is someone who places a bet.	Wetter/in
put (it) [pʊt]	to express s.th. in words	sich ausdrücken
putting ['pʌtɪŋ]	I like ~.	Minigolf auf Rasen
refuse [rɪ'fju:z]	The prisoner refused to answer the policeman's questions.	sich weigern
regularly [,reɡjʊləlɪ]	I go swimming ~, every Tuesday and Thursday.	regelmäßig
report [rɪ'pɔ:t]	There was an interesting ~ on the radio last week about bucket-shop package holidays.	Bericht, Berichterstattung
resign [rɪ'zaɪn]	The bank manager resigned because of the financial scandal.	zurücktreten, kündigen
retire [rɪ'taɪə]	I'd like to ~ before I'm 65.	sich pensionieren lassen
scattered ['skætəd]	There will be ~ showers in the south-west.	vereinzelt
season ['si:zn]	Winter is the coldest ~ of the year.	Jahreszeit
snap (a cold…) [ə 'kəʊld snæp]	A ~ is a sudden period of very cold weather.	Kälteeinbruch
snow [snəʊ]	Are you a ~ lover?	Schnee
snow [snəʊ]	When did it last ~ for Xmas?	schneien
snowdrift ['snəʊdrɪft]	Hundreds of car drivers and their passengers had to spend the night in their cars because of the ~s on the motorway.	Schneeverwehung
snowflake ['snəʊfleɪk]	I'll win my bet if there's only one ~ tomorrow.	Schneeflocke
sound [saʊnd]	Why don't we go out for a meal? – Yes, that sounds a good idea.	klingen, sich anhören
special offer [,speʃl 'ɒfə]	Two weeks in Spain for £200? That really is a ~.	Sonderangebot
spider ['spaɪdə]	a black insect with eight legs	Spinne
spokesman ['spəʊksmən]	A White House ~ has said the President will visit Berlin later this year.	Sprecher
spring [sprɪŋ]	~ is the first season of the year.	Frühling
straight away [,streɪt_ə'weɪ]	immediately	sofort
strange [streɪndʒ]	Listen! Can you hear that ~ noise coming from the cellar?	seltsam
suffer (from) ['sʌfə]	I hope we don't have to ~ another heatwave next summer.	leiden (unter)
sunburnt ['sʌnbɜ:nt]	I fell asleep in the sun and got ~.	einen Sonnenbrand bekommen
thunderstorm ['θʌndəstɔ:m]	Our dog is afraid of ~s. He always hides under the bed.	Gewitter
tour operator ['tʊər_ˌɒpəreɪtə]		Reiseveranstalter
update ['ʌpdeɪt]		neuester Stand
viewing ['vju:ɪŋ]	Last night's ~ wasn't very good.	Fernsehen

Unit 8

accept [ək'sept]	Please ~ my apologies.	annehmen, akzeptieren
adult ['ædʌlt]	These films are suitable for ~s only. / His behaviour is not particularly ~.	Erwachsene(r), erwachsenengemäß (-gerecht)
advise [əd'vaɪz]	I ~ you to see a doctor.	raten
announce [ə'naʊns]	He ~d the winners of the Oscars.	verkünden, ankündigen

article ['ɑːtɪkl]	An ~ in a magazine.	Artikel, Beitrag
attic ['ætɪk]	The room under the roof is the ~.	Dachboden
believe [bɪ'liːv]	to believe in Father Christmas	glauben an
beware of [bɪ'weə]	~ pickpockets in big cities.	sich vor etwas hüten, in Acht nehmen
boot [buːt]	You put suitcases in the ~ of the car.	Kofferraum
busker ['bʌskə]	A person performing music in a public place.	Straßenmusikant
childhood ['tʃaɪldhʊd]	She had an unhappy ~.	Kindheit
clock in and out of work [klɒk 'ɪn ən 'aʊt əv 'wɜːk]	People in this company have to clock in and out. / What is clock-in time at your office?	stempeln; Arbeitszeit auf einer Zeitkarte eintragen
cross [krɒs]	They ~ed the border from Germany to France.	überqueren, hinübergehen
customs ['kʌstəmz]	At the airport you have to go through ~.	Zoll
declare [dɪ'kleə]	Have you got anything to ~? Whisky? Cigarettes?	verzollen
demand (on ...) [dɪ'mɑːnd]	You must show your passport ~.	auf Verlangen
dock worker ['dɒk ˌwɜːkə]	He works as a ~ in Hamburg.	Hafenarbeiter
doll [dɒl]		Puppe
elderly ['eldəlɪ]	Rather old, past middle age. He's very active for an ~ man.	ältere(-r, -s)
electrician [ˌɪlek'trɪʃn]		Elektriker
entry ['entrɪ]	No entry!	Eingang; Kein Eingang!
feed [fiːd]		füttern; einwerfen
fiction ['fɪkʃn]	A type of literature describing imaginary events and people.	Erzählliteratur
food poisoning ['fuːd ˌpɔɪzənɪŋ]		Lebensmittelvergiftung
give up [gɪv ˈʌp]	Please ~ this seat if an elderly person needs it.	freimachen, jmd. überlassen
got that (I've ...) [gɒt]	I understand.	Verstehe.
hit [hɪt]		schlagen
human ['hjuːmən]		menschlich
hunt [hʌnt]		jagen, auf die Jagd gehen
lane [leɪn]	A country ~.	Weg
lead [liːd]	You have to keep a dog on a ~ in the park.	Leine
litter ['lɪtə]	Small pieces of rubbish left lying round a place so as to make it untidy.	Papier und Abfälle
necessities [nə'sesɪtɪz]	For some people air-conditioning belongs to the basic ~ of life.	das Notwendigste zum Leben
non-fiction [ˌnɒn'fɪkʃn]		Sachbücher
notice ['nəʊtɪs]	He didn't ~ the hole and so he fell in.	bemerken, wahrnehmen
novel ['nɒvl]	As a student she read a lot of ~s.	Roman
obstruct [əb'strʌkt]	Parked cars ~ed his view of the road.	verdecken, im Weg sein, blockieren
once more [ˌwʌns 'mɔː]		noch einmal
opposite ['ɒpəzɪt]	Big is the ~ of small.	Gegenteil
penalty ['penəltɪ]	A punishment for breaking a law or rule. Do not drop litter. – Penalty £25.	Strafe
persuade [pə'sweɪd]	Please try and ~ her to come with us. / She finally ~ed us that she was telling the truth.	überreden; überzeugen
queue [kjuː]	A line of people or vehicles. Is this the ~ for the bus? / By 7 o'clock a long ~ had formed outside the cinema.	Warteschlange
rather (I'd ...) ['rɑːðə]		Ich würde lieber …
reason ['riːzn]		Grund
refrain from [rɪ'freɪn]	Customers are kindly requested to ~ smoking.	auf etwas verzichten
remember [rɪ'membə]	When is her birthday? I can't ~.	sich an etwas erinnern
remind [rɪ'maɪnd]	The teddy ~s me of my childhood.	jmd. an etwas erinnern
report [rɪ'pɔːt]		berichten
request [rɪ'kwest]	Visitors are requested to be careful.	bitten, ersuchen
rescue ['reskjuː]	She fell in the water but a friend ~d her.	retten
retired [rɪ'taɪəd]	A person having ~ from work.	pensioniert
room [ruːm]		Zimmer
search for [sɜːtʃ]		suchen
shelf [ʃelf]		Regal
skipping rope ['skɪpɪŋ ˌrəʊp]	Jumping with a ~ is good exercise.	Springseil
strict [strɪkt]	She's very ~ with her children.	streng
stuff [stʌf]	I need some ~ to clean the frying pan.	etwa: Zeug, Mittel
suddenly ['sʌdnlɪ]		plötzlich
support [sə'pɔːt]	She ~s Hamburger SV.	unterstützen; Sie ist HSV-Anhängerin.
thick [θɪk]	a thick soup, a thick book	dick
touch [tʌtʃ]		berühren
track [træk]	The racing cars were driving round the ~.	Bahn
travel abroad [ˌtrævl ə'brɔːd]	They often ~ to visit their family.	ins Ausland reisen
treasures ['treʒəz]	There are some wonderful ~ in the museum.	Schätze
trunk [trʌŋk]	She packed all her books in a big ~.	Truhe
used to [juːstə]	I ~ smoke but now I don't.	hier: früher etwas getan haben
valid ['vælɪd]	A ~ passport. / The point you make is perfectly ~.	gültig
well-known [ˌwel'nəʊn]	The president is a ~ man.	bekannt

Vocabulary – Unit by Unit

Vocabulary Unit by unit

Unit 9

achieve [ə'tʃiːv]	He ~d first place in the race.	erreichen
advantage [əd'vɑːntɪdʒ]	He has the ~ of a steady job. / They took full ~ of the hotel's facilities.	Vorteil, Vorzüge
advertisement [əd'vɜːtɪzˌmənt]	She saw the ~ for the job online.	Inserat, Anzeige
applicant ['æplɪkənt]	A person who applies for a job or a place on a course. There were over 100 ~s for the manager's post.	Bewerber(in)
application [ˌæplɪ'keɪʃn]	He sent in his ~ for the job yesterday.	Bewerbung
approach [ə'prəʊtʃ]	She has a positive ~ to her work.	Einstellung
attachment [ə'tætʃmənt]	You can send ~s with e-mails.	Anhang
ban [bæn]	Airlines ~ smoking on short flights.	verbannen
be aware of [ə'weə]	Are you aware of the danger? / I don't think you're aware (of) how much this means to me. / She became aware that sth. was burning.	sich einer Sache bewusst sein
be willing ['wɪlɪŋ]		bereit sein
become [bɪ'kʌm]		werden
benefit ['benɪfɪt]	Knowing a language can be a great ~.	Vorteil, Nutzen, Gewinn
candidate ['kændɪdeɪt]		Kandidat(in), Bewerber(in)
career [kə'rɪə]	She chose an academic ~.	Karriere, Laufbahn
coach [kəʊtʃ]	a luxury bus	Reisebus
commission [kə'mɪʃn]	She works on ~.	auf Provisionsbasis
company ['kʌmpəni]	BMW is a big ~.	Firma
competitive [kəm'petətɪv]	Our firm is no longer ~ in world markets. / A shop offering very ~ prices.	wettbewerbsfähig
computer-literate [kəm'pjuːtə 'lɪtrət]	My son can use a computer but I'm not ~.	fähig sein, mit einem Computer umzugehen
congratulate [kən'grætjuˌleɪt]	I ~d her because it was her birthday.	beglückwünschen
consumer [kən'sjuːmə]		Verbraucher
contact ['kɒntækt]		Kontakt aufnehmen
cookery ['kʊkəri]	She liked ~ when she was at school.	Kochen
couple ['kʌpl]	Ann and Bill are a nice ~.	Paar
CV (curriculum vitae) [siː 'viː/kə,rɪkjʊləm 'viːtaɪ]	When you apply for a job you send in your ~.	Lebenslauf
degree [dɪ'griː]	She's got an engineering ~.	Diplom, Abschluss
disadvantage [ˌdɪsəd'vɑːntɪdʒ]		Nachteil
discover [dɪs'kʌvə]		entdecken
economics [ˌiːkə'nɒmɪks]	He studied ~.	Volkswirtschaftslehre, Betriebswirtschaftslehre
expand [ɪk'spænd]	The Managing Director wants to ~ his company.	erweitern, ausweiten, wachsen
expansion [ɪk'spænʃn]		Erweiterung, Ausweitung, Vergrößerung
experience [ɪk'spɪərɪəns]	He has three years ~ of working in a bank.	Erfahrung
extension number [ɪk'stenʃn ˌnʌmbə]	Phone me at the office, I'm on extension 291.	Apparatnummer
fact [fækt]		Tatsache
gain [geɪn]	I ~ed a lot of experience in my first job.	gewinnen, erreichen, bekommen
immediately [ɪ'miːdɪətli]	I need it ~, not in five minutes.	sofort, unverzüglich
include [ɪn'kluːd]	Your job responsibilities will ~ answering the telephone.	einschließen
join [dʒɔɪn]	She ~ed the Deutsches Theater.	sich anschließen, sich beteiligen, mitmachen
line [laɪn]	a dog food line	hier: Produktlinie, Sortiment
make a decision [dɪ'sɪʒn]		Entscheidung treffen
make a fool of yourself [meɪk ə 'fuːl əv jə'self]	You are a beginner. Don't worry if you ~.	sich blamieren
manner ['mænə]	The secretary had a friendly personal ~.	Art
matter ['mætə]	It doesn't ~.	Es macht nichts./Ist schon gut.
membership ['membəʃɪp]		Mitgliedschaft
monthly ['mʌnθli]		monatlich
motivated ['məʊtɪveɪtɪd]		motiviert
move [muːv]	She ~d from New York to Berlin.	umziehen
nervous ['nɜːvəs]		nervös
obtain [əb'teɪn]		bekommen, erhalten
opportunity [ˌɒpə'tjuːnəti]	I had no ~ to discuss it with her. / A company promoting equal ~ for women.	Gelegenheit; Möglichkeit; Chancengleichheit
organize ['ɔːgənaɪz]		organisieren
pay rise ['peɪ raɪz]		Gehaltserhöhung
post [pəʊst]	The ~ was advertised in the newspaper.	Arbeitsstelle, Job
pressure ['preʃə]	To work under ~.	Druck

promotion [prə'məʊʃn]	The process of raising sb. to a higher position or more important job. The new job is a ~ for her.	Beförderung
prospects ['prɒspekts]	~ for promotion are good.	Aussichten (auf eine Beförderung)
recruitment [rɪ'kru:tmənt]	The process of finding new people to join a company. The company's ~ policy is not very transparent.	Einstellung von Personal
referee [ˌrefə'ri:]	Mr Brown agreed to be her ~ if the company asked about her work.	jmd. als Referenz dienen
responsibility [rɪˌspɒnsɪ'bɪlɪtɪ]	The food is the ~ of the cook.	Verantwortung
roster ['rɒstə]	The monthly ~ involves a week of night duty.	Dienstplan
salary ['sælərɪ]	A fixed regular payment. Has your ~ been paid into your bank account yet?	Gehalt
skills [skɪlz]	The ability to do sth. well. His job requires great ~s and attention to detail.	Fähigkeiten
smart [smɑ:t]	You look ~ in your new suit. / A ~ restaurant. / He's one of the smartest students in class.	schick, vornehm; klug, gewitzt
staff [stɑ:f]	He's head of department with a ~ of 10.	Belegschaft, Mitarbeiterschaft
stifle ['staɪfl]	It was hot. The air nearly ~d her.	ersticken, erdrücken
succeed [sək'si:d]	Our plan ~ed. / She's determined to ~ in life.	gelingen, Erfolg haben
take a year off [teɪk ə jɪə 'ɒf]		sich ein Jahr beurlauben lassen
tip [tɪp]	You give the waiter a ~ for good service in a restaurant.	Trinkgeld
unemployment [ˌʌnɪm'plɔɪmənt]	The state of being without a paid job. The rising level of ~ is very disturbing.	Arbeitslosigkeit
utilities [ju'tɪlətɪz]	A service provided for the public, e.g. electricity, water or gas supply. The administration of public ~ is not very cost-effective.	Versorgungsbetriebe, versorgungs- wirtschaftliche Einrichtungen
virtual experience ['vɜ:tjʊəl eks'pɪərɪəns]	Children who play computer games a lot seem to enjoy ~s.	virtuelle Erfahrungen, Erlebnisse
working environment		Arbeitsklima

Revision 3

armchair [ɑ:m'tʃeə]	I need a comfortable ~ to relax in.	Sessel
awful ['ɔ:fəl]	Nothing but rain, what ~ weather!	schrecklich
car registration number [kɑ: redʒɪ'streɪʃən 'nʌmbə]		Autokennzeichen
change [tʃeɪndʒ]	I'm getting married next month, but I'm not changing my name.	ändern (lassen)
dig [dɪg]		graben
edit ['edɪt]		redigieren, herausgeben
editor ['edɪtə]		Herausgeber/in, Lektor/in
expand [ek'spænd]	I would like to ~ my teaching experience.	erweitern, ausbauen
experience [eks'pɪərɪəns]	Have you got any ~ in Personnel Management?	Erfahrung
fog [fɒg]	Don't drive in the ~ without your fog lamps on.	Nebel
gain [geɪn]	I ~ed a lot of experience in my first job.	gewinnen
glasses ['glɑ:səz]	I think I need new ~.	Brille
health insurance [helθ ɪn'ʃɔ:rəns]	Is ~ very expensive in your country?	Krankenversicherung
identity card [aɪ'dentɪtɪ kɑ:d]	You can travel to the UK with your German ~.	Personalausweis
in time [ɪn taɪm]	I got to the station at 8.25, just ~ for the 8.28 train.	rechtzeitig
obtain [ɒb'teɪn]		erwerben
on schedule [ɒn 'ʃedju:l]	Does public transport always run ~ in your country?	fahrplanmäßig
passport ['pɑ:spɔ:t]	Have you ever lost your ~ on holiday?	Reisepass
referee [refə'ri:]	Can I name you as my ~?	Referenz
remind (s.o. of s.th.) [rɪ'maɪnd]	Could you please ~ me of my appointment tomorrow?	erinnern (an)
report (to) [rɪ'pɔ:t tu:]	Do you have to ~ to the authorities when you move house?	sich melden (bei)
residence permit ['rezɪdəns 'pɜ:mɪt]		Aufenthaltserlaubnis
shy [ʃaɪ]		schüchtern
smoothly ['smu:ðlɪ]	How are things at the office? Is everything running ~?	glatt, reibungslos
work permit [wɜ:k 'pɜ:mɪt]	Is it easy to get a ~ in your country?	Arbeitserlaubnis

Unit 10

agenda [ə'dʒendə]	What's on the ~ for today's meeting?	Tagesordnung
airport ['eəpɔ:t]	How are you getting to the ~? – We're taking a taxi.	Flughafen
alike [ə'laɪk]	The twins don't look ~, do they?	ähnlich
amount [ə'maʊnt]	Driving is no fun with the ~ of traffic on the roads.	Menge
anywhere ['enɪˌweə]	Are you going ~ at the weekend?	irgendwohin
area ['eərɪə]	Which ~ of London do you live in?	Gegend
bay [beɪ]	I live on one side of the ~ and work on the other.	Bucht

Vocabulary Unit by unit

beforehand [bɪˈfɔːhænd]	It's often cheaper if you buy your ticket ~.	im voraus
bike [baɪk]	How do you come to the English class? - By ~.	Fahrrad
boom (out) [buːm aʊt]		dröhnen
burglar alarm [ˈbɜːglə əlaːm]	Have you got a ~ in your house?	Alarmanlage
burglar-proof [ˈbɜːglə pruːf]	Our doors and windows are absolutely ~.	einbruchsicher
burn [bɜːn]	Be careful, the iron is hot! Don't ~ yourself.	(ver)brennen
cab (AE) [kæb]	In New York the ~s are yellow.	Taxi
cancel [ˈkænsl]	Tomorrow's meeting has been ~led.	streichen, absagen
chairperson [ˈtʃeəpɜːsən]	I'd like to introduce Sheila Wright, our new ~ for the coming year.	Vorsitzende/r
change [tʃeɪndʒ]	Have you got ~ for the bus?	Kleingeld, Wechselgeld
cheap [tʃiːp]	Is public transport ~ in your country?	billig, preisgünstig
convenient [kənˈviːnɪənt]	For Sally public transport is not so ~.	günstig
crawl [krɔːl]	There's nothing worse than ~ing through town by car.	kriechen
crowded [ˈkraʊdɪd]	I hate travelling on a ~ underground. Don't you?	überfüllt, voll
defence [dɪˈfens]	I'm interested in a home ~ system. What have you got?	Verteidigung
development [dɪˈveləpmənt]	For me it's been the ~ in medicine.	Entwicklung
difficult [ˈdɪfɪkʌlt]	I hope it wasn't ~ to find us.	schwer, schwierig
dishwasher [ˈdɪʃˌwɒʃə]	I find a washing machine more important than a ~. What about you?	Spülmaschine
distance [ˈdɪstəns]	I don't mind driving long ~s.	Entfernung
drive [draɪv]	I hate driving in the rush-hour.	(Auto) fahren
driveway [ˈdraɪvweɪ]	Our garage is so full that we have to park our car in the ~.	Einfahrt
easy [ˈiːzɪ]	For me it's a lot easier to take the car.	einfach, leicht
efficient [ɪˈfɪʃənt]	The public transport system in Hong Kong is very ~.	leistungsfähig
emit [ɪˈmɪt]		(Geräusch, Geruch) abgeben
end up [end ʌp]	I ended up paying too much because the driver had no change.	damit enden, dass ...
enjoy [enˈdʒɔɪ]	I ~ working in the garden. I find it so relaxing.	genießen
enter [ˈentə]	The intruder ~ed the house through the garage.	betreten; hineintreten
estimated [ˈestɪmeɪtɪd]	What's the ~ cost of the new motorway?	geschätzt
exciting [ekˈsaɪtɪŋ]	I didn't really like that film. It wasn't very ~.	aufregend
expensive [ekˈspensɪv]	I hardly ever take a taxi. It's too ~.	teuer
fare [feə]	What's the ~ to the airport?	Fahrpreis
fast [faːst]	Do you drive a ~ car? / How ~ do you drive?	schnell
fellow student [ˈfeləʊ ˈstjuːdənt]	Come along and meet my ~s.	Mitschüler, Kommilitone, Mitlernender
ferry [ˈferɪ]	In Sydney lots of people go to work by ~.	Fähre
fire brigade [ˈfaɪə brɪˈgeɪd]	What number do you call for the ~ in your country?	Feuerwehr
get stuck [get ˈstʌk]	Sorry, I'm late. I got stuck in a traffic jam.	stecken bleiben
goose (geese, pl.) [guːs / giːs]		Gans
guard dog [gaːd dɒg]	What do you think is better: geese or ~s?	Wachhund
grade [greɪd]	My school ~s in Maths weren't very good.	Note
hairdryer [ˈheədraɪə]	Is there a ~ in the hotel room?	Fön
hardly ever [haːdlɪ evə]	I ~ go by bus.	kaum (jemals)
height [haɪt]	What ~ are you? - 1 metre 85.	Körpergröße; Höhe
high-density [haɪ ˈdensɪtɪ]		dicht
intruder [ɪnˈtruːdə]	Mrs Watson thought she heard an ~ and called the police.	Eindringling
invention [ɪnˈvenʃən]	What do you think has been the most important ~?	Erfindung
iron [aɪən]	I don't know. That's the second ~ I've bought this year.	Bügeleisen
item [ˈaɪtəm]	How many ~s are there on the agenda?	Tagesordnungspunkt
line [laɪn]	In most towns you'll find a separate bus and taxi ~.	Fahrbahn
local [ˈləʊkl]	Our ~ facilities are very good.	örtlich
locate [ləʊˈkeɪt]	Can you help me? I'm trying to ~ the Cool Water Company.	finden
mind [maɪnd]	I don't ~ travelling by train. / Would you ~ shutting the window?	etwas dagegen haben; etwas ausmachen
public [ˈpʌblɪk]	Do you use ~ transport?	öffentlich
prefer [prɪˈfɜː]	I ~ taking the underground because it's faster.	bevorzugen, etwas lieber tun
receipt [rɪˈsiːt]	Can I have a ~, please?	Quittung
reimburse [riːɪmˈbɜːs]	You need a receipt if you want to ~ the fare from your company.	erstatten lassen
relaxing [rɪˈlæksɪŋ]	Do you find travelling by bus ~?	erholsam
river [ˈrɪvə]	Our friends have just bought a house by the ~.	Fluss
roadside [ˈrəʊdsaɪd]	Taxis don't stand at the ~ in USA.	Straßenrand
round [raʊnd]	Would you like to fly ~ the world?	um
rush-hour [ˈrʌʃ aʊə]	I hate driving in the ~.	Berufsverkehr
savings [ˈseɪvɪŋz]	The old lady next door kept all her ~ under her bed.	Ersparnisse
smoke [sməʊk]	The house was full of ~ when the firemen arrived.	Rauch
sweet [swiːt]	I don't really like eating ~ things.	süß

take (a cab) [teɪk ə kæb]	Is it cheap to ~ a cab in New York?	mit (einem Verkehrsmittel) fahren
technology [ˌtekˈnɒlədʒɪ]	Do you think that ~ has given us only good things?	Technologie
traffic jam [ˈtræfɪk ˌdʒæm]	Sorry, I'm late. I got stuck in a ~.	Verkehrsstau
transport [ˈtrɑːnspɔːt]	Do you use public ~?	Verkehrsmittel
travel [ˈtrævl]	How do you ~ to work?	fahren
tube [tjuːb]	When you're in London, you should take the ~. It's faster.	U-Bahn (in London)
twin [twɪn]	My sister and I are ~s. We were born on the same day.	Zwilling
underground [ˈʌndəˌɡraʊnd]	Most Londoners call the ~ the tube.	U-Bahn
uncomfortable [ʌnˈkʌmpftəbl]	I don't find public transport ~. Do you?	unbequem, ungemütlich
wake-up call [weɪk ʌp kɑːl]	Would you like a ~, sir?	Weckruf
walk [wɔːk]	How do you come to the English class? – I ~.	zu Fuß gehen
weight [weɪt]	What ~ is the baby? – 3.3 kilos.	Gewicht
wire [waɪə]	The alarm is made of an electric ~ system.	Draht
world [wɜːld]	We're going on a trip round the ~.	Welt

Unit 11

aerosol [ˈeərəsɒl]		Spraydose
afterwards [ˈɑːftəwədz]	If you've got a sore head, go out for a walk and ~ you'll feel much better.	nachher, hinterher
avoid [əˈvɔɪd]	If people were more careful, most accidents in the home could be avoided.	vermeiden
aware of (be ...) [əˈweə]	Mrs Chalmers wasn't ~ the smell of gas from the kitchen.	sich einer Sache bewusst sein
borough [ˈbʌrə]		Stadtgemeinde
cabinet [ˈkæbɪnət]	Have you got any aspirin? – Yes, there's some in the bathroom ~.	Schrank
carpet [ˈkɑːpɪt]	That's a beautiful Persian ~. You don't hoover it, do you?	Teppich, Teppichboden
carrier-bag [ˈkærɪə bæɡ]	In British supermarkets you get plastic ~s without paying.	Tragetasche
challenge [ˈtʃælɪndʒ]	Taking part in the Ben Nevis run would be a real ~ for most people.	Herausforderung
check-up [ˈtʃek ʌp]	People over 35 should have a medical ~ once a year.	Untersuchung
chimney [ˈtʃɪmnɪ]	As a child I always believed that Father Christmas came down the ~.	Schornstein
chips [tʃɪps]	Fish and ~ is a very popular meal in Britain.	Pommes frites
connection [kəˈnekʃn]	There's a strong ~ between smoking and heart disease.	Verbindung
contestant [kənˈtestənt]	The ~ with the highest number of points wins tonight's star prize.	Teilnehmer, Kandidat
cotton [ˈkɒtən]	My husband wears nothing but ~ socks.	Baumwolle
cubicle [ˈkjuːbɪkl]	Would you like to try on that dress, madam? There's a ~ right over there.	Kabine
DIY [ˌdiː aɪ ˈwaɪ]	Do-It-Yourself	Heimwerken
domestic appliance [dəˈmestɪk əˈplaɪəns]	The most popular ~ is a fridge.	Haushaltsgerät
double glazing [ˌdʌbl ˈɡleɪzɪŋ]	~ helps to keep out cold and noise.	Doppelverglasung
entranceway [ˈentrənsweɪ]	All ~s should be kept well lit.	Eingang
eventually [ɪˈventʃʊəlɪ]	We waited ages for a taxi. ~ we got one in Green Street.	endlich
exercise [ˈeksəsaɪz]	Daily ~ helps to keep you fit.	Bewegung
food poisoning [ˈfuːd pɔɪzənɪŋ]	Always wash your hands before preparing food to avoid ~.	Lebensmittelvergiftung
free-range [ˈfriːreɪndʒ] eggs	I always buy ~ even though they are more expensive.	Eier von freilaufenden Hühnern
frequent [ˈfriːkwənt]	~ hairwashing is not good for your hair.	häufig
fry [fraɪ]	We don't ~ fish any more, we grill it. It's much better for your health.	in der Pfanne braten
generally speaking [ˌdʒenrəlɪ ˈspiːkɪŋ]	~ it's Martin who does the washing.	im allgemeinen
greengrocer [ˈɡriːnɡrəʊsə]	I prefer to buy my fruit and vegetables at the ~'s.	Obst- und Gemüsehändler
greenish [ˈɡriːnɪʃ]	not completely green	grünlich
guideline [ˈɡaɪdlaɪn]	The ~s for keeping noise to a minimum are really quite easy to follow.	Richtlinie
hankie [ˈhæŋkɪ]	Stop sniffing, Joan. Haven't you got a ~?	Taschentuch
honest [ˈɒnɪst]	To be quite ~, I usually let the water run when I'm cleaning my teeth.	ehrlich
Inland Revenue [ˌɪnlənd ˈrevənjuː]		Finanzamt
case (just in ...) [ˌdʒʌst ɪn keɪs]	Take an umbrella with you ~ it rains!	falls; für alle Fälle
local council [ˌləʊkl ˈkaʊnsl]	Our ~ wants to build a new shopping centre in the middle of town.	Stadt-, Gemeindeverwaltung
luggage [ˈlʌɡɪdʒ]	We always take too much ~ with us on holiday.	Gepäck
match [mætʃ]	Haven't we got any ~es to light the candles?	Streichholz

Vocabulary – Unit by Unit **197**

Vocabulary Unit by unit

meantime (in the ...) ['mi:ntaɪm]	Mrs Brown, you call for an ambulance, and ~ we'll try to make your husband as comfortable as possible.	in der Zwischenzeit
mind [maɪnd]	Mind the step!	aufpassen
neighbourhood ['neɪbəhʊd]	Unfortunately, we live in a very noisy ~.	Gegend, Viertel; Nachbarschaft
non-returnable [ˌnɒnrɪ'tɜ:nəbl]	I'm glad to see that fewer drinks are sold in ~ bottles.	Einweg-
operation [ɒpə'reɪʃn]	The ~ of a new machine can be hard to learn.	Bedienung
overspend ['əʊvəspend]	This year I'm really going to try not to ~ on holiday.	zuviel ausgeben
patience ['peɪʃəns]	You need ~ when you go to see the doctor.	Geduld
Pilgrim Fathers [ˌpɪlgrɪm 'fɑ:ðəz]	The ~ sailed from England to the USA in 1620.	die Pilgerväter
plug [plʌg]	You need an adaptor for German ~s in Britain.	Stecker
power station ['paʊə steɪʃn]	Without ~s there wouldn't be any electricity.	Kraftwerk
receive [rɪ'si:v]	Thank you for your letter which I received yesterday.	erhalten
replace [rɪ'pleɪs]	We've had this washing-machine for 25 years now. Don't you think it's time to ~ it?	ersetzen
response [rɪ'spɒns]	There was no ~ to my question.	Antwort
rev [rev]		(einen Motor) aufheulen lassen
safety ['seɪftɪ]	On a plane it's important to listen to the ~ instructions.	Sicherheit
see eye to eye [si: ˌaɪ tə ˌaɪ]	She has never seen ~ with her sister.	mit jmd. einer Meinung sein
shaver ['ʃeɪvə]		Rasierapparat
slam [slæm]	And don't ~ the door when you go out!	zuknallen
socket ['sɒkɪt]	In Britain you're not allowed to have an electrical ~ in the bathroom.	Steckdose
sound [saʊnd]	Stop sounding that horn: you'll waken the whole neighbourhood.	hupen
soundproof ['saʊndpru:f]	They can't hear what you're saying: they're in a ~ cubicle.	schalldicht
spill [spɪl]	Don't fill that glass too full or you'll just ~ it.	verschütten
squeeze [skwi:z]	Every morning I ~ an orange and drink a glass of fresh juice.	ausdrücken
suggestion [sə'dʒestʃn]	Has anyone got a ~ for next year's holiday?	Vorschlag
suppose [sə'pəʊz]	I don't ~ there's any warm water left, is there?	annehmen
sweep [swi:p]	Do you have to ~ the pavement outside your house?	kehren, fegen
tend [tend]	The children ~ to stay up late when there's no school.	dazu neigen
tile [taɪl]	I like those bathroom ~s with the roses on them.	Kachel, Fliese
tissue ['tɪʃu:]	I don't like washing hankies, so I always use ~s.	Papiertaschentuch
trim [trɪm]	I don't want my hair cut too short. Can you just ~ it a bit, please?	nachschneiden
unbleached [ˌʌn'bli:tʃt]	We only sell ~ coffee and tea filters.	ungebleicht
upright ['ʌpraɪt]		aufrecht, senkrecht
vacuum cleaner ['vækjʊəm kli:nə]	I think we definitely need a new ~; I just can't get the carpets clean with this one.	Staubsauger
vote [vəʊt]		Abstimmungsergebnis; Stimme
wealthy ['welθɪ]	Millionaires may not all be happy, but they're certainly ~.	reich, wohlhabend
well-meant [ˌwel'ment]	I know your advice is ~, but I'm old enough to make my own decisions.	gutgemeint
wink [wɪŋk]	I didn't sleep a ~ last night.	etwa: Ich habe kein Auge zugetan.
wire ['waɪə]	Are you wired for cable TV?	anschliessen
worn [wɔ:n]		abgetreten; abgetragen

Unit 12

accompanied [ə'kʌmpənɪd]	The children weren't ~ by an adult.	begleitet
account [ə'kaʊnt]	I tried to give the police an accurate ~ of what had happened.	Darstellung, Bericht
actress ['æktrəs]	I was surprised when they chose an American ~ to play Bridget.	Schauspielerin
amenity (amenities, pl.) [ə'mi:nɪtɪ]	Would you like to spend a holiday in a place with no modern ~?	öffentliche Einrichtungen
apply [ə'plaɪ]	The questions on the back of the form only ~ to citizens of non-EU member states.	gelten; zutreffen
appropriate [ə'prəʊprɪət]	Do you think these clothes are ~ for a business lunch?	passend, angemessen
back up [bæk 'ʌp]	The policeman wouldn't have believed me if you hadn't backed up my story.	unterstützen, bestätigen
battle ['bætl]	Do you think the Scots painted their faces before they went into ~?	Schlacht
beg [beg]	Even today you still see people begging for money on the streets of London.	betteln
box office ['bɒks ˌɒfɪs]	I've booked the seats, and we can collect the tickets at the ~.	Theater-/Kinokasse
catch up with [kætʃ ʌp wɪð]	The taxi finally caught up with the train in Dumbarton.	einholen
chess [tʃes]	Do you play ~?	Schach
classmate ['klɑ:smeɪt]	Do you ever see any of your old ~s?	Mitschüler/in

credit ['kredɪt]	to believe	glauben
dash [dæʃ]		hier: Rennen
despite [dɪs'paɪt]	He finally became successful ~ his bad school grades.	trotz
dice [daɪs]	Do you take a set of ~ with you on holiday?	Würfel
disgust [dɪs'gʌst]	a strong feeling of dislike	Ekel; Empörung
distance ['dɪstəns]	What ~ is it to the nearest railway station?	Entfernung
embarrassed [ˌem'bærəst]	Charlie was very ~ when he saw his mother.	verlegen
entertainment [ˌentə'teɪnmənt]	What do you do for ~?	Unterhaltung
fault [fɒlt]	It's not my ~ you missed the plane!	Schuld
feel guilty [fiːl 'gɪlti]	Don't ~. It's not your fault.	ein schlechtes Gewissen haben
firewood ['faɪəwʊd]	They didn't even have enough money to buy ~.	Brennholz
force [fɔːs]	He was ~d to leave school when his parents died.	zwingen
former ['fɔːmə]	My ~ boss was much friendlier than the one I have now.	ehemalig, früher
funeral ['fjuːnərəl]	Why are you wearing a black tie? Are you going to a ~?	Beerdigung
get rid of [rɪd_əv]	Hi, Mark. How are you feeling? – Terrible. I still haven't got rid of this cold.	loswerden
glance [glɑːns]	He glanced at his watch as he left the room.	einen kurzen Blick werfen
guardian ['gɑːdɪən]	His uncle became his ~ when his parents died.	Vormund
habit ['hæbɪt]	She has an annoying ~ of biting her fingernails.	Gewohnheit
hangover ['hæŋəʊvə]	I shouldn't have had so much to drink last night. I've got the most dreadful ~.	Kater
housekeeper ['haʊskiːpə]	I would love a ~, but I can't afford one.	Haushälterin
in pursuit of [ɪn pə'sjuːt əv]	The police were ~ the bank robbers all the way through town.	auf Verfolgungsjagd
introductory [ɪntrə'dʌktri]	The chairman opened the meeting by making a few ~ remarks.	einführend, einleitend
item ['aɪtəm]	Add some ~s to the list.	Gegenstand
leading role ['liːdɪŋ rəʊl]	Do you know who plays the ~ in Bridget Jones's Diary?	Hauptrolle
matter (a ... of) ['mætər_əv]	The storm destroyed a whole street of houses in ~ minutes.	hier: innerhalb von
miner ['maɪnə]	Billy's father and brother were ~s.	Bergarbeiter
misery ['mɪzəri]		Elend
option ['ɒpʃən]	You only have one ~.	Wahl, Möglichkeit
orphan ['ɔːfən]	He became an ~ at the age of 16.	Waise
over-indulgent ['əʊvə ɪn'dʌldʒənt]	Do you think Mrs Dukes was an ~ mother?	allzu nachgiebig, nachsichtig
overtake [əʊvə'teɪk]	They finally overtook them on the road to the airport.	überholen
paw [pɔː]	That's a clever dog. Give me your ~.	Pfote
peer [pɪə]	Who's that peering in the window?	starren
petition [pə'tɪʃn]	Young families in the area have petitioned the local council to build a playground for their children.	ersuchen
portable ['pɔːtəbl]	Have you got a ~ TV?	tragbar
poverty ['pɒvəti]		Armut
require [rɪ'kwaɪə]	Young people under the age of 18 ~ the signature of a parent or guardian.	benötigen
ring-leader ['rɪŋ liːdə]	The police have finally arrested the ~ of the gang which has been stealing car radios.	Anführer
rough [rʌf]	In the cold weather my hands soon get quite ~.	rauh
ruin ['ruːɪn]	His father's early death ruined his hopes of studying medicine.	zerstören
scarcely ['skeəsli]	After their first meeting Elsie and Fred could ~ wait to see each other again.	kaum
scenery ['siːnəri]	The ~ in the film was fantastic.	Landschaft
set off [set 'ɒf]	Last year I ~ on holiday without my passport!	aufbrechen, sich auf den Weg machen
skip [skɪp]	The little girl skipped up to her grandfather with pleasure.	hüpfen, springen
sow [səʊ]	You should ~ seeds in the morning or in the evening.	sähen
spectacles ['spektəklz]	Have you seen my ~ anywhere? – Yes, they're on your nose!	Brille
startle ['stɑːtl]	Sorry, did I ~ you?	erschrecken
stupid ['stjuːpɪd]	What a ~ thing to do!	blöd, dumm
suit [suːt]	The cards used in card games come in two red ~s and two black ~s.	Farbe
surge [sɜːdʒ]	I felt a ~ of pity for the old beggar and gave him £5.	Aufwallung, Sympathiewelle
survey ['sɜːveɪ]	Our class ~ shows that most people watch TV on Saturday evening.	Umfrage; Untersuchung
toy [tɔɪ]	My favourite ~ as a child was a little black and white dog.	Spielsache
trace [treɪs]	The police have found no ~ of the burglars.	Spur
trusty ['trʌsti]	My dog Sam has been my ~ friend for 10 years now.	treu
unaccompanied [ˌʌnə'kʌmpənɪd]	No ~ children are allowed into the hotel swimming pool.	unbegleitet
unashamedly [ˌʌnə'ʃeɪmɪdli]	When I handed the beggar 50p, he ~ asked for more.	unverschämt, ohne Scham
warrior ['wɒrɪə]	Mel Gibson plays a famous Scottish ~ in this film.	Krieger
waste [weɪst]	What a ~ of time and money!	Verschwendung
whine [waɪn]	If you leave a young dog alone for too long, it'll start whining.	jaulen; jammern

Vocabulary Unit by unit

wipe out [waɪp]	The forest fires have already wiped out half a dozen campsites.	ausrotten, zerstören
wonder ['wʌndə]	I ~ed where the children had got the money for the cinema.	sich fragen

Revision 4

alarm [əlɑ:m]	Sorry I'm late. I didn't hear the ~.	Wecker
chain of events [tʃeɪn əv ɪ'vents]		Reihe von Ereignissen
collection-box [kə'lekʃən bɒks]	In church people put money in the ~.	Kollekte
cross one's mind [krɒs wʌnz maɪnd]	It suddenly crossed my mind that she might be right.	einfallen
fund-raising [fʌnd 'reɪsɪŋ]		Geldmittelbeschaffung
handsome ['hænsəm]	He was the most ~ man she had ever seen.	gutaussehend
serial rapist [,sɪərɪəl 'reɪpɪst]		Serienvergewaltiger
speech intention ['spi:tʃ ɪn,tenʃən]		Redeabsicht
square-shouldered [skweə ʃəʊldəd]		breitschultrig
voluntary [vɒlʌntrɪ]	Our local hospital is looking for some ~ workers.	freiwillig

Vocabulary Alphabetical Order

A

ability *(Revision 1)*
abroad *(Revision 2, Unit 7)*
accelerator *(Unit 2)*
accept *(Unit 3, 8)*
accommodation *(Revision 2)*
accompanied *(Unit 12)*
according to *(Unit 7)*
account *(Unit 12)*
accountant *(Unit 9)*
achieve *(Unit 9)*
activity *(Unit 1)*
actor *(Unit 2)*
actress *(Unit 12)*
add (up to) *(Unit 1)*
additives *(Unit 1)*
admit *(Unit 1)*
adult *(Unit 2, 8)*
advantage *(Unit 9)*
advertisement *(Unit 9)*
advertising executive *(Unit 2)*
advice *(Unit 7)*
advise *(Unit 8)*
aerosol *(Unit 11)*
afford *(Unit 1, 7)*
afterwards *(Unit 11)*
agenda *(Unit 10)*
ago *(Unit 3)*
air traffic controller *(Unit 6)*
air-conditioned *(Unit 4)*
airline *(Unit 4)*
airport *(Unit 10)*
alarm *(Revision 3, 4)*
alike *(Unit 10)*
allergic to *(Unit 1)*
amazing *(Unit 6)*
ambulance *(Unit 5)*
amenity (amenities, pl.) *(Unit 12)*
amount *(Unit 7, 10)*
announce *(Unit 8)*
anyway *(Unit 6)*
anywhere *(Unit 10)*
appear *(Unit 3)*
applicant *(Unit 9)*
application *(Unit 1, 9)*
application form *(Unit 1)*
apply *(Unit 12)*
appointment *(Revision 2)*
approach *(Unit 9)*
appropriate *(Unit 12)*
archery *(Revision 1)*
architectural *(Unit 6)*
area *(Unit 1, 10)*
armchair *(Revision 3)*
around *(Unit 1)*
arrest *(Unit 5)*
art gallery *(Unit 4)*
article *(Unit 8)*
asleep *(Unit 5)*
assistance *(Revision 1)*
attachment *(Unit 9)*
attack *(Unit 2)*
attend *(Unit 3)*
attic *(Unit 8)*
authorities *(Unit 6)*
autumn *(Unit 7)*
available *(Unit 4)*
average (of) *(Unit 1)*
avoid *(Unit 12)*
awful *(Revision 3)*

B

back *(Unit 1)*
back up *(Unit 12)*
bacon *(Unit 2)*
ban *(Unit 9)*
bank clerk *(Unit 2)*
bar *(Unit 2)*
barbecue (to have a ...) *(Unit 7)*
bark *(Unit 3)*
battle *(Unit 12)*
bay *(Unit 10)*
be afraid *(Unit 1)*
be aware of *(Unit 9, 11)*
be entitled *(Unit 7)*
be fit *(Unit 2)*
be fond of *(Unit 1)*
be lucky *(Unit 3)*
be married *(Unit 1)*
be of assistance *(Revision 1)*
be on a business trip *(Unit 1)*
be responsible for *(Unit 3)*
be sure *(Unit 5)*
be under someone's feet *(Unit 6)*
be willing *(Unit 9)*
be worth *(Unit 1)*
be wrong *(Unit 1)*
beach *(Unit 4)*
beat *(Unit 7)*
beauty treatment *(Revision 2)*
become *(Unit 9)*
beforehand *(Unit 10)*
beg *(Unit 12)*
beginning *(Unit 6)*
behaviour *(Unit 3)*
behind *(Unit 1)*
believe *(Unit 8)*
benefit *(Unit 9)*
bet *(Unit 7)*
beware of *(Unit 8)*
bid *(Unit 6)*
bike *(Unit 10)*
biodegradable *(Unit 6)*
biting *(Unit 7)*
blank *(Unit 3)*
boil *(Unit 7)*
bookmaker *(Unit 7)*
boom (out) *(Unit 10)*
boot *(Unit 8)*
born-again Christian *(Unit 3)*
bother *(Unit 2)*
box of chocolates *(Unit 2)*
box office *(Unit 12)*
braking equipment *(Unit 2)*
branch *(Unit 2)*
break down *(Unit 6)*
break in *(Unit 5)*
breathe *(Unit 5)*
breed *(Unit 7)*
bright *(Unit 7)*
budget *(Unit 4)*
building *(Unit 4)*
burglar alarm *(Unit 10)*
burglar-proof *(Unit 10)*
burn *(Unit 10)*
busker *(Unit 8)*
busy *(Unit 2)*
by mistake *(Unit 5)*

C

cab (AE) *(Unit 10)*
cabin staff *(Unit 4)*
cabinet *(Unit 11)*
can of coke *(Unit 2)*
cancel *(Unit 10)*
candidate *(Unit 9)*
car park *(Unit 2)*
car registration number *(Revision 3)*
care *(Unit 7)*
care (to take ...) *(Unit 1)*
career *(Unit 9)*
carefully *(Unit 1)*
carpet *(Unit 11)*
carrier-bag *(Unit 11)*
carton of orange juice *(Unit 2)*
case (in any ...) *(Unit 1)*
catch *(Unit 6)*
catch up with *(Unit 12)*
cause *(Unit 6)*
celebrate *(Revision 2)*
celebrate *(Unit 4)*
celebration *(Unit 4)*

200

central heating (Unit 2)
century (Unit 1)
certain (Unit 6)
CFC (Unit 7)
chain (Revision 4)
chain of events
    (Revision 4)
chairperson (Unit 10)
challenge (Unit 11)
champion (Unit 6)
change (Unit 3,
    Revision 3, Unit 10)
charge (Unit 5)
charity organisation
    (Unit 2)
chart (Unit 7)
cheap (Unit 10)
check (Unit 1)
check-up (Unit 11)
cheerful (Unit 3)
chess (Unit 12)
chest (Unit 3)
chief (Unit 6)
childhood (Unit 8)
chimney (Unit 11)
choice (Unit 3)
choose (Unit 1)
chop down (Unit 6)
cider (Unit 3)
citizen (Unit 3)
clam (Unit 6)
classmate (Unit 12)
clear (Unit 4, 7)
climb (Unit 6)
clock in and out of work
    (Unit 8)
cloud (Unit 7)
clue (Unit 1)
coach (Unit 9)
cold (Unit 6)
collect (Unit 1)
collection-box
    (Revision 4)
college (Unit 7)
collide with (Unit 4)
column (Unit 3)
commentary (Unit 2)
commission (Unit 9)
commit (Unit 5)
community (Unit 1)
commuter (Unit 1)
company (Unit 9)
compare (Unit 1)
competition (Unit 6)
competitive (Unit 9)
complain (Unit 4)
comprehensive school
    (Unit 1)
computer-literate (Unit 9)
confirm (Unit 2)
congratulate (Unit 9)
connection (Unit 5, 11)
consumer (Unit 9)
contact (Unit 9)
contestant (Unit 11)
continue (Revision 1)
continue (Revision 1,
    Unit 7)
convenient (Unit 10)

cookery (Unit 9)
copy (Unit 2, 6)
cordless (Unit 5)
corner (Unit 2)
cottage (Unit 4,
    Revision 2)
cotton (Unit 11)
count (off) (Unit 1)
countersign (Unit 3)
countryside (Unit 1)
couple (Unit 5, 9)
cover (Unit 4)
crate (Unit 2)
crawl (Unit 10)
credit (Unit 12)
crime (Unit 5)
crisps (Unit 2)
cross (Unit 8)
cross one's mind
    (Revision 4)
crowd (Unit 3)
crowded (Unit 10)
cruise (Unit 6)
cubicle (Unit 11)
Cup Final (Unit 2)
currency (Unit 4)
current (Unit 2)
current affairs
    (Revision 1)
currently (Unit 3)
customs (Unit 8)
CV (curriculum vitae)
    (Unit 9)

D

damage (Unit 6)
dash (Unit 12)
dawn (Unit 5)
debts (Unit 5)
decide (Unit 2)
declare (Unit 8)
decrease (Unit 6)
defence (Unit 10)
degree (Unit 4, 9,
    Revision 3)
deliver (Unit 5)
delivery (Unit 5)
demand (for) (Unit 7)
demonstration (Unit 4)
describe (Unit 3)
description (Unit 3)
design (Unit 6)
despite (Unit 12)
destroy (Unit 5)
details (Unit 4)
develop (Unit 7)
developer (property ...)
    (Unit 6)
development (Unit 10)
diary (Unit 6)
dice (Unit 12)
dictionary (Unit 1)
die (Unit 4)
different (Unit 4)
difficult (Unit 10)
dig (Revision 3)
disadvantage (Unit 9)
disagree (Unit 6)

disappointed (Unit 6, 7)
discover (Unit 9)
disgust (Unit 12)
dishwasher (Unit 1, 10)
distance (Unit 10, 12)
divide (Unit 6)
diving (scuba ...) (Unit 6)
divorced (Unit 1)
DIY (Unit 11)
dock worker (Unit 8)
doll (Unit 8)
domestic appliance
    (Unit 11)
double glazing (Unit 11)
draft beer (Unit 3)
draughtsman (Unit 3)
dress (Unit 7)
drive (Unit 10)
driveway (Unit 10)
driving licence (Unit 5)
drizzle (Unit 7)
drought (Unit 7)
drums (Unit 3)
during (Unit 1, 7)

E

earn (Unit 1)
easy (Unit 10)
eavesdrop (Unit 15)
eavesdropper (Unit 5)
economics (Unit 9,
    Revision 3)
edit (Revision 3)
editor (Revision 3)
efficient (Unit 10)
elderly (Unit 8)
election (Unit 3)
electrician (Unit 8)
embarrassed (Unit 12)
emergency (Unit 5)
emit (Unit 10)
employ (Unit 3)
enchanted (Unit 3)
enclose (Unit 1)
end up (Unit 10)
enjoy (Unit 10)
enjoyable (Unit 4)
enter (Unit 10)
entertainment (Unit 12)
entranceway (Unit 11)
entry (Unit 8)
environment (Unit 6)
equal (Unit 7)
equipment (Unit 1)
escape (Unit 5)
especially (Unit 4)
estimated (Unit 10)
eventually (Unit 11)
exactly (Unit 5)
except (Unit 3)
exchange (Unit 1)
excitement (Unit 2, 5)
exciting (Unit 10)
exercise (Unit 11)
expand (Unit 9,
    Revision 3)
expansion (Unit 9)
expect (Unit 7)

expensive (Unit 10)
experience (Unit 9,
    Revision 3)
extend (Unit 7)
extension number
    (Unit 9)
extravagance (Unit 2)

F

face (Unit 7)
facilities (Unit 1)
fact (Unit 9)
faint-hearted (Unit 2)
fair and square (Unit 7)
fairly (Unit 7)
false (Unit 2)
famous (Revision 2)
fare (Unit 10)
fast (Unit 10)
father-in-law (Unit 1)
fault (Unit 12)
favourite (Unit 1)
feed (Unit 8)
feel guilty (Unit 12)
fellow student (Unit 10)
female (Unit 1)
ferry (Unit 10)
fiction (Unit 8)
fine (Unit 5)
fire brigade (Unit 10)
fireman (Unit 5)
firewood (Unit 12)
fit (Unit 1)
flat (Unit 1)
flight attendant (Unit 4)
float (Unit 5)
foaming (Revision 1)
fog (Revision 3)
food poisoning (Unit 8, 11)
for supper (Unit 4)
force (Unit 12)
forecast (Unit 7)
forehand (Unit 2)
foreign language (Unit 3)
foreigner (Unit 3)
forget (Unit 2)
former (Unit 12)
found (Unit 6)
foursome (Unit 1)
four-wheel-drive (Unit 5)
free (Unit 2)
free-house pub
    (Revision 2)
free-range (Unit 11)
freezer centre (Unit 3)
freezing-point (Unit 7)
frequent (Unit 11)
fridge (Unit 3)
frighten (Unit 6)
fry (Unit 11)
fun (Unit 6)
fund-raising (Revision 4)
funeral (Unit 12)

G

gain (Unit 9, Revision 3)
gaze (Unit 5)

gear (Unit 7)
generally speaking
    (Unit 11)
get (here) (Unit 1)
get married (Unit 6)
get rid of (Unit 7, 12)
get stuck (Unit 7, 10)
get tired of (Unit 4)
get up (Unit 1)
give a statement (Unit 5)
give up (Unit 7, 8)
glance (Unit 12)
glasses (Revision 3)
glow (Unit 5)
go down (Unit 3)
goal (Unit 5)
goose (geese, pl.)
    (Unit 10)
got that (I've ...) (Unit 8)
government (Unit 7)
grade (Unit 10)
greengrocer (Unit 11)
greenish (Unit 11)
grid (Unit 2)
groceries (Unit 3)
grow up (Revision 2)
guard dog (Unit 10)
guardian (Unit 12)
guess (Unit 3)
guideline (Unit 2, 11)

H

habit (Unit 12)
habitat (Unit 6)
hairdryer (Unit 10)
ham (Unit 2)
hand something in
    (Unit 5)
handsome (Revision 4)
hangover (Unit 12)
hankie (Unit 11)
hardly ever (Unit 10)
harmful (Unit 6)
hate (Unit 3)
have a go at something
    (Unit 6)
have sth. left over
    (Unit 2)
headache (Unit 2)
headline (Unit 7)
headquarters (Unit 6)
health insurance
    (Revision 3)
healthy (Unit 7)
heaven (Unit 3)
height (Unit 10)
hesitate (Revision 1)
high-density (Unit 10)
highlight (Unit 7)
hit (Unit 8)
Hold on! (Unit 2)
hold up (Unit 5)
hole in the ozone layer
    (Unit 6)
honest (Unit 11)
honey (Unit 2)
horrified (Unit 5)
hosepipe (Unit 7)

Vocabulary – Alphabetical Order

Vocabulary Alphabetical Order

host (Unit 4)
housekeeper (Revision 1, Unit 12)
however (Unit 1)
hug (Unit 5)
huge (Unit 7)
human (Unit 8)
hump (Unit 2)
hunt (Unit 8)
hurt (Unit 4)
husband (Unit 1)

I

identification (Unit 5)
identity card (Revision 3)
illegally (Unit 5)
imagine (Unit 1)
immediately (Revision 1, Unit 7, 9)
improve (Unit 1)
in advance (Unit 4, Revision 2)
in fact (Unit 1)
in pursuit of (Unit 12)
in the meantime (Unit 12)
in time (Revision 3)
in trouble (Unit 5)
include (Unit 9)
increase (Unit 5)
Inland Revenue (Unit 11)
inside (Unit 2)
install (Unit 5)
insurance (Unit 5)
interested (Unit 4)
intonation (Unit 4)
introduce (Unit 1, 5)
introductory (Revision 1, Unit 12)
intruder (Unit 10)
invent (Unit 4)
invention (Unit 10)
investigate (Unit 5)
investment adviser (Unit 2)
invitation (Unit 6)
invite (Unit 6)
iron (Unit 10)
issue (Unit 5)
item (Unit 10, 12)

J

jacket (Unit 3)
jail (Unit 7)
jar (Unit 2)
job applicants (Unit 3)
join (Unit 5, 9)
journey (Unit 1)
jump (Unit 2)
jumper (Unit 1)
just in case (Unit 11)
just over (Unit 1)

K

kick (Unit 2)
kids (Unit 3)
kiss (Unit 5)
kite (Unit 4)

L

lack (of) (Unit 7)
lane (Unit 8)
last (Unit 5)
launderette (Unit 6)
law and order (Unit 5)
lawn (Unit 5)
lay (Unit 6)
lazy (Unit 1)
lead (Unit 2, 8)
leading role (Unit 12)
lease (Unit 1)
library (Unit 3)
life (bird ...) (Unit 6)
lift (Unit 7)
like (Unit 7)
likely (Unit 7)
line (Unit 9, 10)
line worker (Unit 1)
link (Unit 4)
liquor store (Unit 5)
litter (Unit 8)
liver (Unit 3)
local (Unit 10)
local council (Unit 11)
locally (Unit 1)
locate (Unit 10)
lock (Unit 5)
look at (Unit 1)
look forward to (Unit 1)
look up (Unit 3)
lost property office (Unit 5)
loud (Unit 3)
luck (Unit 7)
ludo (Unit 1)
luggage (Unit 11)

M

magazine (Unit 7)
maintenance (Unit 1)
majority (Unit 7)
make a decision (Unit 9)
make a fool of yourself (Unit 9)
make arrangements (Unit 6)
make yourself at home (Revision 2)
manner (Unit 9)
map (Unit 2)
match (Unit 11)
matter (Unit 9)
matter of (Unit 12)
mean (Unit 6)

meanness (Unit 2)
media (Unit 6)
meet (Unit 6)
member (Unit 1)
membership (Unit 9)
mention (Unit 6)
message (give s.o. a ...) (Unit 1)
met office (Unit 7)
mind (Unit 10, 11)
miner (Unit 12)
misery (Unit 12)
miss (Unit 5, 7)
missing (Unit 1)
mist (Unit 5, 7)
mixed up (Unit 6)
monthly (Unit 9)
moonlight (Unit 5)
mortgage (Unit 1)
motivated (Unit 9)
motorway (Unit 7)
move (Unit 7, 9)
mow (Unit 5)
murderer (Unit 5)

N

national lottery (Unit 6)
necessary (Unit 1)
necessities (Unit 8)
neighbourhood (Unit 11)
nephew (Unit 1)
nervous (Unit 9)
net (Unit 2)
niece (Unit 1)
non-fiction (Unit 8)
non-returnable (Unit 11)
not ... anymore (Unit 6)
notice (Unit 4, 8)
novel (Unit 8)
nuisance (Unit 6)
nurse (Unit 4)

O

obstruct (Unit 8)
obtain (Unit 9)
obvious (Unit 3)
occasional (Unit 7)
occupation (Unit 1)
octopus (Revision 2)
offer (Unit 7)
officer (Unit 3)
on demand (Unit 8)
on schedule (Revision 3)
once more (Unit 8)
operate (Unit 3)
operation (Unit 11)
opponent (Unit 3)
opportunity (Unit 9)
opposite (Unit 8)
option (Unit 12)
order (Unit 3)
organize (Unit 9)
orphan (Unit 12)

outing (Revision 1)
out of order (Unit 2)
outside (Unit 2)
outskirts (Unit 7)
over-indulgent (Unit 12)
overtake (Unit 12)
over there (Unit 1)
overtime (Unit 1)
overspend (Unit 11)

P

packet (Unit 2)
pain (Unit 4)
particularly (Unit 4)
pass (Unit 4)
passport (Revision 3)
patience (Unit 11)
pavement (Unit 1)
paw (Unit 12)
pay rise (Unit 9)
peace (Unit 3)
peaceful (Unit 4)
peer (Unit 12)
penalty (Unit 8)
percentage (Unit 1)
performance (Unit 3)
perhaps (Unit 1)
persuade (Unit 5)
pet (Revision 1)
petition (Unit 12)
PhD (Unit 3)
phone card (Unit 2)
pick up (Unit 3, 5, 6)
pickpocket (Unit 4)
pierced (Unit 3)
Pilgrim Fathers (Unit 11)
pillow (Unit 5)
pineapple (Unit 2)
place a bet (Unit 7)
pleasant (Unit 7)
please (Unit 6)
please yourself (Unit 4)
plug (Unit 11)
polite (Unit 6)
popular (Unit 2)
portable (Unit 12)
post (Unit 9)
pottery (Unit 2)
poverty (Unit 3, 12)
power station (Unit 11)
practically (Unit 7)
pray (Unit 3)
predict (Unit 6)
prediction (Unit 7)
prefer (Unit 2, 7, 10)
present (Unit 1)
pressure (Unit 9)
prevent (Unit 5)
prevention (Unit 5)
primary school (Unit 1)
print (Revision 3)
prison (Unit 5)

probably (Unit 1)
profit (Unit 5)
promotion (Unit 9)
proper (Unit 1)
property (Unit 3)
prospects (Unit 9)
protect (Unit 6)
proud (Unit 4)
public (Unit 5, 10)
punch (Unit 5)
puncture (Unit 6)
punishment (Unit 5)
punter (Unit 7)
puppet play (Unit 4)
put (Unit 7)
putting (Unit 7)

Q

questionnaire (Unit 2)
queue (Unit 8)

R

racing (Unit 2)
racket (tennis ...) (Unit 2)
railway station (Unit 1)
range (Revision 1)
rapids (Revision 1)
rate (Unit 3)
rather (Unit 1)
real (Unit 3)
realise (Unit 3)
really (Unit 3)
reason (Unit 8)
receipt (Unit 10)
receive (Unit 11)
recent (Unit 1)
recently (Unit 4)
reception (Revision 1)
recognize (Unit 5, 6)
recruitment (Unit 9)
reef (Unit 6)
referee (Unit 2, 9, Revision 3)
reflect (Unit 5)
refrain from (Unit 8)
refuse (Unit 7)
regret (Unit 1)
regularly (Unit 7)
reimburse (Unit 10)
relationship (Unit 1)
relaxing (Unit 10)
remain (Unit 5)
remember (Unit 1, 8)
remind (Unit 8)
rent (Unit 1, 4)
replace (Unit 11)
report (Unit 7, 8)
request (Unit 8)
require (Unit 12)
rescue (Unit 8)
research (Unit 6)

202

residence permit *(Revision 3)*
resign *(Unit 7)*
resort *(Unit 4)*
response *(Unit 11)*
responsibility *(Unit 9)*
retire *(Unit 7)*
retired *(Unit 8)*
returnable *(Unit 6)*
reunification *(Unit 4)*
rev *(Unit 11)*
reward *(Unit 5)*
ride *(Unit 2)*
ring *(Revision 1)*
ring-leader *(Unit 12)*
rise *(Unit 4)*
river *(Unit 10)*
roadside *(Unit 10)*
robbery *(Unit 5)*
room *(Unit 8)*
roster *(Unit 9)*
rough *(Unit 12)*
round *(Unit 10)*
rubbish *(Unit 6)*
ruin *(Unit 12)*
rules *(Unit 2)*
rules and regulations *(Unit 8)*
run off with *(Unit 3)*
run out of *(Revision 2)*
rush-hour *(Unit 10)*

S

safety *(Unit 11)*
salad *(Unit 2)*
salary *(Unit 9)*
save *(Unit 5, 6)*
savings *(Unit 10)*
scarcely *(Unit 12)*
scattered *(Unit 7)*
scenery *(Unit 12)*
scholarship *(Unit 3)*
score (no score) *(Unit 1, 2)*
seafood *(Revision 2)*
search for *(Unit 8)*
season *(Unit 7)*
season ticket *(Unit 1)*
security guard *(Unit 2)*
see eye to eye *(Unit 11)*
seize *(Unit 5)*
seldom *(Unit 3)*
semi-detached *(Unit 1)*
sensible *(Unit 4)*
serial rapist *(Revision 4)*
serious *(Unit 4)*
set *(Unit 5)*
set off *(Unit 12)*
shake hands with *(Revision 2)*
shame (what a ...) *(Unit 6)*
shaped like *(Unit 6)*

share *(Unit 6)*
shaver *(Unit 11)*
shelf *(Unit 8)*
sheriffs office *(Unit 5)*
shift *(Unit 1)*
shoot *(Unit 4)*
shout *(Unit 4)*
shy *(Revision 3)*
signature *(Unit 1)*
similar *(Unit 1)*
sister-in-law *(Unit 1)*
site *(Unit 6)*
skills *(Unit 9)*
skip *(Unit 12)*
skipping rope *(Unit 8)*
slam *(Unit 11)*
slice *(Unit 2)*
slide *(Revision 2)*
smart *(Unit 9)*
smell *(Unit 3)*
smile *(Unit 3)*
smoke *(Unit 10)*
smoothly *(Revision 3)*
snap *(Unit 7)*
snore *(Unit 1)*
snorkelling *(Unit 4)*
snow *(Unit 7)*
snowdrift *(Unit 7)*
snowflake *(Unit 7)*
soap *(Unit 2)*
socket *(Unit 11)*
soft *(Unit 5)*
solicitor *(Unit 2)*
sore (leg) *(Unit 1)*
sound *(Unit 4, 7, 11)*
soundproof *(Unit 11)*
sow *(Unit 12)*
space *(Unit 4)*
spare *(Unit 1)*
special offer *(Unit 7)*
spectacles *(Unit 12)*
speech intention *(Revision 4)*
spend *(Unit 2)*
spicy *(Unit 4)*
spider *(Unit 7)*
spill *(Unit 11)*
spoil yourself *(Unit 4)*
spokesman *(Unit 7)*
spring *(Unit 7)*
square-shouldered *(Revision 4)*
squeeze *(Unit 11)*
staff *(Unit 9)*
startle *(Unit 12)*
stationery *(Unit 5)*
steer *(Unit 11)*
stifle *(Unit 9)*
stockbroker *(Unit 1)*
stop-over *(Unit 6)*
straight away *(Unit 7)*
strange *(Unit 7)*
stranger *(Unit 3)*
stressful *(Unit 4)*

strict *(Unit 8)*
stuff *(Unit 8)*
stupid *(Unit 12)*
succeed in *(Unit 9)*
successful *(Unit 1)*
suddenly *(Unit 8)*
suffer (from) *(Unit 7)*
suggestion *(Unit 11)*
suit *(Unit 4, 12)*
suitable *(Unit 1)*
sun roof *(Unit 5)*
sunburnt *(Unit 7)*
support *(Unit 8)*
suppose *(Unit 11)*
surge *(Unit 12)*
surprise *(Unit 3)*
survey *(Unit 12)*
sweep *(Unit 11)*
sweet *(Unit 3, 10)*
swirling *(Revision 1)*
sympathetic *(Unit 4)*

T

take (a cab) *(Unit 10)*
take a year off *(Unit 9)*
take care *(Unit 1)*
take part in *(Unit 5)*
take place *(Unit 6)*
taste *(Unit 3)*
tax *(Unit 1)*
teach *(Unit 2)*
technology *(Unit 10)*
tend *(Unit 11)*
thatched roof *(Unit 1)*
thick *(Unit 8)*
thief *(Unit 5)*
thirsty *(Unit 2)*
threaten *(Unit 5)*
three times *(Unit 3)*
throw *(Unit 2)*
thunderstorm *(Unit 7)*
tie *(Unit 1)*
tile *(Unit 11)*
tin *(Unit 2)*
tip *(Unit 9)*
tissue *(Unit 11)*
touch *(Unit 8)*
tour operator *(Unit 7)*
towel *(Revision 1)*
toy *(Unit 12)*
trace *(Unit 12)*
track *(Unit 8)*
traffic jam *(Unit 10)*
transport *(Unit 10)*
travel *(Unit 10)*
travel abroad *(Unit 8)*
treasures *(Unit 8)*
treat yourself to sth. *(Unit 4)*
trim *(Unit 11)*
true *(Unit 2)*
trunk *(Unit 8)*
trusty *(Unit 12)*

tube *(Unit 2, 10)*
turtle *(Unit 6)*
twin *(Unit 10)*

U

umbrella *(Unit 5)*
unaccompanied *(Unit 12)*
unashamedly *(Unit 12)*
unbleached *(Unit 11)*
uncomfortable *(Unit 10)*
underground *(Unit 10)*
unemployed *(Unit 5)*
unemployment *(Unit 9)*
unfortunately *(Revision 2)*
unit *(Unit 2)*
unless *(Unit 3)*
unreal *(Unit 5)*
unspoilt *(Unit 4)*
until *(Unit 6)*
unusual *(Unit 2, 4)*
update *(Unit 7)*
upright *(Unit 11)*
urban *(Unit 11)*
urgent *(Unit 2)*
use *(Unit 2)*
used to *(Unit 2, 8)*
useful *(Unit 1)*
ususal (as ...) *(Unit 6)*
utilities *(Unit 9)*

V

vacuum cleaner *(Unit 11)*
valid *(Unit 8)*
valuable *(Unit 5)*
value *(Unit 3)*
variety *(Revision 3)*
vary *(Unit 3)*
veal *(Unit 4)*
vegetable *(Unit 1)*
vet *(Unit 1)*
viewing *(Unit 7)*
village *(Unit 1)*
violence *(Unit 3)*
virtual experience *(Unit 9)*
visitor *(Unit 6)*
voice *(Unit 5)*
voluntary *(Revision 4)*
volunteer *(Unit 2)*
vote *(Unit 11)*

W

wait (I can't ...) *(Unit 6)*
wake-up call *(Unit 10)*
walk *(Unit 10)*
wallet *(Unit 2)*
warning *(Unit 2)*
warrior *(Unit 12)*
waste *(Unit 6, 12)*

water *(Unit 6)*
wealthy *(Unit 11)*
wear *(Unit 4)*
wedding anniversary *(Unit 4)*
weight *(Unit 10)*
welcome *(Unit 3)*
well-known *(Unit 8)*
well-meant *(Unit 11)*
what about ...-ing *(Unit 2)*
What's the trouble? *(Revision 1)*
whether *(Revision 1)*
whine *(Unit 12)*
whistle *(Unit 2)*
whole time *(Unit 3)*
wife *(Unit 1)*
wink *(Unit 11)*
wipe out *(Unit 12)*
wire *(Unit 10, 11)*
witness something *(Unit 5)*
wonder *(Unit 1, 12)*
word stress *(Unit 5)*
work permit *(Revision 3)*
working environment *(Unit 9)*
world *(Unit 10)*
worn *(Unit 11)*
worry *(Unit 1)*

X

x-ray *(Revision 3)*

Acknowledgements

The authors and publishers are grateful to the following copyright owners for permission to reproduce artworks, photographs, illustrations and texts. It has not been possible to identify the sources of all the material used and in such cases the publishers would welcome information from copyright owners.

Cover: top: Corbis/Ariel Skelley; bottom: MHV/DigitalVision (London, Thamse River)
page 11: photo: BMW AG, München **page 17:** photo: The Allan Cash Photolibrary, London **page 21:** photos: © Richard Tenczer **page 22:** photo top: © Inter-Topics/Galella (Gérard Depardieu); photo middle: © dpa/Andreas Altwein (left: Sabine Christiansen; right: Sir Peter Ustinov); photo bottom: dpa, Frankfurt (Robbie Williams) **page 24:** photo: Big Spender © Good Housekeeping/Trevor Leighton. – The National Magazine Company. International Editions and Library Department, London **page 29:** text: "I'm just going out for a moment" by Michael Rosen. From: The Hipo Book of Hilarious Poetry, Scholastic Publications Ltd, London **page 30:** photo top: Atmosphere Postcards/Bob Croxford; photo middle left: BlueBox/Tibor Bognàr; photo bottom right: laif/Klover **page 33:** text: "I'm in love with a big blue frog" Musik & Text: Noel Paul Stookey, Peter Yarrow, Mary Allin Travers, Les Braunstein © by Neworld Media Music Publishers. Für D/CH/GUS und osteurop. Länder (ohne Baltikum), Türkei und Länder des ehem. Jugoslawien: Neue Welt Musikverlag GmbH & Co.KG **page 36:** text: "Statements after an arrest under the immorality act" by Athol Fugard, 1974, 1984. Reprinted by permission of Oxford University Press **page 40:** photos: The Allan Cash Photolibrary, London **page 43:** photos: Sue Morris, Schwindegg **page 45:** photo: Erna Friedrich, Ismaning **page 50:** text: "Saved by an eavesdropper". From "Good Housekeeping" May 1995. Reprinted by permission of Sandra McElwaine, Washington D. C., USA **page 51:** photo: MHV/Dieter Reichler **page 52:** text: "Wednesday Morning 3am". Musik und Text: Paul Simon. © by Paul Simon Music, New York **page 56:** photos: Sue Morris, Schwindegg **page 60:** photo: Cornelia Dietz, Ingolstadt **page 61:** photo: Erna Friedrich, Ismaning **page 66:** photo right: Master Builder's Hotel. © Weidenfeld & Nicolson Ltd.; photo left: Barnaby's Picture Library/Norman Price **page 69:** photo: IFA/Jon Arnold Images **page 71:** Please not that players of The National Lottery in the United Kingdom must be 16 years of age or more. The UK National Lottery "crossed fingers" logo is owned by The United Kingdom Secretary of State for National Heritage. The Lottery ticket and playslip are reproduced with the permission of Camelot Group plc, operator of the UK National Lottery. **page 74:** photos: dpa, Frankfurt (top left: Queen Sylvia; middle left: Sting; bottom left: Sean Connery; bottom right: J. K. Rowling **page 75:** cartoon: Graphic Syndication, Hampshire, England **page 76:** laif/Specht **page 78:** photo left: f1 online/Thomas Nühnen; photo right: Alexandra Bünger, Hamburg **page 79:** photo top: © Mattel; photo bottom left: © 2003 The LEGO Group; photo bottom right: © Margarete Steiff GmbH **page 80:** photo top middle: © Partner für Berlin/FTB-Werbefotografie; photo top right: © dpa Frankfurt; photos middle left and right: Sue Morris, Schwindegg; photo bottom: © Presse- und Informationsamt des Landes Berlin/W. Gerling; **page 83:** photo: © Archiv SyndiCAT, München (Margarita de Arellano) **page 84:** text: Rebecca Cripps/Marie Claire/Robert Harding Syndication, London; photo: Gillie Scrivens/Marie Claire/Robert Harding Syndication, London **page 85:** photo: MHV/Dieter Reichler **page 96:** photo: MHV/MEV **page 98:** cartoon: "Creature Feature"/Dave Follows **page 103:** cartoon: "Wizard of ID" by Parker & Hart **page 110:** Electric Cinema/photo left: © The Ronald Grant Archive, London; Cinedom/photo right: © Tibor Magaslaki, Köln **pages 111/112:** cover: © Paul Cox and Penguin Books, London; text: © David Lodge. Permission of Curtis Brown Group, London **page 113:** photo: Interfoto, München **page 114:** photo: by permission of the Citizen's Theatre, Glasgow **page 115:** R. Howe, München **page 117:** photo: "Billy Elliot – I will dance" © DIF Deutsches Filminstitut **page 118:** text: from "Father Frank" by Paul Burke. Reproduced by permission of Hodder and Stoughton Limited **page 121:** Macmillan Guided Readers **page 123:** photo: Sue Morris, Schwindegg **page 126:** photo: MHV/Dieter Reichler